REFLECTIONS OF REVOLUTION

Reflections of Revolution demonstrates the increasing interdisciplinarity emerging from cultural and historical studies. Taking the French Revolution as its focus, the book examines the tremendously diverse and intellectually exciting cultural reactions to the events of 1789.

This collection of essays represents an important new body of scholarship. The cultural effects of the French Revolution are examined by scholars who bring their own concerns and intellectual orientation to bear upon the art and literature of the Romantic period. It is the first full-length study to unite a series of ideas, approaches and subject areas which are crucial to a proper understanding of the period.

Editors: **Alison Yarrington** is Senior Lecturer in Art History at Leicester University. **Kelvin Everest** is A. C. Bradley Professor of Modern Literature at Liverpool University.

Contributors: David Bindman, Fred Botting, Angus Easson, Gavin Edwards, Chris Jones, Nigel Leask, Claudine Mitchell, David Punter, William Ruddick, William Vaughan and Richard Wrigley.

REFLECTIONS OF REVOLUTION

Images of Romanticism

Edited by

Alison Yarrington
and Kelvin Everest

London and New York

First published 1993
by Routledge
11 New Fetter Lane, London EC4P 4EE

Simultaneously published in the USA and Canada
by Routledge
29 West 35th Street, New York, NY 10001

Phototypeset in 10 on 12 point Baskerville by
Intype, London
Printed in Great Britain by
Butler & Tanner Ltd, Frome

British Library Cataloguing in Publication Data
A catalogue record for this book is available from the British Library.

Library of Congress Cataloging in Publication Data
Reflections of revolution : images of Romanticism /
edited by Alison Yarrington
and Kelvin Everest.
p.   cm.
Papers from a conference held at the University of Leicester in July 1989.
Includes bibliographical references and index.
1. English literature—French influences—Congresses. 2. France—
History–Revolution, 1789–1799—Literature and the revolution—Congresses.
3. English literature—19th century—History and criticism—Congresses.
4. Revolutionary literature, English—History and criticism—Congresses.
5. France—History—Revolution, 1789–1799—Influence—Congresses. 6. Great
Britain—Civilization—French influences—Congresses. 7. France in
literature—Congresses. I. Yarrington, Alison. II. Everest, Kelvin.
PR129.F8R43   1993
820.9′008—dc20   92–13300

ISBN 0–415–07741–9

Contents

CONTENTS

Notes on contributors

David Bindman is Professor of History of Art at University College, University of London. He is the author of *Blake as an Artist* (1977), *Hogarth* (1981) and *Shadow of the Guillotine: Britain and the French Revolution* (1989).

Fred Botting is Lecturer in the School of English, University of Wales, Cardiff. He is the author of *Making Monstrous: Frankenstein, Criticism and Theory* (1991).

Angus Easson is Professor of English at Salford University. His most recent publications include *Elizabeth Gaskell: The Critical Heritage* (1991) and an edition of Gaskell's *Mary Barton*. He is joint editor of volume 7 of the Clarendon Press *Letters* of Charles Dickens.

Gavin Edwards is Senior Lecturer in the Department of English, St David's University College, Lampeter. He is the author of *George Crabbe's Poetry on Border Land* (1990) and the editor of *George Crabbe: Selected Poems* (1991). He has also published on Shakespeare and Blake.

Chris Jones is Lecturer in English at the University of Wales, Bangor. He has co-edited two volumes of discursive prose: *The Romantic Age in Prose* (1980) and *The Victorian Age in Prose* (1988); he is the author of *Radical Sensibility: Literature and Ideas in the 1790s* (1993).

Nigel Leask is Fellow and Director of Studies, Queens' College, Cambridge. He is the author of *The Politics of Imagination in Coleridge's Critical Thought* (1988) and *British Romantic Writers and the East: Anxieties of Empire* (1993).

Claudine Mitchell is Henry Moore Scholar in the Department of Fine Art, University of Leeds. Her most recent research has investigated women's art practices.

David Punter is Professor and Head of English Studies at Stirling University. His most recent publications include *Blake: Selected Writings* (1988) *The Romantic Unconcious: A Study of Narcissism and Patriarchy* (1989).

William Ruddick is Honorary Fellow of the University of Manchester where he was Lecturer in English until 1990. He is editor of J.G. Lockhart's *Peter's Letters to His Kinsfolk* (1977) and is co-author of the exhibition catalogue *Joseph Farington* (1977). He is currently editor of *The Charles Lamb Bulletin*.

William Vaughan is Professor of the History of Art at Birbeck College, University of London. He is author of *Romantic Art* (1978), *German Romanticism and English Art* (1979) and *German Romantic Painting* (1980).

Richard Wrigley is Senior Lecturer in Art History at Thames Valley University. He is the author of *The Origins of French Art Criticism: from the Ancien Régime to the Restoration* (1993) and a member of the editorial group of the *Oxford Art Journal*.

Acknowledgements

We would like to thank all those who contributed to the French Revolution and British Culture conference which was held at Beaumont Hall, Leicester University in July 1989, the event which prompted this collection of essays. In particular we would like to express our gratitude to Dr Jane Aaron and Dr Shearer West who co-organized the conference and to Mrs Margaret Lintern-Ball, Mrs Brenda Tracy, Dot Rowe, Bob Proctor and Naomi Summer who assisted. Additional thanks go to Professor Mike Freeman, Ian Maclachlan and Dr Nigel Wood for advice on the final manuscript.

1

Introduction

Alison Yarrington and Kelvin Everest

The essays which make up this volume are drawn from the wide range of papers delivered at a conference on 'The French Revolution and British Culture', organized at the University of Leicester in July 1989. The conference was conceived as a co-operative venture by the departments of English and History of Art at Leicester, and although the emphasis throughout the conference fell on cultural products and their meanings, discussion returned constantly to the great sweep of political events in France which formed the intellectual focus of the Romantic epoch in Britain.

The essays collected here offer no all-embracing or theoretically elaborated account of the relationship between political and cultural events, but they do provide a rich and varied body of commentary and reflection on the detailed interactions and shaping influences at play in the British cultural reaction to the Revolution. One obvious common quality shared by all the essays, however, is an insistence on the complexity and multiple determinations of specific cultural practices and products. The underlying and immediate historical contexts are always inescapable, for all forms of writing, and across the whole range of representational idioms, but their particular forms and effects have nevertheless to be understood primarily in the context of the precise conditions and stages of development of those cultural practices which make response and representation possible. The meanings of events and movements in France are therefore inflected and articulated for Britain in ways which are fundamental to lines of development in *British* culture; the meanings are effectively created by the prevailing preoccupations and intellectual heritage of the observing culture. They are not carried over in any unmediated way from the social and historical matrix of their origin in the Revolutionary situation in France itself.

These essays also clearly demonstrate a further condition of meaning for the British cultural response to the French Revolution; for just as prevailing conditions and preoccupations in British Romantic culture shape for it the meaning of its social and historical experience, so present-day interpreters of Romantic culture bring into play their own formative concerns and intellectual orientation. David Punter's essay, for example, points to the

1

heavily mediated character of Romantic culture for the late twentieth-century critic:

> It would be easy to assume that reactions to massive international events, and particularly revolutionary upheavals, can be modelled on cause and effect; a nearby monarch is executed, and certain consequences in the cultural sphere flow from that. But life is not so simple; and so events get modelled or traced onto other sources of, for example, alienation or anguish, and the products are always mixed . . . one could say that these products, mediated as they are through the pre-existence of language, are always *contaminated*.

And, as David Punter's own essay itself shows, the mediating pre-existence of language – which we can understand to include all the frameworks and structures which we may bring to bear on the act of interpretation – operates now to shape cultural meanings from the perspective of, for example, psychoanalysis and Kleinian child psychology.

David Punter's essay focuses in detail on aspects of Romantic cultural production which involve representation of 'the body in fragments', and seeks by a deployment of various sources in psychoanalysis and psychoanalytic history to explain these recurrent concerns as instances of a thwarting in the healthy development of consciousness which has large-scale social consequences. Another essay which very frankly and directly brings present-day theoretical formations to bear on Romantic culture – and with a similar effect of homogenizing Romantic cultural experience with our own present-day intellectual milieu – is Fred Botting's vivid discussion of monsters, in debate about the Revolution generally, but more particularly in Mary Shelley's *Frankenstein*. This discussion draws freely on the work of post-structuralist theorists to expose the contradictions which are superficially concealed, but which are rather disruptively emergent, in the apparently unifying discourses of Romantic culture. 'Monsters', manifestly deviant and transgressive in their very conception, draw attention to the limits of normative discursive practice, and thereby define its limiting and excluding boundaries. In wry self-consciousness of its own discursive 'monstrosity' as an instance of critical practice, Fred Botting's essay offers a suggestive and provocative articulation of one vital element in current thinking about the nature and genesis of meaning in culture.

A different perspective entirely is provided by other essays in the collection, which work in a distinct British tradition of closely detailed analysis of art and ideas in their social and historical contexts, where these contexts are assumed as a relatively stable and accessible object of knowledge, and are also seen as integral to a continuing development of national culture and political interests. Nigel Leask adopts this approach in his study of Coleridge's early scheme of a 'Pantisocracy' to be established on the banks of an ideally envisaged river in rural North America. By careful attention to questions of intellectual history and cultural context, Nigel Leask traces the origins, development and significant subsequent mutations of some important early political ideas of Wordsworth and Coleridge, and provides an illuminating perspective in particular on their relation to the influential formulations of the 'Preface' to the *Lyrical Ballads*. In a more narrowly focused but none the less suggestive discussion, William Ruddick surveys the potent and pervasive tree symbolism of the Revolutionary period, and notes some hidden political resonances in the language of natural description. A larger context, and one that was of important and direct concern to the Romantic culture itself, was that of 'Sensibility'. Chris Jones analyses this complex amalgam of political, stylistic and emotional components, and discriminates carefully amongst its cultural forebears and affiliations, and in particular its association by the 1790s with French principles. The radical dimension of Sensibility, as a polemical counter in both radical and conservative texts, is brought out very clearly, to illuminate the density of encoded political implication and reference of so much British writing in the immediate aftermath of the early phases of the French Revolution.

Gavin Edwards's essay on Crabbe also seeks to uncover some of the covert literary forms taken by the 'war of ideas' in Britain in the revolutionary period, a war between 'polarized sets of moral and political principles' which pervaded social and intellectual life to an extraordinary extent. Crabbe's ostensibly domestic narrative *Tales* of 1812 are shown to involve, whether consciously or not, a constant slippage between disorder in the household and in the State. The two realms are linked implicitly by metaphor, but Gavin Edwards argues beyond this observation to demonstrate the indirect and displaced manner by which revolutionary revaluations of experience could be negotiated by British writers at the level of kindred and local-domestic economic relationships.

As the emphasis in most of these essays would indicate, the impact of the French Revolution on British culture was first registered in the last decade of the eighteenth century. Nevertheless the reactions, for example, of first generation Romantic poets, became part of an intellectual development with major importance for those of the second generation such as Shelley and Byron; so that the apostasy of their literary forerunners itself became a part of the Revolutionary impact, and helped to shape and alter its meanings for a new generation. This process, of constant refinement in focus, becomes a central line of development in Britain throughout the nineteenth century. The Revolution is constantly reappraised, but in ways which continually take also on board the successive phases and modes of reception which intervene between the evanescent historical event, and the new contemporary moment of interpretation. Angus Easson's intriguing account of Dickens and Carlyle explores just one complex but also representative instance of the constant replenishment and modification of the meanings of the French Revolution in nineteenth-century intellectual life.

As recently as 1757 and Hume's essay, 'Of the standard of taste' it was possible for profound aesthetic comment to be attempted on the basis that the principles of taste were 'universal, and nearly, if not entirely, the same in all men' (Hume 1965: 17). Art had a goal in view and so artists deployed finite (and teachable) means to attain it, even if it was all but impossible to *demonstrate* the validity of superior skills. When lecturing in the Royal Academy, Reynolds felt that 'the internal fabrick of our minds' as well as 'the external form of our bodies' was 'nearly uniform'. Due to this 'general similitude' which ran 'through the whole race of mankind', high art was capable of definition and transmission (*Discourse VII*, delivered 1776, Wark 1959: 131). The French Revolution signalled the decay of such Enlightenment optimism and proclaimed an alternative hope: that there were new things to be said that were not reducible to matters of disembodied form, but rather to the symbolic imagination and more personal myth-making. Note the distance from Reynolds and even the radicalism of Hume in Delacroix's *Journal* entry of 27 March 1824, where he describes the 'interesting discussion at Leblond's about the genius of outstanding men': 'Dufresne said something very sensible, that what made a man really noteworthy was a completely personal and unique vision. . . . Therefore great souls can be bound by no rules: these can only be of use to people whose sole talent is acquired' (Delacroix 1932: I, 64). Burke found the Revolution, as has often been recognized, a tragicomedy, as if the more accepted generic traits of life (and of Royal Academy imprimatur) were flouted by history: 'Everything seems out of nature in this strange chaos of levity and ferocity, and of all sorts of crimes jumbled together with all sorts of follies' (Burke 1790: 92).

The visual arts of the Revolutionary/Romantic period may be representational, but, if the iconoclasm of the *sans-culottes* runs parallel with artistic innovation, then an analysis of these sets of images demands a painstaking contextualization, where a faith in the transmissible and familiar items of established academic discourse is bound to be shaken. Hence it is perhaps only possible to appreciate the full significance of the private symbolism of William Blake, for example, by undertaking a study such as David Bindman's ' "My own mind is my own church": Blake, Paine and the French Revolution', which opens the images up to overdetermined historical influences, the writings of Thomas Paine in particular.

Bindman examines the problematic question of Blake's responses to events in France: the military expansionism of the Girondin government, Robespierre's 'Republic of Virtue' and his cult of *L'Etre suprême*. The execution of the French royal family which evoked such widespread revulsion in Britain, left Blake seemingly unmoved. Blake adopted contradictory responses of abhorrence and admiration to Paine's writings during the period 1791–8, as evidenced by his pencil annotations of 1798 to Bishop Watson's *An Apology for the Bible in a Series of Letters addressed to Thomas*

4

Paine (1796), a paradox in his responses to the French Revolution which is the focus for Bindman's essay. Taking as his starting point the letterpress volume *The French Revolution* (1791) and the well-established genre of the Bastille poem, Bindman charts the nature of Blake's radicalism during this period using a revealing selection of the texts and designs. He argues that in *America* (1793) the debates between Urizen and Orc 'are conducted in terms of the Burke–Paine controversy'; thus Burke's sense of the French Revolution as a 'Promethean aberration' which transgressed the natural order is parodied in the Albion Angel's initial reply to Orc. Specifically Bindman sees Blake responding to the Painean analysis of the relationship between power and religion and the process of distortion of the Christian message through the 'veil' of ceremonial in plates 5 and 10 of *Europe* (1794). Despite these close correlations between image and texts the essential dichotomy between Paine's and Blake's understanding of the role of rational principles within revolution and post-revolutionary states remains distinct.

The call for a new range of individualistic rights demands new visual codes, but even Blake was effectively 'gagged' during the period following 1793 as a consequence of his need to maintain a professional status as an artist and engraver and the continuing support of radical Whigs such as Joseph Johnson and Henry Fuseli. A thorough account of the period must therefore include areas where idealism fails and more pragmatic concerns intrude. Blake, for example, was in every sense a marginal figure within the art establishment of the day with a limited audience for his work. Placed against his situation were those British artists whose aspirations and output made them more part of the mainstream of high art as channelled through the Royal Academy. Both those who promoted the interests of this institution, itself under Royal patronage, and those who were protected by it were thus, necessarily, in rivalry with their counterparts in France. One example of how a lack of individual political sensitivity at a time of widespread paranoia about republican sympathizers could cut short a promising career in this most publicly prestigious area of art practice – history painting – is the case of the Anglo-Irish artist, James Barry. Initially nurtured by the Royal Academy during the brilliant early years of his career (his 'genius' was later acknowledged by Blake in his 'Annotations' [1808] to Reynolds's *Discourses*), he was appointed Professor of Painting there in 1782. Barry's subsequent loss of office and expulsion from the Academy in 1799 was undoubtedly the result of intemperate behaviour towards his colleagues, but it must also be seen as equally due to his radical political sympathies, as William Vaughan argues in his essay ' "David's Brickdust" and the rise of the British School'. His role as 'traitor' to the institution of the Academy had become part of a mythology signified simply by reference to his name. This eponymous betrayal stigmatized his work during the first half of the nineteenth century; an example of the myth overmastering the man. An instance of this usage is provided by the aspirant history painter Benjamin Robert Haydon (in conversation with Martin Arthur Shee) in July 1826 who claimed that he was 'heaped with calumnies, anonymous letters, had everything put upon [his] shoulders, was accused of envy and hatred, called a Barry . . .' (Haydon 1963: 3, 117). Haydon's tenacious pursuit of art at its highest level, which, whilst a student at the Royal Academy had been fuelled by the teachings of Fuseli, was never to be rewarded by public recognition commensurate with his ambition or effort. The possible advantages for history painters which might have accrued from war (as they had in France) with a demand for works to express and promote national pride never materialized, but then the ground for such State patronage to flourish was already virtually barren (take for example the failure of the Academy's pre-war scheme of 1773 for the decoration of the interior of St Paul's Cathedral with history painting). The recipients of government patronage of the arts during the French wars were the sculptors who were commissioned to produce a series of national monuments to the British officers who died in the conflict. Thus St Paul's became the site of a hall of fame which celebrated the fine art of sculpture rather than that of history painting. Alternative, 'Utopian' schemes to stimulate the patronage of history painting through an appeal to patriotic pride similarly failed to attract support from the State or the public. John Opie's proposal for a Temple of Naval Virtue modelled upon the Pantheon in Rome to be internally decorated with scenes from British naval history was first promoted in 1799 and was later to form the basis for Haydon's own proposals for a Nelson monument for Trafalgar Square in 1839. More extraordinary still was the scheme promoted by Major John Cartwright for the *Heironauticon*, designs for which were exhibited in London during 1800 and which again included history painting alongside sculpture as part of a vast architectural complex to celebrate British naval victory. This lack of State sponsorship for history painting at a time when it was flourishing in France was a continuing source of anger and irritation for British artists. The identification of an emergent national school which had been promoted under the aegis of the first President of the Royal Academy, Sir Joshua Reynolds, meant that British artists were therefore necessarily antagonistic towards and resentful of the highly successful and more established French Academy. This was to become particularly acute at a time when the two countries were at war. Central to this antipathetical attitude to French history painting was hostility towards its chief protagonist during the Revolutionary and Napoleonic years, Jacques-Louis David.

David's direct political engagement in the Revolution and his role as regicide was seen by British artists to have tainted his art and to have worked directly against the moral and aesthetic 'universal' purity of the artist's mission as defined within the *Discourses*. Taking as his starting point the reaction to Benjamin Robert Haydon in 1841 to the possible 'contagion' of foreign schools upon national art, Vaughan elucidates the development of the British school and the role of history painting within it. Whilst Haydon's xenophobic responses to the revolutionary art of David were made at a time when the immediate threat of 'infection' in High Art came from the contemporary German history painters rather than the artists of Revolutionary and Napoleonic France, he nevertheless saw both as stemming from the same aberrant root. Vaughan examines the reservations which British artists had about David's art recognizing that this defensive reaction may actually have had a formative effect upon the development of artistic practice in Britain. The varying responses of artists such as Barry, West, Opie, Flaxman and Turner are contextualized in this way.

What emerges most clearly is the significant difference between what we might now take as the expression of Revolutionary principles in France and how they were heard in Britain. The last two essays in this collection are concerned with the wider structures that specific revolutionary acts engendered. Mitchell's essay 'Spectacular fears and popular arts: a view from the nineteenth century' is concerned with the resilience of the Marat–Corday myth within nineteenth-century histories of the French Revolution. This is traced through an investigation into the complex interplay between popular art-forms – such as James Gillray's political prints – with literary histories and the elevated language of history painting found in the dramatic displays of Madame Tussaud's waxworks museum and the Musée Gréven. In these deliberately blood-curdling public spectacles the keynote is a superficial historical veracity, politically coded, in which Marat and Corday became polarized as symbols of good and evil. Corday, representing the bourgeois individual hero(ine) was seen to be pitted against the disruptive power of the people embodied by the corrupt body of Marat, 'the enemy of the whole human race' as described in the *Biographical Sketches* which publicized Tussaud's travelling exhibition to Edinburgh of 1803. The Marat–Corday theme made a later appearance in the public arena of the Royal Academy exhibition of 1852 in the wake of the political uncertainty provoked by the revolutions in France of 1848–51. In this context Ward's painting *Charlotte Corday Going to Execution* was a timely reminder of the destruction of individual liberty which could result from the chaos of popular revolution. In the painting the juxtaposition of the feminine Corday against the de-feminized *sans-culotte* is a telling promotion of the feminine ideal which, like Blake's earlier watercolour *The Penance of Jane Shore* (1793), illustrates the ultimate victory of innocence and virtue over despotic power. Thus Marat, the embodiment of evil assassinated by 'the avenging angel' Corday, provided a potent instance of the intervention of Divine Providence for the nineteenth-century viewer. The image was a lasting one for, as Mitchell points out, the image of the dismembered Marat: 'embodied at primary level, a politically coded language, which maintained its significance during the revolutionary struggles of the nineteenth century'. The presentation of Marat–Corday in successive histories: Gironville (1798), Tussaud's *Memoirs* (1838) edited by Hervé, Lamartine (1847) and Bougeart (1865) alongside the visual imagery of the Salon paintings of David, Baudry and Weerts were cumulative, consolidating a very potent myth. The allusion to such works within the tableaux at the Musée Grévin appeared 'true' and immediate – far more so than any achieved by the language of High Art. When such forms were combined with the real, in this instance Marat's bathtub, an even greater sense of reportage resulted. As Mitchell concludes: 'Such spectacles of horror emerged from the fear the people's power inspired in the bourgeoisie which found its foremost expression in the nineteenth-century conception of the French Revolution as the "tyranny of the mob".'

Such emotive vocabulary has a visual equivalent in caricature and parody, but as Richard Wrigley's contribution to this collection makes plain, there is a fine division between the 'vandalism' of the mob and the political idealism that motivates iconoclasm. In his essay 'Breaking the code: interpreting French Revolutionary iconoclasm' he moves away from the traditional preoccupations of art historians with the problems of artistic production confined to a limited number of works to consider the wider use of the visual arts during the Revolutionary period in France. To do this he has focused upon the positive meanings of iconoclasm: 'because it requires us to make sense of the diverse forces which lay behind such moments of censure'. He thus revises the traditional view that during the Revolutionary period the old was unthinkingly destroyed to make way for the new in France, examining the historical evidence which leads us, for example, to the vivid conclusion that the Jacobin Republic, long seen as an instigator of disorder, in fact 'acted comprehensively to prevent the opportunistic depredations of vandalism'.

The term 'iconoclasm' can also have a more abstract reference than the usual associations with image-breaking normally allow. Wrigley favours this, as he finds in this instance plentiful traces of the traditions supposedly replaced. This new synthesis contains the old, *sous rature* as Derrida would now phrase it, where the erased still exists 'in dialogue' with the new, inclusive of impulses to conserve and thus appropriate as well as to displace.

The explosion of bicentenary activities in Britain during 1989 made abundantly clear the continuing and still vital nature of commemoration. It is usually the rule with anniversaries, however, that the past is approached in a ritual act of celebration and remembrance. We hope that this collection is a contribution to reassessment as well, so that in viewing the past we may also become acutely aware of the present.

BIBLIOGRAPHY

Burke, E. (1790) *Reflections on the Revolution in France and on the Proceedings in Certain Societies in London Relative to that Event*, ed. Conor Cruise O'Brien, Harmondsworth, Penguin Books, 1968.

Delacroix, E. (1932) *Journal de Eugene Delacroix*, ed. André Joubin, rev. edn, 3 vols, Paris, Plon.

Hume, D. (1965) 'Of the standard of taste' from *Of the Standard of Taste and Other Essays*, ed. John W. Lenz, Indianapolis, Bobbs-Merrill Corp. Inc.

Pope, W. B. (ed.) (1963) *The Diary of Benjamin Robert Haydon*, 5 vols, Cambridge, Mass., Harvard University Press.

Wark, R. (ed.) (1959) *The Discourses of Sir Joshua Reynolds*, rev. edn, San Marino, California, Huntington Library; New Haven and London, Yale University Press, 1981.

2

Parts of the body/parts of speech: some instances of dismemberment and healing

David Punter

I need to begin with two apologies or disclaimers. First, I am sorry about the ponderous length of my title. In fact, I shall not be saying a great deal about 'parts of speech', although I think there are connections there which would bear further elaboration; but 'parts of the body' and 'dismemberment and healing' are indeed themes to which I want to pay attention. Second, I am not entirely sure about the place of this essay in a collection addressing 'The French Revolution and British culture', because this raises complex theoretical issues. It is an essay which is about the French Revolution, and it is also about British culture; but the problem comes when one tries to single out the French Revolution as an isolated, privileged object of attention. I shall be talking about various writers, including Blake, Coleridge and Keats, and I shall be trying to describe some of their poetry as I see it; clearly, within the constellation from which that poetry emerges the French Revolution is writ large, as large, say, as the Second World War was to writers writing within it or some few years afterwards; but whether it was the major determining factor in specific structures of imagery is, as always, much harder to determine.

The problem towards which I am trying to point is essentially one of politics and psychology. It would be easy to assume that reactions to massive international events, and particularly revolutionary upheavals, can be modelled on cause and effect: a nearby monarch is executed, and certain consequences in the cultural sphere flow from that. But life is not so simple; and so events get modelled or traced onto other sources of, for example, alienation or anguish, and the products are always mixed. To use an imagery to which I shall return later, one could say that these products, mediated as they are through the pre-existence of language, are always *contaminated*, which is to say that patternings along the thin red line of the ego, or consciousness, are constantly at the mercy of that which is truly objective; which, following Jung, I take to be the unconscious (Jung 1957: 250).

This essay springs from work which I have been doing on the Romantic writers and their responses to historical events; and I want to begin by recapitulating some of that work, which is already available in other formats.[1] I will be brief. A lot of my work in recent years has been on Blake and on the Gothic novelists; and one persistent theme which can be identified in these writings which span the closing years of the eighteenth century is the theme of the body in fragments. I am well aware that this is a theme which has been approached by Lacan; but I have personally found it less useful to refer to his work on body-images than to Melanie Klein's work on the function of the part-object in the development of maturity.

Klein is not an easy thinker to understand; and the difficulty is compounded by her appalling prose style. Nevertheless, to put it at its simplest, what can be found in Klein, among other things, is an account of how consciousness is formed through a process of infant development which begins in a world of part-objects, and principally, of course, the breast. Klein goes on to say that healthy development of the individual depends on a process of transition whereby these part-objects come to be perceived as parts of a human whole; and if this does not happen, then various kinds of thwarting and frustration occur. (See, for example, Klein 1975a: 25–42, 1975b: 262–89.) Klein provides us with various examples of this thwarting at the individual level in her case histories, and particularly her case histories of children; but I would want to suggest examples where this thwarting has social consequences. One is the powerful and obvious instance of the kind of non-recognition of human wholeness which lies behind the pornography of the tabloid newspapers; another is the symbolism of the bomb and the nuclear missile. I take these to be examples writ large of arrested development, although it is probably fair to say that the perpetrators of these cultural and human distortions would not pay much attention to me if I told them that; and perhaps this sense in part accounts for the otherwise culpable timidity of psychoanalysts when they are faced with global evidences of their private speculations.

To return to the literature of the late eighteenth century: one thing which became obvious to me after reading Klein was that the numerous scattered part-objects of Gothic fiction are not meaningless, and I have worked specifically on Horace Walpole's *Castle of Otranto* (1764) in terms of the gigantized hands, helmets and other physical and physically related objects which strew the ground in this crude yet emblematic Gothic tale. The case of *Frankenstein* (1818) is equally obvious, but much more interesting; what we have here, seen from a Kleinian viewpoint, is a classic error of the instrumental psyche: the notion that one can take the part-objects (and you may remember the appalling description of the monster at the moment when he is brought to life) and put them into some kind of mechanical relation to each other without considering the real acts of affection and trust which infants perform when they are deciding that mummy's face really does hang together, and that daddy, even though

11

perhaps less omnipresent, nevertheless constitutes an integrated whole, even if to imagine it takes a great deal of psychic energy; for psychic energy goes mostly into filling in gaps in the presented account of the world.

I have thought also quite a bit about Blake, and particularly about the floating part-objects which populate his world: the spine and bones of Urizen; the floating blood-filled globes which seem to have a great deal to do with the bad breast in Kleinian terms, the breast which does not succour but holds the hovering threat of plague and damnation. Blake's version of the perfect body seems, I think, to be perpetually strung between two poles: on the one hand there is the perfect body of Albion, which is however always in the past; and then there is the task of rebuilding the body of the future from the alienated bits and pieces, the produce of Frankenstein's charnel-house, which happen to be, as it were, at hand. The fact that almost all of Blake's mythic figures have two names reflects this dual status: past integration and future integration are perpetually severed by the problems of the present, by the impossibility of bringing together the fragments of a shattered life.

I go on from these analyses to suggest that one factor among others which enhances this awareness, or inescapability, of fragmentation during these years is the French Revolution; but I would like to leave that hanging for the moment, and to turn instead to Coleridge's poem 'Christabel', written in 1797, which seems to me to be emblematic of these problems of the shattering of the body and of the difficulty of physical and historical integration which composed a significant part of the experience of the 'Romantic' writers.

In 'Christabel', we find motifs of sleeping and waking curiously inter-twined, figuring in a rebus along which inscriptions are ceaselessly chang-ing as the dream squirms through the processes of primary and secondary revision. These forms of revision are, of course, elided with the notion of 're-presentation' of historical material. Sir Leoline – the lion, the straight clear line of tradition, blood, all that is known along the line of the ego's secure integrity – is 'weak in health,/And may not well awakened be' (ll. 118–19), while Christabel and Geraldine explore together the night-world, the realm of the specular other, the curiosity of symbiosis. He has for his defence only the 'toothless mastiff bitch' (l. 7) who lies 'fast asleep' (l. 146) as, on another scene, as Freud puts it, the narrative of the 'mark' is played out, the narrative which thoroughly British Sir Leoline and his last remaining defender can know only in and as dream, as that which produces the 'angry moan' (l. 148) of disturbance and impotence in the sleep of the unguarding dog.

Yet, as Coleridge points out, who can 'know' the source of this disturb-ance: 'what can ail the mastiff bitch' (ll. 149, 153) (as, of course, it will also ail Keats's pale knight)? Who, indeed, is more asleep here, as Christabel and Geraldine pass the father's room, the space of a linear, undisturbed feudal history, freighted with armorial bearings, the sleep as in a crusader's death with the dog at the lion's feet; as they bypass the threshold of a weakened consciousness, it is *they* who are asleep, as 'still as death, with stifled breath' (l. 171), and so the problem of historical cognition enters into the hall of mirrors and generates a redoubled consciousness. The twined images of sickness and guarding, the guarding of British tradition against a dark maid, are thus again redoubled: Geraldine is she who 'ails' as she sees the ghost of Christabel's dead mother, who comes in dream to 'guard' Christabel against that which we must name as contamination, the contamination of the unconscious, the Typhoid Mary of the dream of revolution, palace upheaval.

It is the unlocation, the de-centredness, of the danger, the 'sickness unto death', which is here forced upon us in these tremors of the disordered psyche, and which prefigures the coming textual break, the failure of parts of speech and of speech itself, which is a break in the ordering of the ego's defences but also, as elsewhere in Coleridge, the break in textuality derived from the pressure of the unassimilable Other of the text.

And the break is not long in coming, for Christabel has passed under a double sign. The arrangements of patriarchy, the passing down of the Name-of-the-Father, are already, we may surmise, disrupted at the site of Christabel's absent mother; revolutionary behaviour is sanctioned in the inner world because there is a severing of the organic link. The advent of Geraldine comes as an intimation of the half-world into which the supremacy of the reasoned ego is passing, and thus it is that Christabel lies down to thoughts of 'weal and woe' (l. 239), and cannot sleep: 'so half-way from the bed she rose' (l. 242), prefiguring in turn the 'half-ness' which will be the vision of uncertainty offered by the new order represented by Geraldine:

> Her silken robe, and inner vest,
> Dropt to her feet, and full in view,
> Behold! her bosom and half her side –
> A sight to dream of, not to tell!
> O shield her! shield sweet Christabel!
>
> Yet Geraldine nor speaks nor stirs;
> Ah, what a stricken look was hers!
>
> (ll. 250–6)

Within this bedroom, which is itself disputed social territory, the property of the old knight and also Christabel's sanctuary, what occurs across this crucial textual juncture which is also a historical hiatus is a complexity of regard, of the look, in which is coded the problem of cognition. And this complexity interweaves further the theme of cultural guarding, through a knot in which the term 'guardianship' may be entered as the signifier of the 'holding for' and 'being held in thrall' which become key motifs in Romanticism.

For who is looking at Geraldine? The author, clearly, since he seizes this opportunity to apostrophize and to share his 'guardianship' of Christabel, and thus of a presumed innocence, with the reader. And yet in doing so, and in thrusting Christabel away from the contaminated heart of the poem, it is of course he who takes on the 'sacred' task of historical interpreter, and guarantees our immunity by risking the effects of contact with images welling from repressed contents, which might indeed have to do with the impotence of the masculinist *ancien régime*. And yet again in this imperative address, this call to arms against invasion, this changing of the guard, there is a further interweaving in the readerly position, for clearly the role on offer to us is one which is already filled, by the ghost of Christabel's mother; and we are thereby confronted proleptically with a banishment in the course of which we shall be made to feel Geraldine's power, and to experience also a dealing with this question of contamination by history; or by the objective; or by the unconscious.

How shall Geraldine pass on her mark, her 'différance'? Can these effects of the unconscious be controlled and consigned to the abyss which brought them forth, or will they, in their pressings up against us, mark us also?

What is at stake here is precisely a hovering on the brink of a palace revolution. It is under an oak that Geraldine claims to have been met by unknown assailants, under that tree which above all else during this period stood for British imperviousness to foreign influence and, of course, also for the raw material of British naval mastery. It is also under that oak that Geraldine says she encountered the lion; as it is in a world of solid English emblems and heraldry that the disturbances of Keats's narrative poems will enact their forebodings of a rotting away of the social foundations. The question for us becomes one of the boundary, in a redoubled sense: the contested boundary between ego and its self-created enemies, but mapped within a wider structure of invasion which takes on an orbit which necessarily crosses the English Channel and confronts us with the 'majesty' of a different revolution.

I have dwelt upon 'Christabel' at such length because it seems to me to be typical of a large subgenre of Romantic poetry which is concerned with history and, particularly, with the problem of how to overcome a historical break, the wider equivalent of a psychic trauma; and I take it that the incompleteness of the poem itself is further evidence of the historical difficulty which it faces. What is also important about 'Christabel', I think, is that it tries to confront this problematic area very much in terms of the body, but a body which is fragmented, stained, contaminated; a body which threatens a fearful contagion and is at the same time only half-complete.

And this emphasis on the damaged body is something which we can refer back to the rhetoric of the Revolution itself, on both sides of the Channel. Just to take a few examples: a famous address of the Jacobin clubs in 1793, at a time when Dumouriez was supposedly marching on Paris, refers to Paris as a prone and defenceless body to be protected, and speaks of the forces of reaction whose 'parricidal hands tear your vitals!' (Postgate 1962: 42). Burke, never afraid of an extravagant metaphor, writes in *Reflections on the Revolution in France* (1790) of the 'body' of Britain as so far uncorrupted by the French contagion; 'in England', he says,

> we have not yet been completely embowelled of our natural entrails . . . We have not been drawn and trussed, in order that we may be filled, like stuffed birds in a museum, with chaff and rags, and paltry, blurred shreds of paper about the rights of man.
>
> (Burke 1790: 182)

The imagery here is very close to that of *Frankenstein*; it concentrates on a body which is no longer informed, held together, by natural means but is instead reconstructed artificially. The contrast is between the body where the parts are linked organically together and the body which is animated though essentially dead; there are shades here of the peculiar mode of life in death which preoccupied Coleridge and the Gothic writers, and which had to do, I would say, with a fear of how the body might be reconstructed after an unassimilable break – a break the sense of which became, of course, intensified later by the execution of the French king.[2]

Burke makes the point even more clearly in a speech he gave on Army Estimates in February 1790, when he compares the French Revolution with the Glorious Revolution; or rather, when he at considerable length rebuts such a comparison, saying that in the case of the Glorious Revolution

> the state flourished. Instead of lying as dead, in a sort of trance, or exposed, as some others, in an epileptic fit, to the pity or derision of the world, for her wild, ridiculous, convulsive movements, impotent to every purpose but that of dashing out her brains against the pavement, Great Britain rose above the standard even of her former self.
>
> (Cobban 1960: 72)

The 'body' of France is thus conceived as animated by an 'epileptic', or galvanic, energy which is a savage parody of real life; the purposive organization and proportions of the live body have disappeared and been replaced by a meaningless activity in which the body-parts no longer correspond to an internal integration.

There are many parallel examples in Blake, which I have no room to discuss here, but just to take one: in 'Night the Eighth' of *Vala, or, the Four Zoas* (1795–1804) we find one of many instances where the dream of the

15

perfect body of Albion is 'haunted' by a different vision of the body, a vision which is carried on the identity and activity of Urizen. In this text, as in many others of Blake's, it is not the souls of the dead which come back to haunt us but the severed elements of the living body, the globes of blood, the hurtling bones, the senses floating on their unrooted filaments. Urizen tries to form a shape out of the shattered body, to put together these unaccommodated part-objects through investing them with a semblance of organic desire:

> Horrible hooks & nets he form'd, twisting the cords of iron
> And brass, & molten metals cast in hollow globes, & bor'd
> Tubes in petrific steel, & ramm'd combustibles, & wheels
> And chains & pullies fabricated all round the Heavens of Los
>
> (Night the Eighth, ll. 92–5)

This is, I think, easily recognizable as an exercise of phallic violence, filling the hollow globes (the breasts, the womb) with the fluids of masculine industry, of political planning, in order to expel the feminine, to 'tear bright Enitharmon/To the four winds' (ll. 98–9): under the guise of making the future, what occurs is an unmaking, but to Urizen's own horror this very unmaking, this further ravaging of the body, produces its own shape:

> Terrified & astonish'd, Urizen beheld the battle take a form
> Which he intended not: a Shadowy hermaphrodite, black & opake;
> The soldiers nam'd it Satan, but he was yet unform'd & vast.
> Hermaphroditic it at length became, hiding the Male
> Within as in a Tabernacle, Abominable, Deadly.
>
> (ll. 102–6)

So the attempted expulsion of the feminine encounters the forms of resistance, as it is twisted into a 'hiding' and implanting of the masculine, as the male is hidden literally in this text: Blake deleted 'male' in the second of these lines and wrote 'hermaphrodite' over it, the hermaphrodite standing precisely for the failure of real differentiation which occurs when the body has been reduced to the mere sum of its parts. But what Urizen cannot achieve in the way of narcissistic perfection occurs under a more diffuse agency later in *The Four Zoas*, when the terrifying 'globes', which carry also the signification of Vala, of the planet earth, of ecological integration, of maternal nourishment, and thus of the image which would allow the part-objects to cohere, are banished.

There are several ways in which one could pursue this line of imagery further. One would be through a close examination of Blake's 'The Mental Traveller' (*c.* 1803), which is in one sense a narrative of recurring revolution, but in which relationships through the affections are gradually replaced by hardened, crystallized simulacra of relationships, feelings are replaced by 'gems & gold' (l. 46), as revolution cuts off the body and

16

substitutes a graven image. Another path to be followed would be through French literature and the tradition of violence traced by Wallace Fowlie among others, leading eventually to, for example, Lautréamont, whose world is awash with body-parts and chimeras, some of them clearly historically related (Fowlie 1969: 20–36).

Turning back to the Revolution itself, we can trace in its actual culture and rhetoric an awareness of the problem of the historical break, the hiatus, and of the difficulty of reconstructing a body which will accommodate the future. For where are the materials for this future body to come from if the succession of the generations has been abolished, chopped off by execution and a symbolic castration of the authority of the father? 'A revolution', as one provincial revolutionary was saying in 1793,

> is never made by halves; it must either be total or it will abort. All the revolutions which history has conserved for memory as well as those that have been attempted in our time have failed because people wanted to square new laws with old customs and rule new institutions with old men . . . REVOLUTIONARY means outside of all forms and all rules; REVOLUTIONARY means that which affirms, consolidates the revolution, that which removes all the obstacles which impede its progress.
>
> (Hunt 1984: 27)

It is this thinking, of course, which has to regard the body of the past as a mere impediment to development; no image can be derived from it which we would want to imitate, and thus we are left in a world without mirrors, where the only available relationship to the body of the past is one half of the infant's reaction, based on punishment and a revenge which is unexplained because of the denial of the fantasized damage to the body of the parents which is at the root of the ambiguities of maturation (see Klein 1973: 65–93). At the political level, we have Robespierre's explanation of the positive purposes of the Terror:

> in this situation the first maxim of your policy must be to guide the people with reason and the people's enemies with terror. . . . Terror is nothing other than justice, prompt, severe, and inflexible; it is therefore an emanation of virtue. . . . Break the enemies of liberty with terror, and you will be justified as founders of the Republic. The government of the revolution is the despotism of liberty against tyranny.
>
> (Hunt 1984: 46)

None of the old men of Tiananmen Square could have put it better.

In more imagistic terms, what this brings us to is the series of attempts by the leaders of the Revolution to find a national image which would hold together this new body politic, embodied in, for example, David's

17

Hercules. One contemporary editor draws out the symbolism of the Hercules figure thus: because 'Homer called the kings of his time "mangeurs de peuples" [people-eaters], we will write on the figures of the French sans-culottes these words: "Le Peuple Mangeur de Rois" [The People, Eater of Kings]' (Hunt 1984: 108).

So Hercules stands in this context for a reversal of the process of body integration, as a symbol for vengeance and the severing of body-parts; but he is also much more than this. Lynn Hunt, in *Politics, Culture and Class in the French Revolution*, gives us a splendid analysis of the evolving meanings of the Hercules figure, which hinges not so much on the 'eater of kings' theme as on Hercules' role in gathering together the shattered fragments into a single massive body. In doing so she touches on the unavoidable problem of reification which accompanies the search for an overarching symbol:

> When they chose Hercules for the seal of the Republic, the radicals committed themselves to the view that some sort of representation of sovereignty was necessary. In Hercules they sought the most 'transparent' representation possible, a kind of diminishing point of representation. . . . It was an image-representation of the people provided by the people's representatives, and as such it inherently included the representatives' interpretation of the people. This implicit interpretive element threatened to reestablish in cultural form the very relationship of political authority . . . that the radicals were promising to abolish.
>
> (Hunt 1984: 99–100)

What Hunt is touching on here, looked at from another perspective, is the inevitable ambiguity of a process of healing through the image which succeeds a period marked by an internalized imagery of dismemberment. For healing to occur, there must be a vantage-point, a process of general acceptance, which presupposes a new fiction of the united body. But the danger is that this new, man-made and indeed insistently male body may, in another guise, be a monstrous creation like that of Urizen. Hunt quotes Fouché at the end of June 1793 describing the victory of the people of Paris over the Girondins in this fashion:

> the excess of oppression broke through the restraints on the people's indignation. A terrible cry made itself heard in the midst of this great city. The tocsin and the cannon of alarm awakened their patriotism, announcing that liberty was in danger, that there wasn't a moment to spare. Suddenly the forty-eight sections armed themselves and were transformed into an army. This formidable colossus is standing, he marches, he advances, he moves like Hercules, traversing the

Republic to exterminate this ferocious crusade that swore death to the people.

(Hunt 1984: 101)

And when the actual statue of Hercules first appeared in the festival of 10 August 1793, the president of the Convention explained it in terms which specifically remind us of the necessity of 'reuniting' and 'reattaching', as he put it, that which has been severed (Hunt 1984: 107).

But the revolutionaries themselves were aware of the dangers of hypostatization which accompanied the emergence of an image of physical healing and conjoining, and of course other experiments were tried, particularly around the evolution of a female image of Liberty. This was the theme of the famous Festival of Reason of November 1793, and it is interesting that the innovation of this festival which was most noted at the time was that, instead of dealing in statues, Liberty was represented by a living woman. A contemporary commentator glosses this thus:

> One wanted from the first moment to break the habit of every species of idolatry; we avoided putting in the place of the holy sacrament an inanimate image of liberty because vulgar minds might have misunderstood and substituted in place of the god of bread a god of stone . . . and this living woman, despite all the charms that embellished her, could not be deified by the ignorant, as would a statue of stone.
>
> Something which we must never tire of saying to the people is that liberty, reason, truth are only abstract beings. These are not gods, for properly speaking, they are parts of ourselves.

(Hunt 1984: 64–5)

This redefinition of the gods as parts of the self is interesting in itself (see Hillman 1979), reminding us as it does of Blake's similar comments in *The Marriage of Heaven and Hell* (c. 1790–3) and Hegel's evolving description of the perils of positivity in his early theological writings (see Punter 1982: 105–21). What is more important here though, I think, is the notion that in the form of the living woman contradictions can be healed and sealed; and perhaps, lurking behind this, there is also a sense that forgiveness may be obtained from the only source which is really able to provide that forgiveness, from the imagining of the perfect virgin mother. It is incidentally the case that the idea behind the selection of actual women to represent Liberty in various provincial festivals was supposed to be one of 'typicality'; in fact, it seems as though the selection process rapidly turned into a kind of beauty contest, which is obviously significant in terms of superficial gender relations, but may also have a bearing on the underlying requirement of a 'perfect body', healed of all flaws and faults, to represent the newly

19

emergent State and at the same time to absolve us of the consequences of our envious attacks on the mother. (See Klein 1961: 157–61.)

It is worth also noticing that some of the British political rhetoric, particularly in the early years of enthusiasm for the Revolution, is cast in parallel terms. One example would be from a letter to Burke written in 1791 by Sir Brooke Boothby, in which he speaks of how:

> Every humane mind will anticipate with heart-felt satisfaction the approach of that day when the race of despots shall have disappeared from the face of the earth; and when, by their rusty coins and mutilated statues, they shall be known to have existed, it shall be said of them as of the giants of old, 'in those days there were tyrants in the land'. . . . But let us turn . . . to the most magnificent spectacle that has ever presented itself to the human eye. A great and generous nation, animated with one soul, rising up as one man to demand the restitution of their natural rights.
>
> (Cobban 1960: 91)

This rhetoric of the fallen giants of old can be immediately paralleled in Shelley, in 'Ozymandias' (1817) and also in the 'Ode to Liberty' (1820) and in parts of *Prometheus Unbound* (1819). The matter of being 'animated with one soul' is, as we have seen, much more problematic.

For the French revolutionaries, the killing of the father-king and his replacement by a female symbol was often quite explicit; there is, for example, a proclamation of 1794 from the department of the Gers which says that 'the French people wants to be and must be only a family of brothers, equally cherished and protected by their common mother' (Hunt 1984: 32). The psychoanalytic signification of this in terms of the primal horde is perhaps too obvious to go into, and the possibility of Oedipal conflict thus set up took, of course, an equally obvious historical route. What would perhaps be more interesting to trace would be the connections between this distortion of the model of the family-in-the-mind and the actual fate of the family under revolutionary circumstances, since one effect of the chaos and terror was clearly to undermine the protective role previously assumed to be an adjunct of the 'head of the family' (cf. Agulhon 1981: 11–37).

We may turn again at this point to Blake. Hunt points out that in the early years of the Revolution there was a general adherence to what we might call the rhetorical structure of comedy; in other words, the fantasized outcome of current discord was taken to be reconciliation, particularly between the king-father and the brother-sons. Naturally, with the execution of the King, this supposed reconciliation became somewhat less tenable, and lines of the imagination which had previously been convergent inevitably opened themselves to the possibility of divergence. We can see the difficulties of Blake's plots, especially in the longer and darker Prophetic

Books, as an endless series of wrestlings with the problems thus created. Although he evolved many different myths to accommodate it, Blake is not in doubt about the sparking event of the Fall, which consisted of a usurpation of power, a distortion of the body of the 'giant man' Albion through hubris on the part, usually, of Urizen, the Prince of Light. But what the outcome will be of the consequent battles is far less clear. *The Four Zoas*, which deals with the struggles of the primal horde in great detail, comes to no resolution; indeed, it is a poem which cannot even take on a definitive shape. One reason for this is that in order to have such a shape, it would have to posit the return to a perfect body, wherein the various senses and faculties represented by the mythic figures would resume or re-invent a harmony; but this question returns us to the problem of Hercules, for that new harmony must have a bodily organization and an order, and to define this organization always runs the risk of re-inventing the king-father, reinstating precisely the shape of authority which the revolution has deconstructed.

So healing, for Blake, is always deferred; and it is interesting to look at some of the other thinking about this process which was around at the time. Some of the ambiguities come out usefully in passages from Schiller where he talks, as he often does, of the necessity for a healing process, a process of reharmonization, which must none the less look back to the giants of the past, the Greeks, for its model. But as has been pointed out about Schiller's conception of the artist, there is still a fatal contradiction which cannot be properly sealed: on the one hand, the writer seeks 'the healing of his own or his society's secret and patent wounds', but on the other,

> the effect of the sentimental artist is not joy and peace, but tension, conflict with nature or society, insatiable craving, the notorious neuroses of the modern age, with its troubled spirits, its martyrs, fanatics and rebels, and its angry, bullying subversive preachers . . . offering not peace but a sword.

Certainly Orc, in Blake, comes bearing a sword; he also comes bearing in his own partial body all the lines of fracture and breakdown which characterize the moment of revolutionary energy, and how this is to be accommodated into a peaceful afterlife remains insoluble without the invocation of a *deus ex machina*; and without also the submergence of all 'différance' in the newly perfect female body of Jerusalem.

Southey, in 1797, was more intransigent on the problem of healing: 'there was a time', he writes, 'when I believed in the persuadability of man, and had the mania of man-mending. Experience has taught me better. . . . The ablest physician can do little in the great lazar house of society; it is a pest-house that infects all within its atmosphere' (Cobban 1960: 376). I think that to get further with this problem of healing, the

21

obvious place to turn is to Keats, the poet-healer. In Keats, we may say, we can find the figure of Narcissus who ignores and covers his wounds in the specular moves of perfection; against him we may range the image of Hephaestos, whose wound is precisely the emblematic guarantor of creative power. The wound of the pale knight, who is also the grounded pale rider, is the outcome and recognition of the impossibility of the search for sources, the knowledge, coded as it is, of the fantasies which prevail in and around the 'elfin grot',[3] which is the substantial and mythic retreat which covers the perpetually unacceptable absence of the womb. And this leads us to Keats's reflexivity about the effects of narcissism in 'Lamia' (1819), where indeed the touch of 'cold philosophy' (l. 230)

> will clip an angel's wings,
> Conquer all mysteries by rule and line,
> Empty the haunted air, and gnomed mine –
> Unweave a rainbow, as it erewhile made
> The tender-person'd Lamia melt into a shade.
>
> (ll. 234–8)

Philosophy has no power to heal:

> On the high couch he lay! his friends came round –
> Supported him – no pulse, or breath they found,
> And, in its marriage robe, the heavy body wound.
>
> (ll. 309–11)

For Keats, I would say, the possibility of healing merges into the imagery of glutting and satiation, whereby the kind of surgical precision which might be necessary to reform the tubercular body disappears into the swoon in which personal and historical pain can be forgotten. The body reappears in Keats in all its material wealth, but, I would say, still strangely without organization, instead at the mercy of its own joyous welter of sense-impressions, a body perfected only in the infantile sense and thus returned to the premature condition before the Fall rather than engaging with the problem of the organization of innocence which so preoccupied many of the Romantics.

These problems of the body to which I have alluded can be spoken of in another way which we may also derive from the psychoanalysts; for in speaking of the incarnate myths of Hercules and Liberty, what we are also speaking of is a problem of containment. The execution of the king, the removal of parental authority, opens up a field in which indeed liberty is possible but cannot be readily differentiated from anarchy; what paradoxically disappears at the same time is the possibility of creating situations safe enough for the work of healing and development to proceed. Thus the rage of the child, that the rejection of authority in the outer world entails a breakdown in the order of the inner world such that the proffered freedom remains forever elusive because all measure disappears as the tension with the enclosing outer is shed.[4]

For further exploration of these problems, again a locus would be in Blake, this time in the *Songs of Innocence and of Experience* wherein, over the years leading up to 1794, we find precisely an agonizing about the relations between inner and outer, such that there is a transplantation of freedom and confinement.[5] In Innocence, the 'pen' becomes the lamb's familiar and protecting realm, variously represented as a 'nest' (in 'Night'), an 'Angel-guarded bed' (in 'A Dream') and a 'green' (in 'The Ecchoing Green' and 'Nurse's Song'). Here there is comfort and security, a containment which safely wards off the outer world, which is itself imaged as dangerous and painful, associated with 'wolves and tygers' ('Night'), a 'lonely fen' (as in 'The Little Boy Found') and a 'tangled' waste wherein one becomes lost, again as in 'A Dream'.

But in Experience this familiar world of enclosure begins to look dangerous, diseased or deceptive and the unknown outer becomes enticing and attractive. In 'The Tyger', for example, the creatures from the night-forest may be 'fearful' but they are also beautiful and bright, whereas the enclosure is now a prison, a place of 'mind-forg'd manacles' ('London'); the bed of roses is 'sick'.

The complexity of Blake's analysis is such that it is not easy to tell in what direction, historically or politically, this structure points. Certainly excessive trust in unvalidated inner truth and excessive attraction to the Orcian wild are both posited as dangers to personality development in other areas of Blake's *oeuvre*; here, though, I think the emphasis is on tensions in the body-image, between the body as that which encloses and protects its own mental contents and the body which opens those contents to damage through its own emotional and physical vulnerability. The perfect body can then only be conceived as an interface, as precisely the primary mode of mediation between tyger and lamb, rather than as the all enveloping sensuous manifold which we find in Keats.

Further development of this stream of imagery during the period would also return us, I think, to the extraordinary symbolic power of the Fall of the Bastille; the letting out into the world of a set of contents whose interpretation is vexed to the present day. Murderers, counterfeiters and a sadist, according to the sources, were the few who proved to be inside the Bastille; but what did they represent? Not crime, certainly, but perhaps incarceration in its Romantic, later to be Byronic, mode; all those parts of experience which may be shut away but which return to haunt us.

On that note, I want to conclude with a brief passage from Helen Maria Williams's *Letters Containing a Sketch of the Politics of France* of 1795. She says:

> In the first days of the Revolution, when Liberty and Property went
> hand-in-hand together, what a moral revolution was instantly effected

throughout Europe, by the sublime and immortal principles which this great change seemed about to introduce into government! But what eternal regrets must the lovers of liberty feel, that her cause should have fallen into the hands of monsters, ignorant of her charms, by whom she has been transformed into a fury, who, brandishing her snaky whips and torches, has enlarged the limits of wickedness and driven us back into regions of guilt hitherto unknown!

(Cobban 1960: 368)

What we have here in Kleinian terms is a spectacular image of the bad mother; the mother who seemed to promise freedom but ends by reinforcing our sense of guilt about the freedom which we long to enjoy. Here the world of 'innocent' exploration of the versatility of the body has been submerged in the punishing moralities of a burdensome adulthood; what proffered itself as a path to maturity has remained entangled in the mire of ancient fears and ambiguous revenges. Dismemberment remains as a dreadful possibility to haunt us, and what is worse it is precisely the figure of forgiveness which has now revealed itself in its 'true' colours as a permanent reminder of the wound, and as the mark on history which will not go away however much we might want to seal ourselves off from the contamination of revolt.

NOTES

1 See, for example, Punter 1989: 1–27 and Punter 1985: 313–34. Since this paper was delivered, these and other thoughts have been gathered together in Punter 1990.
2 I have chosen to write up this paper in very much the form in which it was originally delivered, although various points were made in discussion afterwards. The most important of these, raised by Mary Hamer, concerned the extent to which I concentrate on the symbolism of the execution of the king rather than the queen, and I accept that this is a matter which requires further thought.
3 Keats, 'La Belle Dame Sans Merci', l. 29.
4 See, for example, Milner 1987: 21–38.
5 The following remarks are an abbreviated version of the perceptive analysis in Swingle 1987: 140–1.

BIBLIOGRAPHY

Agulhon, M. (1981) *Marianne into Battle: Republican Imagery and Symbolism in France, 1789–1880*, trans. Janet Lloyd, Cambridge, Cambridge University Press.
Burke, E. (1790), *Reflections on the Revolution in France*, ed. Conor Cruise O'Brien, Harmondsworth, Penguin, 1968.
Cobban, A. (ed.) (1960) *The Debate on the French Revolution 1789–1800*, London, Black.
Fowlie, W. (1969) *Climate of Violence: The French Literary Tradition from Baudelaire to the Present*, London, Secker & Warburg.
Hillman, J. (1979) *The Dream and the Underworld*, New York, Harper & Row.

Hunt, L. (1984) *Politics, Culture, and Class in the French Revolution*, Berkeley, California, University of California Press.

Jung, C. G. (1957) 'The undiscovered self (present and future)', in *The Collected Works of C. G. Jung*, volume 10, ed. Herbert Read, Michael Fordham and Gerhard Adler, 20 vols, London, Routledge & Kegan Paul, 1953–72: 245–305.

Klein, M. (1961) *Narrative of a Child Analysis*, London, Hogarth Press and The Institute of Psycho-Analysis.

—— (1973) 'An obsessional neurosis in a six-year-old girl', in *The Psycho-Analysis of Children*, London, Hogarth Press: 35–57.

—— (1975a) 'On the Theory of Anxiety and Guilt', in *Envy and Gratitude, and Other Works 1946–1963*, London, Hogarth Press: 25–42.

—— (1975b) 'A contribution to the psychogenesis of manic-depressive states', in *Love, Guilt and Reparation, and Other Works 1921–1945*, London, Hogarth Press: 262–89.

Milner, M. (1987) 'A suicidal symptom in a child of 3', in *The Suppressed Madness of Sane Men*, London, Tavistock.

Postgate, R. W. (1962) 'Address of the Jacobins Club, dated April 13, 1793', in *Revolution from 1789 to 1906*, ed. R. W. Postgate, New York, Harper & Row: 41–3.

Punter, David (1982) *Blake, Hegel and Dialectic*, Amsterdam, Rodopi.

—— (1985) 'The sign of Blake', *Criticism* XXVI (4): 313–34.

—— (1989) 'Narrative and psychology in Gothic fiction', in *Gothic Fictions: Prohibition/Transgression*, ed. Kenneth W. Graham, New York, AMS Press: 1–27.

—— (1990) *The Romantic Unconscious: A Study in Narcissism and Patriarchy*, London and New York, Harvester.

Swingle, L. J. (1987) *The Obstinate Questionings of English Romanticism*, Baton Rouge, Louisiana State University Press.

3

Reflections of excess: *Frankenstein*, the French Revolution and monstrosity

Fred Botting

This essay examines the appearance and effect of monsters in British political positions immediately after the French Revolution and analyses some of their reverberations in *Frankenstein*. The project, however, is not one that simply tries to identify *Frankenstein*'s meaning in terms of British exchanges concerned with the French Revolution, it also regards *Frankenstein* as a novel that provides reflections on, as much as reflections of, revolutionary and counter-revolutionary texts. Focusing on the repeated appearances of the monster metaphor, the essay attempts to identify some of the implications of the monster's diverse and prolific animations within different political and literary positions.

At once necessary and terribly dangerous, the figure of the monster takes on a multitude of different forms and functions. Its effects are multiple also: it defines the limits of a position as a threat to the continued existence of that position. Constructed as a figure of transgression, an other that marks out the boundaries of discourse, the monster also begins to disclose internal contradictions within discursive frameworks. Produced by positions that cannot contain them, monsters activate an excessive force which continually poses a challenge to unity, singularity and stability, a threat that demands repeated attempts to reconstitute boundaries from within. The friction involved in this internal and external confrontation, however, engenders a proliferation of monsters, an excess that encourages interrogations and transformations which upset the stability and unity of yet more limits and distinctions. The excess marked by various forms of monstrosity can be described loosely, and perhaps monstrously, as a force of difference between opposed poles that questions the privileged status one pole attempts to sustain by disclosing its dependence on its other. Undermining the system which holds distinctions in place, the tension poses further questions and releases further movements of difference. Monsters are thus produced by and also reveal inherent instabilities: refusing to remain in a fixed space of exclusion or to be contained at the margins of any one position, they pose a permanently shifting challenge and produce the possibility of significant transformations. The excess that is constructed by various positions in order to define their limits also works upon and within them, inhabiting and undermining the fixity of their boundaries.

Frankenstein is not only about the manufacture of a monster. It is, as many critics have noted, a monster itself. Like the natural and unnatural inhuman human life created by Frankenstein out of pieces from various corpses, the novel is composed from an extensive literary corpus: direct citations of Romantic poetry, *Paradise Lost* and myths of Prometheus, references to many literary, philosophical and historical texts, events and figures, as well as traces of many others, all distinguish the novel as an 'assemblage' of fragments, a disunified text that subverts the possibility and implications of textual and semantic coherence. Indeed, the phrase 'my hideous progeny' which the author's 1831 'Introduction' to the novel uses to describe both book and monster, not only equates the two, but draws the author into the scene of commentary and repetition by suggesting a parallel between the writer's and Frankenstein's projects, as well as injecting a note of difference.[1] Unlike Frankenstein, who tries to subject his creation to his will, Mary Shelley makes no such tyrannical gesture: she bids her text-monster farewell and hopes it might 'go forth and prosper' (10). Ironically her creation obeys, engendering a multitude of monsters and mythical monstrosities on the stage, in cinemas and in books.

Many of these reappearances and reproductions of *Frankenstein* are conservatively recuperated in popular culture and mythology, especially in their silencing of the monster, as Chris Baldick argues in his book, *In Frankenstein's Shadow*. For Baldick (1987: 62), the 'eloquent invisibility' of the monster ensures its more radical survival in the liberal confines of literary criticism. Yet, even in the profusion of literary meanings that give form and identity to the monster, strategies of limitation and exclusion still seem to function to contain the interrogative excess of monstrosity as it reflects on all institutions, literary criticism included.

Frankenstein, distinguished by Baldick from its reproductions by means of an opposition of literary tradition and popular culture, does not, however, respect such boundaries since, for many, it is hardly 'literature' at all. Sensational Gothic fiction or a clumsy Romantic novel (Bloom 1965: 613), a 'minor work' (Norman 1970: 408) that is 'not one of the living novels of the world' (Glynn Grylls 1938: 320), *Frankenstein* occupies an unstable place on the boundaries that separate 'literature' and its values from second-rate fiction. It is a monstrous space, itself subject to the excessive effects of monstrosity. For Deleuze and Guattari (1981: 50) literature is also a kind of monster, an 'assemblage'. Composed of disjunctive parts and fragments, 'literature' forms an amalgam of multiplicitous and heterogeneous positions, a form of writing that combines elements and upsets their autonomy, blurring and questioning the artificial distinctions that construct its meaning.

In this context of excess and transgression, it would be presumptuous

27

indeed to adopt a position outside the play of those forces, a position that refuses to acknowledge its own investments, involvements and interests in the texts it reads. It would also be foolish since it would mark another attempt to restrict or recuperate the excessive and dangerous movements of difference that it analyses and is affected by, another Frankensteinian attempt at mastery perhaps. Instead, the theoretical position adopted here, a product of a different French revolution – the revolutions of structuralism and post-structuralism, forms something of a monster itself. As an amalgam or 'assemblage' of disparate elements drawn from a number of French theorists, this paper is situated along lines of intersection and divergence between several theoretical positions. Partially formed in the diverse conjunctions of and differences between various theories, the project attempts, not to restrict or to confine, but to open up possibilities and inhabit a frictional position that both resists closure and produces, in its engagements with revolutions and monsters, questions concerning the differences and power relations involved in politics, literature, theory and reading itself.

Of the multiple and diverse theoretical utterances that have informed this paper, a few can be specified for their direct bearings upon this account of *Frankenstein* and the French Revolution. In the essays 'Preface to Transgression' and 'Language to Infinity', Michel Foucault (1977a, 1977b) considers the way that language displays its monstrous potential to both set and transgress limits and engender a dangerous profusion of self-reflection and doubling. There are certain similarities between Foucault's account of writing and Derrida's description of deconstruction, in 'Signature Event Context', as a 'double gesture, a double science, a double writing'. The doubling effects of deconstruction demand a transgression of the limits imposed on writing by hierarchical binary oppositions: deconstruction must 'put into practice a *reversal* of the classical opposition *and* a general *displacement* of the system' (Derrida 1977: 195). Double gestures thus disturb the stability of oppositions by activating the differences between one pole and its other.

For Jacques Lacan, the construction of subjectivity in language also involves relations of doubling: identifying with its specular image in the mirror, identifying with the Other of language, the subject exists only in relations of difference and desire. Determined by the laws of the symbolic order, the subject is constructed by the effects of signification and is also subject to the shifts, the displacements of desire, within the system of differences that is language (Lacan 1972, 1977a, 1977b). Constituting the limits of subjectivity and meaning, the differences and desires at work in language also transgress and exceed those limits. In and between language and theory, then, a space of reflections appears in a fragmented, mirrored, doubled and interrogative form, a space from which meanings multiply. A similar position is disclosed by the monsters that appear in revolutionary controversies and in *Frankenstein*. From this space of reflections, this position of doubling and monstrosity, it becomes possible to generate different readings of Burke's *Reflections*, radical responses to it and *Frankenstein*'s monsters and doubles.

Burke's *Reflections on the Revolution in France* (1790) exemplifies the diffractions involved in processes of reflection: his text casts its rather partial light on events in France and reflects back on the situation in England and upon its own modes of representation. Monsters proliferate among these reflections. Already a conventional image of the enraged and riotous mob, monsters are also used to signify the French National Assembly's destructive capacity and the Constitution of Republican France (see Burke 1790: 279–80, 313). This written document is opposed to the unwritten 'constitution' of 1688, which Burke sets up as the guardian of English liberty, tradition and good order. Indeed, everything in France is constructed as England's other: 'out of nature', irrational, irreligious and illegitimate, the affairs of France form a 'monstrous fiction' that displays the rightness of English 'good order' as well as the obvious truth of Burke's case (Burke 1790: 124).

This is a most traditional deployment of monstrosity, one which, as Chris Baldick (1987: 10–11), following Foucault, observes, stages vice in order to vindicate virtue, presenting a cautionary tale that warns against the horrors of transgression. The 'monstrous tragi-comic scene' performed in France describes a state of chaos, of revolving and uncontrollable extremes. In Burke's words, 'the most opposite passions necessarily succeed, and sometimes mix with each other in the mind; alternate contempt and indignation; alternate laughter and tears; alternate scorn and horror' (Burke 1790: 92–3). Revolutionary France, moreover, exists as a monstrous fiction in several other senses. It is the invention of 'literary caballers and intriguing philosophers', revolutionary alchemists whose evil imaginations conjure up and attempt to realize their own extreme and perverse ambitions (Burke 1790: 93). Exposing the deceptions of such conspirators in France and England, Burke attempts to forestall revolution in Britain, a revolution advocated publicly in the monstrous fictions of radicals, like Richard Price, that identify with the revolutionary slogans of France.

The monsters constructed in Burke's text as figures that affirm the presence and value of good order in England betray a certain anxiety. Instead of affirming good order they expound the need for, and thus lack of, good order. Burke's final metaphor is telling in this respect. His book, he humbly admits, comes from one who 'when the equipoise of the vessel in which he sails, may be endangered by overloading it upon one side, is desirous of carrying the small weight of his reasons to that which may preserve its equipoise' (Burke 1790: 377). The ship of State in which he sails is already unstable, however, already under threat from forces which are beginning to exceed the bounds of liberal reason. To follow Stephen Blakemore's (1988) analysis of Burke's texts as writings deeply concerned about the maintenance of linguistic propriety and decorum within traditional orders of meaning, the ship might also be interpreted as a figure of conventional discourse upset by radical and revolutionary contestations and appropriations of meaning. These struggles raise the danger of the ship being cast adrift in chaotic seas of signification. In the name of good order, reason, nature, liberty and tradition, Burke's text becomes another monstrous fiction engaged in, and seriously affected by, the 'revolution in sentiments, manners and moral opinions' that it sets out to control (Burke 1790: 175).

Furthermore, the project of preserving 'equipoise' has the opposite effect. Instead of quelling resistance and dissent, the *Reflections* provoked a great many vigorous and diverse responses, responses that extended, rather than contained, the dangerous proliferation of monsters. In his reply to Burke in *The Rights of Man* (1792), Paine attacks the former's 'marvellous and monstrous' method and goes on to criticize the system Burke defends, describing, in the process, the aristocracy as a monster (see Paine 1791–2: 202, 229). From radical perspectives, it is the social system that bears the responsibility for creating monsters. In her response to Burke in *A Vindication of the Rights of Men* (1790), Mary Wollstonecraft castigates the system of hereditary property for making monsters of humans: 'man', she states, 'has been changed into an artificial monster by the station in which he was born' (quoted in Butler 1984: 72–3). For William Godwin, writing a few years later, the 'monstrous edifice' of government by courts and ministers 'will always be found supported by all the various instruments for perverting the human character' (Godwin 1985: 439).

The system that defines its own limits in the construction of monsters thus has its terms challenged and reversed. Burke, a maker of monsters and a supporter of the system that creates them, is made monstrous himself. In this battle of meanings, the monster functions as a double-edged weapon and continues to reproduce at an enormous rate. The *New Annual Register* for 1794 stated that 'the whole system of insurrection lay in the monstrous doctrine of the Rights of Man, and the Corresponding Society composed of the meanest and most despicable of people'.[2] Later, the followers of Godwin and Wollstonecraft were described by the *Anti-Jacobin Review* as the 'spawn of the monster'.[3] As an awful threat that was still at large, disseminating among radical writings, the designation of monsters legitimates their exclusion or suppression as figures dangerously opposed to national unity.

The excessive threat of the French Revolution appears in its capacity to engender other revolutions. Indeed, the word 'revolution', Ronald Paulson argues, underwent a significant change to mean an inversion, a half, or 180 degree, turn (Paulson 1983: 49–50). These turns initiate a momentum that shifts meanings from one pole to the other in a similar manner to the way that the monsters created by Burke challenged the authority of his order of meaning and appropriated and transformed his terms: monster-makers become monstrous in the very act of creating monsters or in the resistance of the monsters they create. In turn, systems of authority attempt to return defiant radicals to their monstrous place. Like the Revolution in France which, in the name of liberty, overthrew tyranny only to repeat tyrannical practices, the revolving momentum of monsters and monster-makers releases forces that exceed the determining limits of binary oppositions and raise the possibility of other positions.

Godwin, for example, rejects the need for any form of government other than rational and individual responsibility in the same text in which he rejects revolution as a useful means of establishing a free, benevolent and just society: 'revolutions', he contends, 'are the produce of passion, not sober and tranquil reason' (Godwin 1985: 252). But, unable to escape the violent and repressive logic of opposition that produces the polarizations of revolution in the name of some fixed and transcendent principle, Godwin's argument returns to bellicose binary distinctions: 'truth will bring down all her forces, mankind will be her army, and oppression, injustice, monarchy and vice, will tumble into a common ruin' (Godwin 1985: 462). The sober and tranquil language of reason cedes to the passionately rhetorical mode of prophetic and apocalyptic vision. Truth constitutes the authority and promise of victory as well as the cause of conflict, the ultimate booty as well as the bugle that begins the battle. Passion returns within the discourse of divine reason and revolutions rotate still more.

The monster, a figure constructed to legitimate the exclusion or suppression of others, betrays their necessity and fecundity. Demarcating the limits of a position, monsters, at the same time, possess the power to interrogate and transgress all limits.

The excessive momentum of revolution and monster-making powerfully affects and is also transformed by *Frankenstein*. This focus on monstrosity and excess necessarily precludes detailed consideration of other readings of the novel's relation to the French Revolution by Ronald Paulson, Lee Sterrenburg and Chris Baldick. Offering many important insights into the relationship between *Frankenstein* and the French Revolution, these critics, particularly Paulson and Sterrenburg, seem to identify a unity too firmly in the conjunction of text, history and biography through recourse to the name of the author. Divided between Burkean conservatism and her family's radicalism, between love and political differences, it is the personal pole that is privileged in Paulson's and Sterrenburg's accounts. These readings are thus forced to contain or exclude the many excesses that surround *Frankenstein*'s production. The multiplicitous impact of the French Revolution, its polarization and dispersion of political positions, as well as the fascinating but complicated biographical archive surrounding Mary

Shelley, all contribute to an overdetermined set of pretexts for the novel and its interpretations.

Frankenstein does not resolve these contradictions and intricate interconnections, but extends and entangles them. Echoes of British Revolutionary debates abound. Victor Frankenstein is educated at Ingolstadt, a town that is also the birthplace of the Illuminati, the secret society founded by Adam Weishaupt. The Illuminati, the Abbé Barruel argues in his conservative account of the French Revolution, were the conspirators responsible for revolutionary agitations. Frankenstein also embodies Burke's fear of revolutionary alchemists or Enlightenment philosophers whose dangerous experiments upset all order by releasing dark and chaotic forces of evil. The monster forms the hideous result, a revolutionary mob that cuts a wake of terror across Europe.

But the monster also speaks, not only to challenge his creator's authority and question unjust human practices, but to claim recognition and human kindness. His argument, that 'misery made me a fiend' (100), echoes the radical descriptions of monsters as socially produced creatures. In opposing Frankenstein, then, the resistance of the monster constructs a relationship that doubles the polemics of Burke and the radicals, and invites a reading in which Frankenstein can be seen, not as a dangerous radical philosopher, but as a pastiche, or even a parody, of paranoid Burkean fictions. *Frankenstein*'s heterogeneous assembly of political positions makes many identifications possible, but refuses to specify a single, recognizable and dominant viewpoint. This is the significant and divergent aspect of *Frankenstein*'s account of the French Revolution. Replaying and extending the structures of reversal that emerge in revolutionary polemics, the novel also represents their totalizing desires, their invocations of some transcendent unity, whether it be Burkean good order or Godwinian rational truth.

Robert Walton, the explorer whose letters begin the novel, sets out to discover the North Pole and the 'wondrous power that attracts the needle' so that he 'may regulate a thousand celestial observations' and 'render their seeming eccentricities consistent for ever' (16). The imagined unity of this world of 'eternal light' excites Walton's aspirations. Victor Frankenstein, similarly, aspires to metaphysical knowledge and imagines he can attain the unity and presence of a singular and privileged pole of significance beyond the bounds of binary oppositions:

> Life and death appeared to me ideal bounds, which I should first break through, and pour a torrent of light into our dark world. A new species would bless me as its creator and source; many happy and excellent natures would owe their being to me. No father could claim the gratitude of his child so completely as I should deserve theirs.

(54)

Transcending human constraints, the superhuman creator envisages a world beyond difference in which his 'new species' exists only to adore the master.

But the others – death, darkness, women, bodies – on which Frankenstein depends in order to steal the secrets of nature and succeed in his illumination of life in full, are not effaced: 'to examine the causes of life', Frankenstein comments, 'we must first have recourse to death' (51). In conjunction with many of the others Victor's project aimed to efface, like women, bodies, sexuality and darkness, death returns with a vengeance in the dream that follows the animation of the monster. As he wakes from his disturbing sleep of dreams, the creator sees the horrible form of his creation approaching him and he flees from this inverted image of his aspirations.

Frankenstein has not achieved the fullness of life and illumination that he projected: he has revitalized the forces of otherness which he hoped to efface. The creature he designed to be beautiful is realized as an ugly and repulsive being. But then how could anything have lived up to the exorbitant ideals of the creator's imagination? Frankenstein's totalizing dream discovers its dependence on systems of difference as the human creator encounters the necessity of monstrosity when, waking from his dream, he repeats the convulsive physical agitations that announced the first stirrings of life in the monster. One turns into other; dreams become nightmares: 'dreams that had been my food and pleasant rest for so long a space were now become a hell to me; and the change was so rapid, the overthrow so complete!' (58–9). This subjective upheaval is described in terms of a revolution: it is Frankenstein's first revolution.

The momentum inaugurated by this overturning is not arrested, but rolls on through the course of the novel in an excessive play of differences that blurs all distinctions and questions all limits. In the next encounter between Frankenstein and monster, in the sublime setting of the Alps, more reversals occur: forced to be a listener, the creator is subjected to the monster's demands for a mate that conclude the latter's story. The shift in their relationship is declared, after Frankenstein has destroyed the half-finished female creature, when the monster exclaims: 'you are my creator, but I am your master; – obey!' (167). Ironically, the creator has just performed an act of resistance.

The ensuing struggle involves both figures in a tense dialectic in which they both try negatively to affirm their lost authority: Frankenstein vows to kill his creation, while the monster destroys almost all the creator's friends and relations. The subsequent confused and mutually sustaining pursuit speeds the novel to an end in which the life-giver attempts to persuade Walton to continue his destructive quest but fails and dies, while the creation announces his intention to kill himself on a funeral pyre at the pole in the only act of self-possession available to him. Fire amid ice, light in darkness, with this promised extinction of the first and last of a new species the novel ends in an entangled assembly of opposites. The hopes of discovering a world of 'eternal light' that began the novel have been overturned by the end, as Walton, reluctantly and disappointedly returning home, gazes at the monster becoming 'lost in darkness and distance' (223).

Yet the novel does not simply describe the collapse of one pole of significance into its other, light into dark, life into death, creation into destruction, it also questions the tensions between oppositional limits and engenders different positions, positions that can criticize and subvert, challenge and transform. From his position as a voyeur on the De Lacey family, the monster learns about the arbitrary system of differences called language; he learns about gender differentiation and learns that humans have more than one identity, since signifiers have different effects. From this position, within and yet outside human orders, he is able to expose the inhumanity of human codes and values since they are the very things that define him as a monster.

An artificial yet natural man, alive yet composed of dead bodies, benevolent and destructive, the monster shifts along the margins of many distinctions. His shifting and excluded situation produces the critical faculty that engenders an excessive array of disturbing effects. For example, when the monster frames the Frankenstein family servant, Justine, for the murder of William Frankenstein, she is found guilty and sentenced to death despite her, and others', testimonies to her innocent character. The verdict, however, for the reader who is aware of the existence of the monster, reflects upon the inadequacy and injustice of judicial institutions. Furthermore, the behaviour of Justine's confessor extends the reflections of monstrosity since he forces her to confess a lie: 'he threatened and menaced,' Justine tells Elizabeth, 'until I almost began to think I was the monster that he said I was' (87). The confessor's actions reflect less on Justine than the clerical institutions that make her a monster.

The proliferation of monsters and the challenging and critical interrogations they provoke extend still further. Elizabeth, Frankenstein's adopted sister and fiancée, deeply upset by Justine's ordeal, learns that vice and injustice are not the 'imaginary evils' she thought they were. In her words, 'misery has come home, and men appear to me as monsters thirsting for each other's blood' (92). A critique of masculinity as much as human inhumanity, Elizabeth echoes some of the monster's own sentiments and goes on to question the possibility of making any distinctions at all in a world in which the limits and authority of any order seem so arbitrary. She exclaims: 'alas! Victor, when falsehood can look so like the truth, who can assure themselves of certain happiness? I feel as if I were walking on the edge of a precipice, towards which thousands are crowding, and endeavouring to plunge me into the abyss' (93). Swept up by the monstrous

34

momentum of interrogative doubt, no bonds are secure and no position is safe.

The uncontainable excess of monstrous otherness transgresses the limits set by any order as it operates along a position's lines of demarcation and resistance. Structurally too, *Frankenstein* opens itself up to the forces of critical reflection that operate in its own fraught bipolar momentum. As a set of broken frames, the narrative encloses the monster's story within Frankenstein's, the latter's being surrounded by Walton's letters, letters that are addressed to his sister on the edges of the text: the reader is at once moved inward to a presumed centre, the monster's account of the De Lacey family, and outwards, to the absent addressee on the margins. But the story at the centre fragments, dispersed by the rage of the monster, while the monster, neither wholly inside and contained by the structure, nor completely outside and excluded from it, appears at the end to confront Walton directly. Inside and outside, centre and margin, have their distinctions subverted by a novel in which the different speakers and writers also occupy the positions of readers and listeners. But, in its refusal of a dominant, authorial overview, the novel does not necessarily equivocate or compromise between the poles it identifies and confuses. Walton's final situation, suspended uneasily between departure and return, success and failure, light and darkness, is divided in such a way that it perpetuates doubts and dilemmas and engenders further questions: the ship may be returning home, but his gaze still attempts to penetrate the darkness into which the monster disappears.

The direction of the monster's disappearance itself engenders doubled effects. Moving in an opposite direction to the middle-class reader to whom Walton is returning, the monster approaches another place on the fractured margins of the text, a position which contrasts with the comfortable and domestic situation in which the text's absent reader, Mrs Saville, is constructed. Dividing the marginal and uncertain identity of the reader, the movement of the monster turns that position into a critical space of reading. Reading thus becomes dangerous and excessive. A space of passive reception, it is also a space from which resistance and transformation can begin. Readers, indeed, become monsters. As one alarmed critic of the enormous popularity of Gothic novels wrote:

> The class of readers, for whom this kind of entertainment is provided, as if no longer capable of deriving pleasure from the gentle and tender sympathies of the heart, require to have their curiosity excited by artificial concealments, their astonishment kept awake by a perpetual succession of wonderful incidents, and their very blood congealed with chilling horrors.[4]

Upsetting the bounds of literary propriety with their insatiable appetites, readers of Gothic fiction eschew taste and decorum with their demands for more and more awful thrills.

Novels were constructed in a similar manner to readers – as monsters. In 1796, a brief review of Matthew Lewis's *The Monk* lamented the waste of the author's talents on the production of a text so irredeemably devoted to excess:

> Lust, murder, incest, and every atrocity that can disgrace human nature, brought together, without the apology of probability, or even possibility, for their introduction. To make amends, the moral is general and *very practical*; it is, 'not to deal in witchcraft and magic, because the devil will have you at last!' We are sorry to observe that good talents have been misapplied in the production of this monster.[5]

Patently exceeding the bounds of literary propriety and taste, *The Monk* displayed its monstrosity and reflected that of the readers of Gothic romances.

The origin for the threatening proliferation of those figures of excess – Gothic tales and their readers – was identified as Horace Walpole's *The Castle of Otranto*. One commentator noted how 'Otranto Ghosts have propagated their species with unequalled fecundity. The spawn is in every novel shop.'[6] Like the phrase 'the spawn of the monster' that was used to describe the followers of Godwin and Wollstonecraft, the 'new species' of fiction created by Horace Walpole's *The Castle of Otranto* reproduced at an alarming rate (Walpole 1764: 12). *Frankenstein*, too, imagines the creation of a 'new species'. But his own 'hideous progeny' resists, subverts and exceeds his control. Like Burke who, Paulson argues, constructed the French Revolution as a Gothic novel, and like Walpole, Frankenstein cannot limit the effects of his monstrous creation. Indeed, the demand for greater thrills and more excessive pleasures subjected authors and the literary establishment to the desires of their readership in a similar manner to the way that radicals demanded liberty and equality from the systems that ruled them. More than passive consumers, readers begin to possess, in their function within the necessary and dangerous conditions of production, a certain power. Consuming, constructing and demanding, they form significant others, figures of difference crucial to the work of creation even as they exist beyond the determinations of authority.

Reading positions, glimpsed and activated among *Frankenstein*'s unstable frames, betray their monstrous power. Neither inside nor outside the novel, necessary yet unknown, absent addressees that produce powerful effects, readers cannot be contained by the limits of a single text. Inhabiting and generating textual contradictions, readers can identify and recognize themselves in parts of the text as passive addressees, but they can also resist such constructions and produce readings that attempt to decide Walton's disturbing dilemma: they can privilege Frankenstein or the monster. Furthermore, as the monstrous and marginal space engenders a surplus of meanings that cannot be limited by the novel's broken frames, so reading positions might multiply and challenge the terms and patterns prescribed in textual representations to interrogate and reactivate issues of difference and power.

Not merely subjected to or positioned by the effects of writing, the construction of readers within the text allots a certain power and resistance to acts of reading and offers subject positions which can be refused, adopted or, even, transformed. Who knows? The writer, for sure, does not. The possibility of adopting different positions, always available in the frictions of textual oppositions and differences, is the partial and yet powerful prerogative of that figure of potential excess, the reader. Readers always might, like the monsters of Gothic fiction and the French Revolution, follow the exciting and unknown lines of excess that operate within the limits in which they are partially constructed, since reading always involves some differences and thus entails the possibility of monstrous literary and political transgressions.

NOTES

1 Shelley 1831: 10. Throughout the essay the reprinted version of the 1831 edition of *Frankenstein* will be used. Further references to the novel will cite the page number in brackets in the text.
2 Cited by Kramnick, 'Introduction' to Godwin 1985: 40.
3 *The Anti-Jacobin Review*, V (1800): 427; quoted in Sterrenburg 1979: 147.
4 Review of *Count Roderic's Castle; or, Gothic Times, Analytical Review* 20 (1794): 489; cited in Napier 1987: vii.
5 Review of *The Monk, a Romance, The British Critic*, 7 June 1796: 677.
6 T. J. Matthias, *The Pursuits of Literature: A Satirical Poem in Four Dialogues*, London, 1797: 87, n. iii; cited in Napier 1987: viii.

BIBLIOGRAPHY

Baldick, C. (1987) *In Frankenstein's Shadow*, Oxford, Clarendon Press.
Blakemore, S. (1988) *Burke and the Fall of Language*, Hanover and London, University Press of New England.
Bloom, H. (1965) '*Frankenstein*, or the new Prometheus', *Partisan Review* 32: 611–18.
Burke, E. (1790) *Reflections on the Revolution in France*, ed. Conor Cruise O'Brien, Harmondsworth, Penguin, 1968.
Butler, M. (ed.) (1984) *Burke, Paine, Godwin, and the Revolution Controversy*, Cambridge, Cambridge University Press.
Deleuze, G. and Guattari, F. (1981) 'Rhizome', *Ideology and Consciousness* 8: 49–71.
Derrida, J. (1977) 'Signature event context', *Glyph* 1: 172–97.
Foucault, M. (1977a) 'Preface to transgression', in *Language, Counter-Memory, Practice*, ed. Donald F. Bouchard, trans. Donald F. Bouchard and Sherry Simon, Oxford, Blackwell: 29–52.
———— (1977b) 'Language to infinity', in *Language, Counter-Memory, Practice*, ed.

Donald F. Bouchard, trans. Donald F. Bouchard and Sherry Simon, Oxford, Blackwell: 53–67.

Glynn Grylls, R. (1938) *Mary Shelley: A Biography*, London, Oxford University Press.

Godwin, W. (1985) *Political Justice*, ed. Isaac Kramnick, Harmondsworth, Penguin.

Lacan, J. (1972) 'Seminar on "The Purloined Letter" ', *Yale French Studies* 48: 38–72.

―――― (1977a) *Ecrits*, trans. Alan Sheridan, London, Tavistock.

―――― (1977b) 'Desire and the interpretation of desire in *Hamlet*', *Yale French Studies* 55/6: 11–52.

Napier, E. (1987) *The Failure of Gothic*, Oxford, Clarendon Press.

Norman, S. (1970) 'Mary Wollstonecraft Shelley', in *Shelley and his Circle 1773–1822*, vol. III, ed. Kenneth Neill Cameron, London, Oxford University Press, 397–422.

Paine, T. (1791–2) *The Rights of Man*, repr. in Paine 1987: 201–364.

―――― (1987) *The Thomas Paine Reader*, ed. Michael Foot and Isaac Kramnick, Harmondsworth, Penguin.

Paulson, R. (1983) *Representations of Revolution (1789–1820)*, New Haven and London, Yale University Press.

Shelley, M. (1831) *Frankenstein, or the Modern Prometheus*, ed. M. K. Joseph, Oxford, Oxford University Press, 1969.

Sterrenburg, L. (1979) 'Mary Shelley's monster: politics and psyche in *Frankenstein*', in George Levine and U. C. Knoepflmacher (eds) *The Endurance of Frankenstein*, Berkeley, Los Angeles; London, University of California Press: 143–71.

Walpole, H. (1764) *The Castle of Otranto*, ed. W. S. Lewis, London, Oxford University Press, 1964.

4

Pantisocracy and the politics of the 'Preface' to *Lyrical Ballads*

Nigel Leask

In the eleventh number of *The Friend*, published from the Lakes in October 1809, Coleridge denied that he had ever been a convert to the principles of Jacobinism (or 'metapolitics', as he dubbed it) because he had always maintained that political participation should be based on a property qualification rather than upon abstract rights. In the same paragraph, he attributed the fortunate fact that his own thinking in the 1790s had been untainted by Jacobinism to his involvement in the Pantisocracy scheme:

> What I dared not expect from constitutions of Government and whole Nations, I hoped from Religion and a small Company of chosen Individuals, and formed a plan, as harmless as it was extravagant, of trying the experiment of human Perfectibility on the banks of the *Susquehannah*; where our little Society, in its second Generation, was to have combined the innocence of the patriarchal Age with the knowledge and genuine refinements of European culture.
>
> (Coleridge 1969: II, 146)

Coleridge's retrospective (and thoroughly *exculpatory*) account of Pantisocracy in 1809 was to set the agenda for subsequent accounts of this episode in his radical youth, depicting it as a Utopian venture unconnected either with the main currents of the 1790s political scene or with his later thinking. The present essay will seek to reconstruct the political theory and context of Pantisocracy by refusing to take as axiomatic the revisionary manoeuvring of the later Coleridge, so anxious publicly to disassociate himself from the radical movement. My argument will elaborate three main points. First, that Pantisocracy was a response to a critical phase of the French Revolution, the collapse of Girondin republicanism, and the ideological predicament of its Dissenting supporters in England. Second, that emigration to the newly independent USA became almost a civic duty for Dissenting intellectuals in furthering the realization of the millennium, Christ's republic on earth, after the failure of republicanism in corrupt Europe. Despite the rationalist basis of Unitarian polemic, Coleridge as author of *Religious Musings* and the *Destiny of Nations* was not alone in his use of the language of radical apocalyptics to describe contemporary political events, as Jack Fruchtman has shown (Fruchtman 1983). In 1784 Richard Price, philosopher, Dissenting minister, and target of Burke's fulminations in the *Reflections upon the Revolution in France* (1790) was persuaded that the 'independence of the English colonies in America is one step ordained by Providence to introduce [the millennium]' (quoted in Fruchtman 1983: 59). Third (as Coleridge's remarks from *The Friend* quoted above obliquely indicate), the principles of Pantisocracy had an enduring significance in the later thought of Coleridge and, by extension, Wordsworth, and are particularly manifest in the suppressed politics of the 'Preface' to *Lyrical Ballads*.

Rational Dissenters in the mould of Richard Price and Joseph Priestley had been quick to identify their own flagging campaign for civil liberties with the early reformist phase of the French Revolution. However, the rise to power of the Jacobin and Robespierreist faction from late 1792 and the systematic liquidation of the Girondins in 1793 destroyed the Dissenters' hopes that the adoption of an enlightened constitution by peaceful means in France would stimulate reform at home. Moreover, the outbreak of war with France in 1793 resulted in their identification as traitors and French fellow travellers, somewhat ironic in the light of their bitter opposition to Robespierre and Jacobin principles as well as to the belligerent Pitt ministry (Pocock 1985: 283). Unitarians like Coleridge and other radical Dissenters found themselves in an ideological cul-de-sac from which emigration seemed to be the most plausible escape. Pantisocracy was one amongst many such emigration schemes, originating in Coleridge's circle in the Unitarian stronghold of Jesus College, Cambridge, in 1794, following the trial and expulsion from the University of Jesus Fellow William Frend the previous year on a charge of sedition. The Unitarian Frend's expulsion was part of a general purge of radical Dissenters by the ascendant Tory evangelical party in the University, led by the Vice-Chancellor, Dr Isaac Milner.

Six years later, when the rising star of Napoleon had made the revolutionary French Republic look more like an expansionist military dictatorship than an egalitarian commonwealth, Wordsworth began the idealization of what he would term the 'perfect Republic of Shepherds and Agriculturists' amongst the Freeholders of Westmoreland and Cumberland. Wordsworth and Coleridge collaborated in a revolt against the standards of literary politeness, claiming, most notoriously, to partake of the linguistic as well as the moral virtues of the 'cottage economy', thereby flouting the conventions of a recognized pastoral mode (Barrell 1980: 137–41). In the 'Preface' to *Lyrical Ballads*, 'the real language of men in a state of vivid sensation' (the linguistic model for the poetry of *Lyrical Ballads*), specified as the language of 'Low and rustic life', is described as a more 'philosophical language than that which is frequently substituted for it by Poets'

(Wordsworth 1974: II, 124). In October 1800, shortly after having completed, with Wordsworth, the first 'Preface' to *Lyrical Ballads*, Coleridge wrote to Humphry Davy that he was planning 'an Essay on the Elements of Poetry; it would in reality be a *disguised* System of Morals and Politics' (Coleridge 1956–71: I, 356). By suggesting that there is a significant continuity between these cryptic politics and those more confidently announced by Coleridge and Southey five years before under the aegis of Pantisocracy, I hope both to refute the sort of 'Burkean' reading of the politics of *Lyrical Ballads* expounded most authoritatively by James Chandler (1984), and approach an explanation of the particularly attenuated, understated and often *visionary* inflection of those politics in 'Preface' and poems alike. The fact that the Wordsworthian 'enclosure' of Grasmere, where 'A blended holiness of earth and sky,/Something that makes this individual Spot,/This small Abiding-place of many Men,/A termination, and a last retreat' is also moralized as a *'Centre'*, a 'Whole without dependence or defect' gives a sense of the way in which Wordsworth's destination is at once essential *and* peripheral (Wordsworth 1977: I, 701). In terms of the poets' ideological trajectory from 1795 to 1800, the principles embodied in this 'mountain republic' had been tailored to fit an emigration from corrupt Europe to republican America, a fact which helps to explain why Wordsworth's is, in David Simpson's expression, a 'poetry of displacement'. My thesis here is that the poets of the Lake School were 'internal emigrants' in a manner which anticipates in many ways the tradition classically described by Raymond Williams in *Culture and Society* (Williams 1958).

The starting point of the Pantisocracy scheme seems to have been a competition between two land-agents of similar political convictions to sell off plots of farmland in America to French and English radicals whose position at home was becoming increasingly dangerous. One of them, Mary Wollstonecraft's lover Gilbert Imlay, canvassed the advantages of Kentucky, whilst the other, Thomas Cooper, projected three sales offices in Europe to dispose of land he had purchased on the eastern branch of the Susquehannah river in Pennsylvania. Cooper had settled there himself the previous year with his father-in-law, the *emigré* Unitarian scientist and Divine Joseph Priestley (Kelley 1930: 218–20; Logan 1930: 1069–84; MacGillivray 1931). The idea of emigration was very attractive to English republicans in 1794; as I have already indicated, in the new wartime climate they found themselves branded as traitors subject to increasing persecution from both official and unofficial sources. The climate of Coleridge's Cambridge was no exception, for the expulsion of Frend was only the start of a war of persecution against Dissenters. Coleridge's undergraduate contemporary Henry Gunning, in his *Reminiscences*, tells us that from the winter of 1793 loyalist mobs, often tacitly encouraged by the Tory lobby in the University, smashed the windows of Dissenting households and burnt effigies of Tom Paine in Market Square. 'Many', he recorded, 'consulted their own safety

41

by leaving Cambridge for America' (Gunning 1854: I, 278). Little wonder that when Coleridge was invited, in October 1794, to 'drink tea and spend the evening' with Dr Thomas Edwards, distinguished editor of Plutarch's *Works* and Fellow of Jesus, together with other radical Fellows of the college, the subject turned to emigration: 'I was challenged on the subject of Pantisocracy, which is indeed the universal topic at this university.' After six hours of heated discussion, Coleridge was pleased to record that his mentors 'declared the System impregnable, supposing the assigned Quantum of Virtue and Genius in the first individuals' (Coleridge 1956–71: I, 118). Nor were the practical details wanting from a scheme which Coleridge in *The Friend* would dismiss as being 'as harmless as it was extravagant' (Coleridge 1969: II, 146). In a book entitled *Some Information Respecting America*, published in 1794, Thomas Cooper provided the English Pantisocrats with the concrete details of land prices, bison, Indians and mosquitoes. Coleridge probably reviewed the book for the *Critical Review* in early 1795; it is just one of the many American travel books devoured by the Pantisocrats Coleridge and Southey in this period (*Critical Review* 13 January 1795: 88–92; Coleridge 1957-: I, 50n).

Significantly it was France, rather than England, which apparently saw the birth of Cooper's Pennsylvania scheme. A French pamphlet unearthed in the Bibliothèque nationale in the 1920s shows that Cooper and Priestley hoped at least initially that the Susquahannah would provide a haven for Girondins fleeing from the ascendancy of Robespierre and the Jacobins after the fateful summer of 1793 (Kelley 1930: 219). Indeed the Girondin leader Brissot de Warville had himself crossed to America in 1788 in the hope of establishing a pure republic in the wilderness; Coleridge quoted from his *New Travels in the United States* (trans. 1792) in the 1795 lecture 'Conciones ad populum' by way of recommending the high private virtues required of the true patriot (Coleridge 1971: 47). Brissot had returned to France for the calling of the States General in 1789, but unlike his follower Cooper was not fortunate enough to get out again before the Jacobin Terror. Cooper and James Watt the younger, his co-delegate to the National Assembly from the Manchester Constitutional Society, were both forced to flee after they had been expelled from the Jacobin club for Brissotin allegiances in late 1792 (Roe 1988: 45). Another young English supporter of the Girondins, William Wordsworth, whose movements in revolutionary France have been carefully reconstructed by Nicholas Roe, had followed the example of his countrymen and left France in December 1792 (Roe 1988: 80–3). Although Wordsworth met the Bristol Pantisocrats in September 1795 when their emigration plan was collapsing, the Girondin milieu with which he had been involved in 1792 may well have made the Pantisocracy scheme quite familiar to him. The *Prelude*, Book X, tells us how meeting Coleridge had restored Wordsworth's confidence in the republican ideas he had imbibed from Michel Beaupuy and other

Girondins, and which had been so badly shaken by the rise of Robespierre and the outbreak of war between England and the young French republic (Wordsworth 1971: 1805, X: 905–1006). In point of fact a group of Girondin *emigrés* did establish their own form of Pantisocracy at Frenchtown, 'not far from the Susquehannah river', as reported by the *Gentleman's Magazine* in June 1795, where 'they have relinquished their titles and have domesticated in the most social manner'. Evidently Cooper's salesmanship was a cut above Gilbert Imlay's.

There is no doubt that Coleridge was attracted by the Unitarian Cooper's ideal portrait of the American farmer, enjoying religious liberty and participation in the sort of republican government which seemed to have failed in both England and France:

> In America a farmer is a landowner, paying no rents, no tythes, and a few taxes; equal in rank to any other rank in the States, having a voice in the appointment of his legislators, and a fair chance, if he deserves it, of becoming one himself.
>
> (Cooper 1794: 72)

Maurice Kelley has suggested that the Pantisocrats were not happy with some of Cooper's proposals, however, and sought an independent colony within easy reach of his settlement (Chard 1972: 103; Kelley 1930: 220; Piper 1962: 66). Whatever the truth of this, clearly Priestley, whose thought was such an important influence on Coleridge and other radical Dissenters in the 1790s, was one of the main attractions of the Susquhennah over Imlay's Kentucky. In September 1794, Coleridge described how he had outlined the scheme to George Dyer, another Cambridge Unitarian whom, he wrote, 'was enraptured; pronounced it impregnable. He is intimate with Dr Priestley, and doubts not that the Doctor will join us (Coleridge 1956–71: I, 98). Dyer would remember Coleridge's enthusiasm in a 'poetical dialogue' called 'The Poet's Fate' published three years later, in which he lamented the plight of the group of mainly Unitarian writers whose works were published by Joseph Johnson:

> ... such as needs must write, should learn to fast;
> ... When hungry, smoke your pipe, or say your prayers;
> Or plough, in learned pride, the Atlantic main,
> Join Pantisocracy's harmonious train;
> Haste, where young love still spreads his brooding wings,
> And freedom digs, and ploughs, and laughs, and sings.
>
> (Dyer 1797, no line numbers)

Dyer's poem, like Coleridge's 1794 sonnet 'Pantisocracy' shows how closely the compromised political ideals of the Dissenters were connected with hopes of emigration at this period. Although Dyer never enlisted in Coleridge and Southey's scheme, he clearly sympathized with its principles;

when Lamb described his friend many years later in his essay 'Oxford in the Vacation', Dyer's absent-mindedness is pardoned on the grounds that 'at that moment, reader, he is on Mount Tabor – or Parnassus – or co-sphered with Plato – or, with Harrington, framing "immortal common-wealths" – devising some plan of amelioration to thy country, or thy species' (Lamb 1962: 13). Southey's Unitarian friend William Taylor of Norwich placed similar emphasis on the fantastical and exotic nature of the plan in an 1803 letter to Southey as author of *Madoc*, which he had not been alone in recognizing as an epical treatment of the Pantisocracy project:

> Do you still think of his imitating the Carthaginian students whom St. Austin mentions in his *Confessions*, and who were to have gone into the back settlements, beyond the blue mountains of Africa, to found a Christian platonical pantisocratical republic, and to become the Mango Capaks and Madocs of the paulo-post-future Tombuctoos?
>
> (Taylor 1843: I, 442)

Taylor's learned jibe recognizes, in its half-serious way, that Pantisocracy was a *colonial*, as well as a radical-democratic enterprise, a fact that although understated in the original 1795 scheme, is quite explicit by 1805, in the published form of Southey's poem *Madoc*. Marilyn Butler has described how the original plan of the poem sent a party of twelfth-century Welsh Bardic 'Unitarians' out to Peru in search of religious and political freedom from Saxon and Catholic tyranny at home: 'The Welsh king Madoc was to have become conflated with Mango Capac, Peru's legendary lawgiver.' The published 1805 version of the poem, however, changed the setting to Aztlan, in *North* America, and dwelt on the religious cruelties of the Aztecs. 'A group of manly white benefactors', to quote Butler again, 'rescue a well-intentioned but feeble native tribe from their nasty, fraudu-lent, power-mad priests and their bloodthirsty serpent god' (Butler n.d.). Southey's shift of emphasis unambiguously places *Madoc* within the cate-gory of nineteenth-century imperialist literature, an accommodation which is a curious variation of the fate of agrarian idealism in the developing Toryism of Wordsworth and Coleridge in the same period.

Southey's friend William Taylor clearly believed that an emigration scheme was still in the air as late as 1803, and that Southey's reluctance to leave Bristol, a western seaport, was connected with this fact. If Taylor was correct, his surmise supports my thesis that the manner in which Wordsworth, Coleridge and Southey regarded their drift to the Lakes after 1799 may have been conditioned by the idea of emigration, and that the bones of Pantisocracy were not finally laid to rest in 1795. Paradoxically, return to the heartland of national probity in the Lake District in an internal and external quest for the True Briton might have originated in a colonial emigration to the periphery, virgin territory inhabited only by noble savages. But just like Southey's colonial shift of emphasis in the later text of *Madoc*, Wordsworth's literary relationship with the Lakeland farmers was transformed from a notion of shared participation in an egalitarian republic to the feudal polity he would describe in the 1818 *Address to the Freeholders of Westmoreland* (Wordsworth 1974: III, 137–228). Perhaps this shift helps to explain De Quincey's otherwise rather odd claim in 1839 that Wordsworth, the 'Little Englander', was in fact the poet *par excellence* for English Empire-builders:

> Wordsworth is peculiarly the poet for the solitary and meditative; and, throughout the countless myriads of future America and future Australia, no less than Polynesia and Southern Africa, there will be situations without end fitted by their loneliness to favour his influence for centuries to come.

> (De Quincey 1970: 144)

Wordsworth's encounters with local figures like the Leech-Gatherer or the Cumberland Beggar do often suggest a visionary internalization of sociability, a nurturing of solitude; the indigenous inhabitants of the Lakes are literally metamorphosed into figures of the landscape. Teasing out the implications of De Quincey's comment, putting race in the place of class, the nature of the encounter between colonizer and colonized in the Anglo-Saxon imperial expansion of the nineteenth century may have been influenced by Wordsworth's ambivalent poetic encounters with the collapsing social fabric of the Lakeland freeholders to a degree which has not yet been appreciated.

As a Unitarian and Necessitarian, Coleridge denied the existence of radical evil or original sin, to which he rather attributed a political and economic cause: 'The real source of inconstancy, depravity, and prostitution, is *Property*, which mixes with and poisons everything good – & is beyond doubt the Origin of all Evil' (Coleridge 1956–71: I, 214). Although Coleridge believed that Christ had unequivocally condemned the possession of private property and urged his disciples to 'aspheterize' or divide up their goods (the term is predictably a Coleridgean coinage) (Coleridge 1971: 228), he was prepared to concede that in the present corrupt state of society, 'such Similarity of Property, as would amount to *moral sameness*, [would] answer all the purposes of Abolition' (Coleridge 1956–71: I, 93). In his recent analysis of Coleridge's political thought, John Morrow overlooks this Coleridgean accommodation in arguing that 'Christian egalitarianism necessitated the abandonment of the independent-property-holder myth that lay at the heart of Harringtonian discourse' (Morrow 1990: 31). The advantage of basing society on the equal possession of property (and not *necessarily* on its abolition), was that it provided a foundation for the development of the private affections, a far surer basis for public benevolence than either Paine's appeal to the 'rights' of man or

spies and censors the slip. But perhaps of more importance was the fact that Coleridge's lectures belonged to a tradition of commonwealth polemic which had, since the seventeenth century, employed the Jewish republic as a paradigm for its own political principles. Because the eventual replacement of the Jewish republic by a monarchy was often used, as John Morrow points out, 'by conservative writers to buttress claims about God-ordained, absolutist monarchy which were essentially, and in some cases overtly, Filmerian', the commonwealth writers regarded the Old Testament account as an object lesson in the evils of monarchy (Morrow 1990: 29). There had been a great deal of discussion about the Jewish theocracy and poetry in the latter half of the eighteenth century, particularly in the wake of Robert Lowth's 1753 *Lectures on the Sacred Poetry of the Hebrews*, translated from the Latin and published by Joseph Johnson in 1787. Lowth had linked the sublimity of the Hebrews' poetry with their egalitarian orders of commonwealth, praising the imagery of a poetry derived from nature and objects of 'common and domestic life' (Lowth 1787: 145). Most important of all, however, Coleridge's account of the Jewish commonwealth which God had established on earth as part of his revelation to man followed Moses Lowman's *Dissertation on the Civil Government of the Hebrews* of 1740, in its turn based on Harrington's commentary on the Mosaic theocracy in *The Art of Lawgiving*, published in 1659. Lowman was a Dissenting minister whose disguised polemic sought to maximize a republican interpretation of the 1688 constitution and expose the corruption to which it was being subjected by the Crown and Anglican Establishment; one can see the attractions of this old commonwealth argument for Unitarians like Priestley and Coleridge in the 1790s, further than ever from achieving civil and political rights by a repeal of the Test Acts (Robbins 1959: 252). True to his sources, Coleridge described how God instituted an Agrarian Law in the division by equal lots of the lands of the Canaanites, creating for the twelve tribes of Israel an immutable commonwealth based upon inalienable tenure and entailment of land. The imposition of a fifty-year jubilee prevented the hoarding of property, as did a ban on commerce and usury. Thus alienation of property and accumulation were both obviated; we need only look as far as Wordworth's description of the Ewbank's dwindling patrimonial fields, 'buffeted with bond,/Interest and mortgages' in *The Brothers* (Wordsworth 1977: I, 407–8) for a picture of the moral effects of these corrupting influences of commercial society. Although this equalized freehold fell short of the ultimate goal of 'aspheterization', it was the best that could be achieved in an imperfect world, for 'the Jews were too ignorant a people, too deeply leavened with the Vices of Aegypt to be capable of so exalted a state of society' (Coleridge 1971: 128). Each man's patrimony of twenty-five acres ensured a responsible and virtuous participation in the body politic. Coleridge was apologetic on God's behalf for the very need to impose the Agrarian Law, a 'coercion' which 'may seem unfavourable to the benevolent principle. But in untutored minds Regulations are necessary to virtuous Habits – and then our Habits supercede the necessity of Regulations' (Coleridge 1971: 129). What is important here is Coleridge's use of the word 'habit', the bugbear of Godwin's *Political Justice* and an important prop of Burke's conservative defence of prejudice, in a context quite opposed to the ideology which Burke supported. By basing moral education on the habits demanded by small ownership, Coleridge was using Hartley's associationist psychology in combination with the Harringtonian Agrarian Law as an alternative to, and an implied critique of, Jacobin abstract rights. We will see below how important this becomes in the politics of the 1800 'Preface' and Wordsworth's 1801 letter to Charles Fox. The 'admirable division of property' of the Jews illustrates Harrington's aphorism that 'good orders [of government] make evil men good, bad orders make good men evil' (Harrington 1977: 838). It also aptly describes Wordsworth's depiction of the moral qualities of the characters of *Lyrical Ballads* in relation to their threatened environment.

The constitutional arrangements of this 'Divine Original' were based on a national congress of Assembly of 24,000 men composed of the members of a rotated militia which thus represented the entire population of the Jewish nation. This was balanced by a senate of 70 elders, the Sanhedrin, which could deliberate and propose, but not enact the laws. These were executed by the Assembly on the basis of a balloted vote. Coleridge adds that this constitution 'provided that every Freeman in the State should by rotation exercise that power the possession of which constituted the security of Freedom' (Coleridge 1971: 130). The similarities between this and the 'form of government' advocated by Wordsworth in the *Letter to Llandaff* are remarkable, although his system is modernized by the substitution of referendums, or a democratic system of representation, for the gigantic Jewish Assembly (Wordsworth 1974: I, 37; Fink 1948: 113), and Wordsworth proposes the Agrarian Law only in order to reject its strict enforcement as impracticable. What is clear is the opposition of this constitutional model to the Hobbesian principles of Robespierre and the dictatorship of the General Will, when, in Aikin's words, 'a majority may lawfully be governed by a minority, upon the pretext of the public good' (Aikin 1823: II, 295). Clearly Pantisocracy would have required a miniature version only of this 'two-tier' Harringtonian and Girondin constitution, although it is easy to see why Coleridge would have been attracted to Cooper's account, quoted above, of the American freeholder having both a voice in the appointment of legislators and the chance of becoming one himself.

The third, and most important feature of the Hebrew commonwealth for the principles of the 1800 'Preface', lies in the issue of the appointment of a spiritual authority, the Levites or priestly caste. Although the self-rule of the people excluded monarchy and the *jure divino* claims of a State church, it was necessary that one of the tribes should abandon its land in order to disseminate knowledge amongst the ignorant Jews and steer them clear of idolatry. Coleridge is very cautious in presenting the Levitical institution, the 'chief objection to the Mosaic Dispensation' from his point of view. It was excusable only because 'the Art of Printing was [not] then discovered, [and] . . . knowledge was vastly more difficult of attainment than it is at present' (Coleridge 1971: 136–7). When Coleridge read Spinoza's *Tractatus Theologico-politicus* in 1797 (if we are to believe the anecdote in the *Biographia Literaria* in which the paranoiac Home Office spy sent to tail Wordsworth and Coleridge at Stowey heard them talking incessantly about 'Spy-nozy') (Coleridge 1983: I, 194; Roe 1988: 234–62), he would have discovered a direct link between the Levites and the corruption of the Jewish commonwealth. Spinoza enthusiastically endorsed the politics of a state whose subjects 'possessed as large a share in the lands as did their chiefs, and were owners of their plots of ground in perpetuity' (Spinoza 1951: 230). The fact that, according to Spinoza's argument, such uniquely democratic orders of commonwealth were the secret behind the 'inspiration' of the scriptures (rather than any direct intervention by God), ensured that the *Tractatus* was one of the great banned books of the eighteenth century which everyone nevertheless read. Spinoza also insisted that priests were quite alien to the body politic; their pedagogic duties 'had orginally been intended for the first born of each family' so that the institution of a separate caste, demanding tithes and taxes, was 'a constant reproach to the people'. This corrupted them into the idolatory of calling for a 'mortal king' to replace their divine ruler (Spinoza 1951: 232–5), which Coleridge described as 'the foulest crime of which human nature is capable' (Coleridge 1971: 133). Priesthood was the fatal flaw which prevented the otherwise perfect Hebrew commonwealth from being immutable. Christ's mission, according to Harrington, Lowman and Coleridge, was to return the fallen Jews, and now also the Gentiles, to the republican purity of the Mosaic dispensation. Or rather, to a *purer* state, by abolishing the flaw of priesthood, a point of special relevance to the Pantisocrats, that 'deeply principled minority' which Coleridge trusted would procure by gradual means the 'Universal Equality' which he termed 'the object of the Messiah's mission' (Coleridge 1971: 218). As he wrote in the second lecture,

> the very name [priest] is no where applied to Christians in the new Testament except in one Text – and there it is said, Ye shall all be Priests – in the same sense as it is elsewhere – Ye shall all be Kings, and, I suppose, if we were all Priests and all Kings, it would be all as one if there were no Priest and no King.
>
> (Coleridge 1971: 137–8)

Strange as it may seem, this 'Pantisocratic' notion of the civic priest is an important clue to understanding the nature of the poet as theorized in the 'Preface' to *Lyrical Ballads*. In Coleridge's career in the 1790s it is only a small shift from the role of Unitarian lay preacher to that of poet. After the Pantisocrats' emigration scheme had collapsed, and plans to estabish a communal farm in Wales had also proved fruitless, Coleridge sought a substitute in the cottage community around Tom Poole at Nether Stowey. 'Shall I not', he wrote in late 1796 'be an Agriculturalist, an Husband, a Father, and a *Priest* after the order of Peace? an *hireless* Priest?' (Coleridge 1956–71: I, 255). Wordsworth found such priests in the Dissenting chapels of Westmorland, characters like 'the homely priest of Ennerdale' in *The Brothers* (Wordsworth 1977: I, 402. 1.17), whose cottage industry is described in an uncharacteristically georgic passage, or the clergymen in *Guide to the Lakes* 'in clothing or in manner of life in no way differing . . . except on the Sabbath day' from the neighbouring freeholders (Wordsworth 1974: II, 200–1). If Wordsworth was eager to show the civic role of priests, he was correspondingly anxious to demonstrate the spiritual probity he found inherent in the labour of the Lakeland farmers and shepherds ('Ye shall all be priests . . .'). In Book VIII of the *Prelude*, he gave literal force to the Christian metaphor of the 'good shepherd', adding a radical and visionary turn to pastoral convention in his account of a shepherd at work high on the distant mountain:

> Or him have I descried in distant sky,
> A solitary object and sublime,
> Above all height! like an aerial cross,
> As it is stationed on some spiry rock
> Of the Chartreuse for worship'
> (Wordsworth 1977: VIII 406–10)

In an article called 'Is verse essential to poetry?' which appeared in the *Monthly Magazine* of July 1796 and which has been recognized as an important source for the 1800 'Preface', the Unitarian minister William Enfield argued that poets suffer from 'that spirit of monopoly . . . so injurious in ecclesiastical and civil society':

> Fancying the inhabitants of this consecrated inclosure [i.e. poetry] a privileged order, they have been accustomed to look down, with a kind of senatorial haughtiness, upon the prose-men, who inhabit the common of letters, as a vulgar, plebeian herd
> (*Monthly Magazine*, July 1796: 453)

Clearly Enfield's point is more cautious than Wordsworth's and Coleridge's, in that he is arguing for an identity between the languages of poetry and prose, rather than demanding that poetic language should be modelled on 'the real language of men in a state of vivid sensation'. But nevertheless it is apparent that the language of criticism is underpinned by a Unitarian polemic contesting the 'motley masquerade of tricks, quaintnesses, hieroglyphics, and enigmas' (to quote Wordsworth again) which mark the spiritual authority of a corrupt national church, or its literary equivalent, the 'poetic diction' of the literary establishment (Wordsworth 1974: I, 162). When Francis Jeffrey wrote in 1802 that Wordsworth's attempt 'to copy the sentiments of the lower orders is implied in his resolution to copy their style' (*Edinburgh Review*, October 1802: 66), he demonstrated his failure to comprehend the nature of a poet's authority in a commonwealth where all men are kings and priests, or for that matter poets. The 'Preface' insists that not only is the poet a 'man speaking to men' but that the language of freeholders 'is a more permanent and a far more philosophical language than that which is frequently substituted for it by Poets' who, like their brethren the usurping priests 'separate themselves from the sympathies of men, and indulge in arbitrary and capricious habits of expression' (Wordsworth 1974: I, 124). This was the principle against which a Tory and Anglican Coleridge directed the main force of his argument in the second volume of *Biographia Literaria* in 1817, for reasons which, it should be by now apparent, were not motivated simply by aesthetic preferences.

To conclude I want to look briefly at Wordsworth's 'naturalization' of the ideas of Pantisocracy and of the Jewish commonwealth in the Lakes and suggest how they were absorbed, in a manner which I have already intimated, into an increasingly conservative programme of culture and politics in the 1800s. In the final years of the eighteenth century, whilst Southey and Colderidge were still considering emigration to America, Italy, Portugal or the south of France (Coleridge 1956–71: I, 553–6), the Wordsworths discovered Pantisocratic values 'Home at Grasmere', in

> This small Abiding-place of many Men,
> A termination, and a last retreat,
> A Centre, come from wheresoe'er you will,
> A Whole without dependence or defect,
> Made for itself, and happy in itself,
> Perfect Contentment, Unity entire.
>
> . . . so here abides
> A power and a protection for the mind,
> Dispensed indeed to other solitudes,
> Favoured by noble privilege like this,
> Where kindred independence of estate
> Is prevalent, where he who tills the field,
> He, happy Man! is Master of the field
> And treads the mountain which his Fathers trod
> (Wordsworth 1977: I, 146–51, 376–83)

The final lines here show the extent to which the idea of Pantisocracy as emigration from a hopelessly corrupt Europe dominated by a surplus rather than a subsistence economy, division of labour and antagonistic class interests affected Wordsworth's 'rediscovery' of the virtues of the Lakeland peasants. The Freeholders, who still farmed a third of the Lake District, were a different species from the Dorset peasantry at Racedown who in 1797 Dorothy had been horrified to find 'miserably poor . . . not at all beyond what might be expected in savage life' (Maclean 1970: 87). But her brother's description of Grasmere as an 'enclosure', however threatened by the encroachments of a larger world, spells out the extent to which the so-called 'Lake school' was, as I have already intimated, an *internal* emigration which permitted the poet to find the civic ideal 'here, now, and in England'. The poet reiterates the point in his 1801 letter to Charles Fox, describing the virtues of the Lakeland 'Statesmen':

> Their little tract of land serves as a kind of permanent rallying point for their domestic feelings, as a tablet upon which they are written which makes them objects of memory in a thousand instances when they would otherwise be forgotten. It is a fountain fitted to the nature of social man from which supplies of affection, as pure as his heart was intended for, are daily drawn.
>
> (Wordsworth 1967: 314)

These passages go a long way to explaining what the 'Preface' to *Lyrical Ballads* means in designating the language of 'low and rustic life' as 'more philosophical' than that of Poets, and the epistemological vagueness of the reason given, that 'such men hourly communicate with the best objects from which the best part of language is originally derived', is clarified in the comparison (Wordsworth, 1974: I, 124). One cannot help feeling that in October 1800 Coleridge, in collaboration with Wordsworth, had *already* written his 'Essay on the Elements of Poetry' which would in reality be 'a *disguised* System of Morals and Politics' (Coleridge 1956–71: I, 356). Given that he had recently been urging Southey to collaborate with him on a 'History of Levellers and the Levelling Principle' which would 'enlighten without offending', we should not need to doubt the nature of the politics being disguised. Pantisocratic principles were *only* presentable in disguise by 1800, although Coleridge hoped that 'Boys & Youths would read such a work with far different Impressions from their Fathers and Godfathers – and yet the latter find nothing alarming in the nature of the Work, it being purely historical' (Coleridge 1956–71: I, 554). The fact that Coleridge was engaged at this time in writing a series of articles for the *Morning Post* criticizing the new French Constitution of 1799 and praising the relative merits of the unreformed British Constitution shows the discrepancy between the public and private politics of the Lake poets around the turn of the century. 'The more delicate superstition of ancestry' he suggested rather cynically, might still counteract the 'grosser superstition of wealth' (Coleridge 1976: I, 55). We know the negative connotations which the word 'superstition' held for Coleridge at this time, but nevertheless we can see here how a qualified acceptance of unequal property and of landed aristocracy as a political expedient to fend off Jacobin dictatorship of the kind which he discerned behind the new Napoleonic Constitution was transforming Coleridge's agrarian republicanism. By the time of writing *The Friend* in 1809, the Kantian distinction between Reason and Understanding provided a bedrock for his critique of Jacobin 'metapolitics' and his philosophical defence of social hierarchies, aristocracy, and unequal landed property:

> But where individual landed property exists, there must be inequalities of Property: the nature of the Earth and the nature of the Mind unite to make the contrary impossible ... To Property, therefore, and to its inequalities, all human Laws directly or indirectly relate, which would not be equally laws in the state of Nature. Now it is impossible to deduce the Right of Property from pure Reason. The utmost which Reason could give, would be a property in *forms* of things, as far as the forms were produced by individual Power. In the *matter* it could give no Property.
>
> (Coleridge 1969: II, 132)

A slight but significant inflection, bulwarked by the new German philosophy, pressed an ideology originally critical of the established political order into the service of the aristocratic landed interest and the legitimation of a burgeoning Empire. Nevertheless the fact is often overlooked that defending the interests of aristocracy and established Church was a position with which Wordsworth was happier than Coleridge in later years. I have argued elsewhere that the latter was driven, in the mid-1820s, to discover what he would call an 'internal theocracy' in a theory of culture and a 'clerisy' which sought to uphold a democratic 'realm of pure reason' in the midst of a hierarchical political realm swayed by pragmatic and partial interests (Leask 1988: 184–219). Wordsworth, on the other hand, was left with the often unenviable task of redefining the part played by his republican experiments in a national and imperial culture defined, most notably in *The Excursion* of 1814, in increasingly traditionalist and Burkean terms. This work of redefinition is finely illustrated in a passage from his *Guide to the Lakes*, written in 1809, which provides a suitable conclusion:

> Venerable was the transition, when a curious traveller, descending from the heart of the mountains, had come to some ancient manorial residence in the more open parts of the Vales, which, through the rights attached to its proprietor, connected the almost visionary mountain republic he had been contemplating with the substantial

frame of society as existing in the laws and constitution of a mighty empire.

(Wordsworth 1974: II, 206–7)

BIBLIOGRAPHY

Aikin, J. (1823) *Memoir of John Aikin M. D.*, 2 vols, ed. Lucy Aikin, London, Baldwin, Cradock & Joy.

Barrell, J. (1980) *The Dark Side of the Landscape*, Cambridge, Cambridge University Press.

Butler, M. (n.d.) 'Welsh nationalism and English poets 1790–1805', unpublished paper.

—— (ed.) (1984) *Burke, Paine, Godwin and the Revolution Controversy*, Cambridge, Cambridge University Press.

Chandler, J. (1984) *Wordsworth's Second Nature*, Chicago and London, Chicago University Press.

Chard, L. (1972) 'Dissenting Republican: Wordsworth's Early Life and Thought in their Political Context', *Studies in English Literature*, 66.

Coleridge, S. T. (1956–71) *Collected Letters*, 6 vols. ed. E. L. Griggs, Oxford, Clarendon Press.

—— (1957–) *Notebooks*, 5 vols, ed. K. Coburn, New York, Princeton, Princeton University Press; London, Routledge & Kegan Paul.

—— (1969) *The Friend*, 2 vols, ed, Barbara Rooke, Princeton, New York, Princeton University Press; London, Routledge & Kegan Paul.

—— (1971), *Lectures 1795 on Politics and Religion*, ed. Lewis Patton and Peter Mann; Princeton, New York, Princeton University Press; London, Routledge & Kegan Paul.

—— (1976) *Essays on his Times*, 3 vols, ed. David Erdman, Princeton, New York, Princeton University Press; London, Routledge & Kegan Paul.

—— (1983) *Biographia Literaria*, 2 vols, ed. W. Jackson Bate and James Engell, Princeton, New York, Princeton University Press; London, Routledge & Kegan Paul.

Cooper, T. (1794) *Some Information Respecting America*, London, Joseph Johnson.

De Quincey, T. (1970) *Recollections of the Lakes and the Lake Poets*, ed. with intro. by David Wright, Harmondsworth, Penguin.

Dyer, G. (1797) *The Poets' Fate: A Poetic Dialogue*, London, Joseph Johnson.

Enfield, W. (1796) 'The Enquirer IV' (anon.). *Monthly Magazine* II (July): 453–6.

Fink, Z. (1948), 'Wordsworth and the English republican tradition', *Journal of English and German Philology* 4: 107–26.

Fruchtman, J. (1983) 'The apocalyptic politics of Richard Price and Joseph Priestley: a study in late-18th century Millennialism', *Transactions of the American Philosophical Society*, 73, 4.

Gunning, H. (1854) *Reminiscences of the University, Town and County of Cambridge, From the Year 1780*, 2 vols, London, George Bell.

Harrington, J. (1977) *Harrington's Political Writings*, ed. J. G. A. Pocock, Cambridge, Cambridge University Press.

Kelley, M. (1930) 'Thomas Cooper and Pantisocracy', *Modern Language Notes* 45: 218–20.

Lamb, C.(1962) *Essays of Elia*, intro. G. Tillotson, London, Melbourne and Toronto, Dent.

Leask, N. (1988) *The Politics of Imagination in Coleridge's Critical Thought*, London, Macmillan.

Logan, E. (1930) 'Pantisocracy and American travel accounts', *Publications of The Modern Languages Association* 45 (ii): 1069–84.

Lowth, R. (1787) *Lectures on the Sacred Poetry of the Hebrews*, London, Joseph Johnson.

MacGillivray, J. R. (1931) 'The Pantisocracy scheme and its immediate background', in M. Wallace (ed.), *Studies in English at University College, Toronto*, Toronto, Toronto University Press: 131–69.

Maclean, K. (1970) *Agrarian Age: A Background for Wordsworth*, Connecticut, Archon Books.

Morrow, J. (1990), *Coleridge's Political Thought: Property, Morality, and the Limits of Traditional Discourse*, London, Macmillan.

Piper, H. W. (1962) *The Active Universe*, London, Athlone Press.

Pocock, J. G. A. (1985) *Virtue, Commerce and History*, Cambridge, Cambridge University Press.

Robbins, C. (1959) *The Eighteenth-Century Commonwealthmen*, Cambridge, Mass., Harvard University Press.

Roe, N. (1988) *Wordsworth and Coleridge: The Radical Years*, Oxford, Clarendon Press.

Saitta, A. (1950–1) *Fillipo Buonarotti*, vol. 2, Rome, Storia e letteratura.

Simpson, D. (1987), *Wordsworth's Historical Imagination: The Poetry of Displacement*, New York, Methuen.

Southey, R. (1965) *New Letters of Robert Southey*, 2 vols, ed. Kenneth Curry, New York and London, Columbia University Press.

Spinoza, B. (1951) *Tractatus Theologico-politicus*, trans. as *A Theological-political Treatise*, by R. H. M. Elwes, New York, Dover Publications.

Taylor, W. (1984) *Memoirs of William Taylor of Norwich*, 2 vols, ed. J. W. Robbards, London, John Murray.

Thompson, E. P. (1969) 'Disenchantment or default? A lay sermon', in Conor Cruise O'Brien and W. D. Vanech (eds) *Power and Consciousness*, New York, New York University Press; London, London University Press: 149–81.

Venturi, F. (1971) *Utopia and Reform in the Enlightenment*, Cambridge, Cambridge University Press.

Williams, R. (1958) *Culture and Society 1780–1950*, London, Chatto & Windus.

Wollstonecraft, M. (1792) *A Vindication of the Rights of Woman*, London and Melbourne, Dent, 1985.

Wordsworth, W. (1967) *Letters of William and Dorothy Wordsworth, Volume I: The Early Years*, ed. E. De Selincourt, revised by Chester Shaver, Oxford, Clarendon Press.

—— (1971), *The Prelude: A Parallel Text*, ed. J.C. Maxwell, Harmondsworth, Penguin.

—— (1974), *Prose Works of William Wordsworth*, 3 vols, ed. W. J. B. Owen and Jane Worthington Smyser, Oxford, Clarendon Press.

—— (1977), *Poems of William Wordsworth*, 2 vols, ed. John O. Hayden, Harmondsworth, Penguin.

5

Liberty trees and loyal oaks: emblematic presences in some English poems of the French Revolutionary period

William Ruddick

Trees have always stimulated the priest's and the poet's imagination, forming an integral part of the traditional body of myth and fable. In ancient times, spirits were supposedly imprisoned in them, oracles spoke from them, and they were frequently thought of as having a life and personality of their own. In Roman and in eighteenth-century poetry, lovers, philosophers and would-be writers of verse can be found reclining beneath them (preferably near a stream) and the eighteenth century enriched the tradition by incorporating figures somewhat resembling Mr Allworthy in Fielding's *Tom Jones*, who walk up hills to share a prospect with oaks and other ancient denizens of the place and to think ennobling thoughts. But the present essay will concentrate on two later, more original attitudes to trees, developing in the French Revolutionary and early Napoleonic periods; considering how the politicizing of certain types of trees in Radical iconography failed to stir the imagination of the majority of English poets of the time, and how a counter-revolutionary view of the tree can be discovered in a number of notable poems of the period.

In the early years of the French Revolution, the Tree of Liberty (usually a poplar or an oak) formed a visual icon at the centre of public celebrations and, in due course, featured in the highly staged-managed pageants of the new Republic. The Tree of Liberty, thus planted and made a central feature of Revolutionary ceremonies in France during the early 1790s, was, we are told, a piece of symbolism taken over from the May Day ceremonies of the *ancien régime*. Sometimes it is described as a more naturalistic replacement for the maypole. 'By mid 1792,' Ray Tannahill claims in a note to *Paris in the Revolution: A Collection of Eye-witness Accounts*, 'over sixty thousand had been planted throughout France, although both trees and liberty frequently wilted in the care of men unaccustomed to handling them' (Tannahill 1966: 124, n. 1). J. M. Thompson's *The French Revolution*, from which Tannahill's note directly derives, also gives the information that the trees themselves were usually 'young oaks or poplars (since its Latin name

59

populus made it appropriate: "peuplier" and "peuple" are close in French' (Thompson 1943: 341).

The planting of a tree of liberty, though often a stage-managed event, could easily open out into universal and spontaneous celebration. A week after Louis XVI's execution of 27 January 1793, in the brief period before the Republic declared war on England, the *Patriote français* newspaper recorded how

> after the ceremonial planting of a Tree of Liberty in the Place du Carrousel, the band played the *Carmagnole* and the *Ça ira*, which so electrified every soul that the municipal officers, headed by the mayor, danced round it; and at seven at night they were still dancing.
>
> (Thompson 1943: 341)

By June 1794 such spontaneities had given way to the highly-organized spectaculars of Robespierre's 'Fête of the Supreme Being'. The Parisian public, purely an audience now, were treated to elaborately symbolic tableaux and pageants, designed in what must in some ways have been like a 1790s precursor to Busby Berkely's production numbers, designed by the painter Jacques-Louis David. Emblematic characters advanced: 'Childhood, adorned with violets; Adolescence with myrtle; Virility with oak; and white-haired Age, with vine and olive leaves'. These improving characters approached 'an immense mountain' which represented 'the altar of the nation'. On its summit rose the Tree of Liberty and the edifying personages already mentioned grouped themselves around it and beneath its branches (Tannahill 1966: 96).

In France the vogue for trees of liberty seems to have waned rapidly with Robespierre's death. They had but a brief popularity in England, too. The Friends of the People, to name only one of the reformist groups of the early 1790s, had begun to mark the anniversaries of the Revolution with the planting of trees of liberty. But it must be assumed that Pitt put a stop to their activities at an early date, for they soon cease to be noted.

The Tree of Liberty appears to have possessed two related associations for the educated English radical mind. On the one hand, it had a central place in visionary scenes of universal brotherhood, liberty, joy and the dance. The notion of the dance as a social unifier, bringing the generations together, had been memorably expressed by Laurence Sterne in the chapter called 'The Grace' near the end of *A Sentimental Journey* in 1768. There the social order is maintained by the authority of the old peasant father who authorizes the scene of family rejoicing. But it is noticeable that when William Blake reworks the situation in his poem 'The Echoing Green' in *Songs of Innocence* in 1789, the authority of the old generation is made to disappear. Blake's rural merrymaking is one in which all ages are united by sympathy and generous affections, and in this scene the oak has its place:

Old John, with white hair,
Does laugh away care,
Sitting under the oak,
Among the old folk.
They laugh at our play,
And soon they all say:
Such, such were the joys
When we all, girls and boys,
In our youth time were seen
On the Echoing Green.

(ll. 11–20)

Later eighteenth-century theorists, however, had an alternative, though related, view. Tom Paine voices it well in his poem of 1775, 'Liberty Tree' (Paine [1776] 1987: 67–8); a call to the Americans to defend themselves against English aggression. In this poem the Goddess of Liberty comes to America with 'a fair budding branch from the Gardens above' which grows and flourishes till 'freemen' come 'unmindful of names or distinctions' to eat their bread in contentment beneath its branches. In *Common Sense*, the pamphlet of a year later, Paine uses the image of the liberty tree again, imagining the beginnings of colonization in America (or any other newly discovered place), when the initial small group of settlers would gather together from time to time to regulate their society:

> Some convenient tree will afford them a State-House under the branches of which, the whole Colony may assemble to deliberate on public matters . . . in this first parliament every man, by natural right, will have a seat.

(Paine [1776] 1987: 67–8)

So the Tree of Liberty's significance as an emblem of 'Liberté, Egalité, Fraternité' is clear enough. But it does not appear to be possible to show that in England, at least, the Liberty Tree ever managed to develop from a man-made philosopher's emblem of ideal qualities into a living symbol endowed with *poetic* intensity and richness. It seems to remain on the one-to-one level of significance we associate with simile and never to go beyond to the intensity and complex possibilities of metaphor.

One can suggest various reasons why this should have been so. To take just one, it cannot have helped the Liberty Tree in its struggle for icono-graphic existence as a living emblem of freedom that it came up against the biblical emblem of the Tree of the Knowledge of Good and Evil, which so firmly associates free thought and self-assertion with guilt. But most important of all, in that period, must have been the overwhelming impact made on the imaginations of the poets of the day by Edmund Burke's use of the tree image in his *Reflections on the Revolution in France* (1790), together

61

with the way his view of the organic development of society through history fused onto the traditional image of the oak, not as a Liberty Tree but as an emblem of national identity and, more specifically, because of the well-known story of the oak at Boscobel, where Charles II hid after the Battle of Worcester, as an emblem of royal survival.

The strength of eighteenth-century ships depended on oak, and oak was readily employed as an emblem of the British character:

> Heart of oak are our ships,
> Heart of oak are our men:
> We always are ready;
> Steady, boys steady;
> We'll fight and we'll conquer again and again.

So goes the refrain of David Garrick's song 'Heart of Oak', sung in *Harlequin's Invasion* (1759) at a time when there were widespread fears of a French invasion. And early in the century, Pope's *Windsor Forest* (the most borrowed-from of poems when patriotism was the eighteenth-century poet's theme) shows Windsor's trees, in Father Thames's vision, uprooting themselves in their enthusiasm for Queen Anne and the British cause, and turning themselves into ships:

> Thy trees, fair Windsor! now shall leave their Woods,
> And half thy Forests rush into thy Floods,
> Bear Britain's Thunder, and her Cross display,
> To the bright Regions of the rising Day
>
> (ll. 385–8)

The vision is appealing, but it is not, it should be noted, one in which a sense of British history plays a part.

When Edmund Burke published his *Reflections on the Revolution in France* on 1 November 1790, the radical publisher Joseph Johnson was kept so busy bringing out replies by Capel Lofft, Mary Wollstonecraft and Tom Paine (among others) that he had to suspend work on the translations from Homer which the poet William Cowper was undertaking. Cowper mentions the fact in a letter, and it seems clear that he read Burke's celebrated book, because the unfinished poem *Yardley Oak* which he worked on in June 1791 not only incorporates Burke's belief that the development of a society is organic, with slow, gradual improvement a possibility in it, but also tries to subvert Burke's viewpoint in a rather interesting way.

Yardley Oak (written 1793, published 1803) shows traces of Cowper's reading of Burke quite clearly. Burke's assertion that 'it is one of the excellencies of a method in which time is among the assistants, that its operation is slow, and in some cases almost imperceptible' (Burke 1790: 280) becomes part of the texture of Cowper's poem, but it undergoes an important modification. Cowper's thought is closer to Gibbon's as he views

62

the slow growth to magnificence of the ancient tree and its slow decline
to hollow-trunked, giant decay:

> Thought cannot spend itself, comparing still
> The great and little of thy lot, thy growth
> From almost nullity into a state
> Of matchless grandeur, and declension thence,
> Slow, into such magnificent decay.
>
> (ll. 86–90)

The oak disproves Burke's assertion that a society and its constitution
develop slowly but surely towards ideal excellence through time. Cowper
sees that they can also decay. He directly links the trees with the kingdom,
but asserts that

> Change is the diet, on which all subsist,
> Created changeable, and change at last
> Destroys them.
>
> (ll. 72–4)

But the ancient tree, though picturesque in its decay, is also still alive; the
kingdom, for all its feebleness, still one 'whose foundation yet/Fails not in
virtue' (ll. 120–1). And a reading of Cowper's letters makes clear what the
poem itself might lead us to suspect: that *Yardley Oak* is also a poem related
to the traditional equation of the oak with the preservation of kingship.
George III had recently recovered his sanity when Cowper worked on the
poem and a Regency, which would have been dominated by Fox, Sheridan,
Burke (ironically in the context of a poem standing up to his view of
history) and other Whigs, in Cowper's view, providentially averted. Yardley Oak, the ancient tree, also symbolizes George III, elderly and shaken,
but healthy still. The problem of what would happen when the King and
the British Constitution finally succumbed to the effects of time was one
that Cowper could not resolve. The poems breaks off, incomplete and
uncompleteable.

An attempt such as Cowper's to subvert the Burkean view of history in
poetry stands out all the more because of its rarity. Rarer still is a poem
concerned with tree emblems which attacks Burke head on. Yet this is
what Coleridge's strange poem 'The Raven', written in 1797, appears to
be doing. 'The Raven' tells a savage story concerning a bird who buries
an acorn which duly grows into a great oak. Amid its branches the bird
builds a nest. Later the tree is felled, the nest and the young birds destroyed
and the wood used to build a ship. This sinks in a storm, and the raven
flies overhead cawing savagely:

> Right glad was the Raven, and off he went fleet,
> And Death riding home on a cloud he did meet,

63

And he thank'd him again and again for this treat;
They had taken his all, and REVENGE IT WAS SWEET!

(ll. 41–4)

It must be admitted that Coleridge appears to be unique within the period in the extent to which he subverts (indeed savages) the traditional symbolism of the oak and its Burkean sophistications in this poem. The precise meaning of his grim little fable is, it must be said, open to dispute. He himself tried to play it down in later years. In 1795 he had stuck his neck out by openly referring to the Liberty Tree in his pamphlet *Conciones ad Populum*, thus laying himself open to a prima-facie case for prosecution for seditious libel (Holmes 1989: 105). But as part of the process of covering up his former radical tracks in the early 1800s, he subtitled the poem 'A Christmas tale, told by a school-boy to his little brothers and sisters' in 1817. But the poem's original significance was clearly far removed from the world of Dingley Dell. Carl Woodring devotes several excellent pages of exposition to it in his *Politics in the Poetry of Coleridge*, finally confessing to finding the poem one 'born in political immediacy rather than in errant moralizing or idle narrative (Woodring 1961: 137) but not ideally precise in its pairing of events and characters within the verse with the political situation in which it was written. Yet the sense that the Burkean old oak, representing the British Constitution under which the 'swine' of placemen feed till its fruits are almost all devoured, is replaced by a new growth in reformist times is clear enough. This new oak of liberty and reform in which the raven nests and rears its young is chopped down by the woodman, Pitt, and its timbers used to bear armaments in warfare. When war ends in disaster and the destruction of the State, with the new oak, wrongly used, shattered and sinking in the storm, the raven rejoices: 'They had taken his all, and REVENGE IT WAS SWEET!' The fable is apocalyptic: its imagery begins with Burke, but ends in a wholly new interpretation of the oak and its symbolism within the context of contemporary political realities.

The 1790s were years in which the British, debarred from Continental travel, were exploring their own country and using their eyes in search of the picturesque and the antiquarian with a new zeal. Ancient trees shared the traveller's attention with ancient buildings. Guide books began to mention them. The artist Joseph Farington, trained by Richard Wilson and an enthusiast for the works of Claude Lorrain (who had made fine studies of Italian oaks in the mid-seventeenth century), was in the van of the new taste: he had, in fact, been making drawings of old trees since the 1760s. But Farington's studies of celebrated ancient oaks, dating from the late 1780s till the early years of the new century (*The Lady Oak near Cressage, Shropshire* (1789), *The Cowthorpe Oak, near Wetherby, Yorkshire* (1801)) show a remarkable sympathy with the signs of age and individuality which distinguished these giant trees. They are quintessentially *English* studies,

64

and studies which incorporate the visible effects of time; and since Farington was a staunch Tory, the trees represent survival and a capacity to
generate interest and sympathy in their old age, rather than to trouble the
spectator with thoughts of the future. They show the same power to speak
for the historic past as Cowper's Yardley Oak, but as witnesses to history
they endow it with the positive power of their yet-living strength. In
Farington's tree studies of the giant oaks, Burke's metaphor for the slow
but certain evolution of the State through history is given a direct visual
correlative.

By 1803, William Wordsworth had moved far from his youthful Revolutionary sympathies, and was finding his way onto the path which would
lead him to the High Toryism of his later years. Though as yet little
advanced along that path, and still unacquainted with Cowper's *Yardley
Oak*, which would not see print till the following year, Wordsworth's eye
was upon the trees, and particularly the ancient trees of his own Lakeland
region. In 1802 his sister Dorothy had lamented the felling of the old trees
around Rydal in her *Journal* (6 May 1802) and it is clear that these ancient
survivals had a strong emotional significance for both the Wordsworths.
So, a year later, William looked at another venerable tree species, the yew,
a family also rich in historical associations, with medieval bowmen and
Crécy, Agincourt and other great moments in earlier struggles against the
French. In the poem 'Yew Trees', Wordsworth offers a tribute to the
power of these old trees to stimulate the historic imagination. His poem
has its resemblances to Cowper, but in its untroubled sense of historic
continuity it comes far closer to Burke: unlike Yardley Oak, the great yew
at Lorton is

> a living thing
> Produced too slowly ever to decay;
> Of form and aspect too magnificent
> To be destroyed.
>
> (ll. 10–13)

The historic sense leads into moral reflections on the capacity of the trees
to contain, as well as suggest, thoughts of time and human mutability.
But above all, the trees form 'a natural temple scattered o'er/With altars
undisturbed of mossy stone' (ll. 29–30): age has endowed them with the
capacity to endure, seemingly without suffering loss. As emblems of the
nation whose history they commemmorate, they stand triumphant. A
glance of comparison at the *Lines Left upon a Seat in a Yew-tree* which
Wordsworth began at Hawkshead School and finished in 1795, with their
simpler moral-reflective framework, will instantly show the extent to which
his historical sense had deepened and achieved a confidence in the existence
of meaningful historical and political perspectives in the interim.

The whole subject of emblematic trees and their utilization in English poetry during the 1790s and the early years of the new century is one which tantalizes by its incompleteness of evidence: one senses that at a time when direct reference to the Liberty Tree was proscribed (though the icon itself was far from forgotten: liberty trees featured prominently in the Irish Rebellion in and around Wexford in 1798, for instance) there may have been much covert use of the symbol which modern writers have failed to distinguish, or which has simply failed to survive because of the ephemeral nature of the original publications. Even in the work of major writers one cannot speak with absolute confidence, but an instance from Wordsworth's *Prelude* may serve to suggest some possibilities.

Shortly after writing about the yew trees in Lorton Vale, Wordsworth reached that point in the composition of his autobiographical poem which involved him in recalling memories of his first visit to France in 1790, when he and his Cambridge friend Robert Jones crossed the country in order to reach the Alps and penetrate into northern Italy. Present-day Wordsworth criticism is much concerned with absences and silences in *The Prelude*, so it seems legitimate to conclude the present discussion by looking at Wordsworth's account of his arrival in France at the time when the French were celebrating the first anniversary of the fall of the Bastille, and also the granting by the King of a new Constitution. The passage has one or two rather unexpected features, and also one or two curious absences:

> Southward thence
> We took our way, direct through hamlets, towns,
> Gaudy with reliques of that festival,
> Flowers left to wither on triumphal arcs
> And window-garlands. On the public roads—
> And once three days successively through paths
> By which our toilsome journey was abridged—
> Among sequestered villages we walked
> And found benevolence and blessedness
> Spread like a fragrance everywhere, like spring
> That leaves no corner of the land untouched.
> Where elms for many and many a league in files,
> With their thin umbrage, on the stately roads
> Of that great kingdom rustled o'er our heads,
> For ever near us as we paced along
>
> (*Prelude*, 1805: VI. 360–74)

The reference to 'that great kingdom' may alert us to a degree of uneasiness on Wordsworth's part. Why, in 1805, when Napoleon's authority over the French was fully established, speak so directly of its former state? And why is the description of the 'reliques of that festival' allowed 'flowers left to wither on triumphal arcs/And window-garlands' but not trees of liberty?

Why should the roads be remembered as fringed with iconographically neutral elms rather than the poplars that a modern reader feels sure must have been by French roadsides even then? Are they, in fact, a later innovation, or was Wordsworth sinking the memory of an emblematically subversive tree?

The uneasiness which appears to mark a passage such as the one just quoted may suggest more widespread problems which the inconographical characteristics of certain trees, gained in the years immediately preceding the French Revolution, possessed for English poets of the 1790s and early 1800s. But not only the Tree of Liberty cast a shadow over poetry; there was also the much deeper and darker umbrage of Burke's ancient and royal oak. Much still may be discovered in this shadowy area of English political and poetical history. Hopefully my own brief investigation may serve to stimulate further exploration of the subject.

BIBLIOGRAPHY

Burke, E. (1790) *Reflections on the Revolution in France*, ed. Conor Cruise O'Brien, Harmondsworth, Penguin, 1968.

Coleridge, W. (1795) *Conciones ad Populum*, Bristol.

Holmes, R. (1989) *Coleridge: Early Visions*, London, Hodder & Stoughton.

Paine, T. ([1776] 1987) *The Thomas Paine Reader*, ed. Michael Foot and Isaac Kramnick, Harmondsworth, Penguin.

Tannahill, R. (1966) *Paris in the Revolution: A Collection of Eyewitness Accounts*, London, Folio Society.

Thompson, J. M. (1943) *The French Revolution*, Oxford, Blackwell.

Woodring, C. (1961) *Politics in the Poetry of Coleridge*, Madison, Wisconsin, Univeristy of Wisconsin Press.

Wordsworth, W. (1977) *Poems, Volume 1*, ed. John O. Hayden, Harmondsworth, Penguin.

——— (1979) *The Prelude 1799, 1805, 1850*, ed. Jonathan Wordsworth, M. H. Abrams and Stephen Gill, New York and London, Norton & Co.

6

Radical sensibility in the 1790s

Chris Jones

Sensibility in the eighteenth century poses an intriguing problem for the historian of ideas. It is not a unitary idea, but an umbrella term covering a wide variety of ideas and attitudes. It poses similar problems to the vexed concept of Romanticism, with which it has direct historical and ideological continuities. Unlike 'Romantic', it was a term widely accepted by its representatives, who felt themselves part of a distinct modern progressive movement. It is linked with the philosophical ideas of Shaftesbury, Hutcheson, Hume, Smith and Butler in the movement from reason to feeling as the ultimate authority in matters of belief. Towards the end of the century the appeals to feeling appear to lose contact with philosophical formulations. The shift from 'sentimental' to 'sensibility' seems to imply this growing instability. Sensibility became a vogue word, contaminated by popular indiscriminate usage, and it also became identified with historical issues. It was associated with the humanitarian campaigns against slavery, for reform in the treatment of prisoners, orphans, child-labourers, and the destitute. It was also implicated in the libertarian ideas of the American and French Revolutions. Most of the early Romantic writers can be associated with the causes of Sensibility in the 1790s, yet during this period Sensibility and its associated vocabulary perished in a storm of abuse and satire, to be replaced by Romanticism, a creed which cultivated an individual vision, commonly of loss and compensation. In this essay I want to investigate the instabilities within the concept which can be ascribed to philosophical and ideological differences and the ways in which they are played out in discursive and imaginative literature.

The demise of Sensibility was principally due to its association with French principles as the Revolution degenerated into the Terror and the rise of a despot. This and the wartime suppression of radical ideas in Britain revealed the schisms in the school of Sensibility. Even on subjects dear to the heart of humanity opinion was not unanimous. Anna Seward, the model of respectable provincial Sensibility, refused to support the Anti-Slavery campaign because she had been persuaded that slavery was essential to Britain's commercial prosperity. She was equally persuadable in her attitude to the French Revolution, veering with every book she read until she became a vituperative critic of all who supported it. Lord Kames, a disciple of Rousseau, campaigned for the abolition of foundling hospitals. Burns, reared in the same culture of Scottish Sensibility, oscillated between celebrating the patriotism of a contented peasantry, willing to perish in faint huzzas for Royal George, and making disparaging comments about belted earls. He was suspected of diverting confiscated cannons to the French and joining in a public rendering of the *ça ira*. Within the philosophical debates of the eighteenth century opinions were divided on subjects such as the priority of the partial or universal affections, the use of reason, and the moral status of the imagination. Even the central notion of Sensibility, that man was capable of benevolence and was naturally drawn towards it, was often understood in a qualified way. Ostensibly benevolent actions could be motivated by a wish for popularity or the 'selfish' desire for the pleasures of beneficence. Evangelicals like Cowper and Hannah More were part of the movement, though they held natural man to be inherently corrupt. Coleridge too distrusted the natural man and relied on the divine power of association to produce a being capable of true benevolence.

The divisions within Sensibility were sites of conflict before the French Revolution, but they split the movement apart in the 1790s. At least three aspects of Sensibility were distinguished by contemporary writers. Self-centred emotional indulgence in 'fine feelings' was attacked by all parties. A conservative Sensibility claimed that man's feelings were fostered by the associations of traditional society and were its principal support. A radical Sensibility continued to trust to innate emotional response to provide the basis of a beneficial social order, and embraced a philosophy which proposed to liberate individual energies. It espoused the libertarian ideals of the Revolution, and continued to use the terms of Sensibility to criticize British institutions.

Many modern studies devalue the radical strain of Sensibility, identifying it with the individualistic, self-indulgent variety, or conflating it with Rationalism.[1] Some have aligned Sensibility with established opinions, especially in the construction of femininity (see Todd 1986: ch. 7, Poovey 1984). Even in Gary Kelly's recent *English Fiction of the Romantic Period* (1989), which treats Sensibility as a critical movement, some confusion appears when at one point he calls it 'that culture of courtliness in disguise' (Kelly 1989: 40). But for many writers Sensibility prompted criticism of things as they are and aspirations towards a better state of society foreshadowed by the French Revolution. Wordsworth presented his dedication to the Revolution as a movement of heart towards the oppressed French peasantry and proclaimed a faith 'of passionate intuition' (*Prelude*, 1805: X, 587) that the Republic would march forward to irresistible universal victory. Coleridge, while distinguishing true benevolence from passive

69

sensibility, used the language of sensibility in attacking the slave trade and the French War.

Helen Maria Williams identified herself with the French cause and broke with Portman Square and the respectable traditions of the Bluestockings. Her *Letters From France* (1792, 1793, 1795) carried Sensibility into imprisonment and massacre. Like Wordsworth and Godwin, she attributed the Terror to the effect of previous oppression and she thought the horror of its bloodiest passages exceeded by the scenes on board a slave-transport. Imprisoned under Robespierre, her sympathy for her fellow sufferers pointedly excluded the Royal family, and she continued to defend the Revolution (see Jones 1989). She might well have inspired Gillray's portrait of Sensibility in the famous *New Morality* print. This shows Gillray's typical French fishwife cradling a dead bird in her arms, while her foot rests on the head of the decapitated monarch. Williams had included in her novel *Julia* (1790) an 'Elegy: On finding a young THRUSH in the Street, who escaped from the Writer's Hand, as she was bringing him home, and, falling down the Area of a House, could not be found' (1790: II, 27). She also defended La Reveillère-Lépaux and the Theophilanthropists whose meeting provided the scene for Gillray's print. For conservatives, the implication of the print was that the votaries of Sensibility, in their fine feelings towards dead birds or mistreated asses, became callously neglectful of the major obligations of social life. They could not imagine that the same feelings which pitied animals might inspire potent indignation against the oppressors of men.

The radical Sensibility of the 1790s was not just an individual humanitarian response to human suffering. It had its roots in ideas of a progressive community based on the benevolist principles of Shaftesbury and Hutcheson, which were developed in social and aesthetic philosophy. Scottish philosophers propounded theories of social progress which started from the assumptions of Hutcheson and linked progress with the liberalization of traditional power relationships. Their theories stressed the progressive nature of man and the natural evolution of his institutions. One of them, John Millar, was a supporter of Fox. In the 1790s he joined the Friends of the People, contributed to the *Analytical Review*, and was persecuted for progressive opinions during the 1790s. Shaftesbury's libertarian republic of letters existed only in the equality of the gentleman's club, but his ideas were developed in a less restrictive context. Shaftesbury's 'final version of the moral sense' was of a '*Sense of Partnership* with Human Kind' and included 'Natural affection, Humanity, obligingness, or that sort of *Civility* which rises from a just *Sense* of the common *Rights* of Mankind, and the *natural Equality* there is amongst those of the same Species' (Voitle 1984: 332, quoting *Sensus Communis*). Both Shaftesbury and Hutcheson criticized customs which had perverted a 'natural' humanity and asserted the individual's capacity to act on a rational apprehension of the good of the widest system of which the individual was a member. It was one of their cardinal points that this extensive benevolence should regulate the partial affections towards kindred. Shaftesbury's conception of the artist as creator could also license the creative and reforming powers of the individual in the social sphere, when guided by an intuitive faculty which grasped the sublime of humanity as well as that of nature.

The line of thought running through Hume and Adam Smith to Burke can be seen as a particularly conservative tradition. Hume speculated on the possible mutations of natural benevolence, but used it to justify prevailing social mores as 'natural'. Smith took this union of Sensibility with the forms of contemporary society and sanctified it by the hidden hand of Providence. Both exalted the private affections distrusted by Shaftesbury and Hutcheson.

Hume, especially when considering aesthetic response, appealed to the contagion of the passions, and Smith feelingly evoked the human desire for unbounded sympathy, yet both explored the mechanisms by which Providence directed this capacity to the limited ends ensuring the stability of society. Hume's account of sympathy in the *Treatise* (1739/40) follows his general empirical argument that more immediate objects are more strongly experienced. Therefore we sympathize more with relations, friends, and countrymen than with strangers, and have difficulty in sympathizing with those whose joys or sufferings have no direct relation to our own. Sympathy is defined as an imaginary participation in the joys or sorrows of the individual who is contemplated, and Hume finds that we sympathize more readily with happiness, especially the happiness of the rich and powerful (Hume 1739/40: 362). In the *Enquiry* (1751), obviously in response to criticism, he remarks that the philosophic man will not 'measure out degrees of esteem according to the rent-rolls of his acquaintance', but a footnote still recognizes that in general, 'power and riches commonly cause respect, poverty and meanness contempt' (Hume 1888: 248). Adam Smith's idea of sympathy is strongly regulative, a means by which the norms of society are upheld. We all look for sympathy and approval in others, in fact, mankind do not wish to be great, but to be beloved; but in order to gain people's sympathy one has to restrain one's demands to those which society, or an 'impartial spectator' will admit (Smith 1759: 22–3). While he recognizes that the tendency to worship the rich and powerful is deleterious to morals, he considers that it serves a more important purpose in maintaining the distinction of ranks and the stability of society. The rich have a positive duty to parade their wealth and encourage the admiration of the vulgar. Charity definitely stops at home, confined to the narrow familial connections which form the basis of society: 'the peace and order of society is of more importance than even the relief of the miserable' (Smith 1759: 226). Price and Reid considered Smith's theory to be a refinement of the selfish system, and certainly there is little optimism about the benevolent propensities of man in Smith's writings. It is only fear

71

of legal punishment (another 'implanted' sense) that prevents universal aggression:

> Men, though naturally sympathetic, feel so little for another, with whom they have no particular connexion, in comparison to what they feel for themselves . . . that if this principle did not stand up within them in his defence . . . they would, like wild beasts, be at all times ready to fly upon him; and a man would enter an assembly of men as he enters a den of lions.
>
> (Smith 1759: 86)

It is easy to see how this type of Sensibility leads to the affirmations of Burke that all our feelings are formed by the habitual associations of the *status quo*, and that any departure from these divinely implanted guides will bring anarchy.

Mackenzie's Harley (*The Man of Feeling*, 1771) answers perfectly to Smith's description of the man of humanity who is an exception in a naughty world, a heart-warming spectacle, but condemned to victimization:

> There is a helplessness in the character of extreme humanity which more than anything interests our pity . . . We only regret that it is unfit for the world, because it must expose the person who is endowed with it as a prey to the perfidy and ingratitude of insinuating false-hood, and to a thousand pains and uneasinesses, which, of all men, he the least deserves to feel, which generally too he is, of all men, the least capable of supporting.
>
> (Smith 1759: 40)

This picture of the man of feeling is an ironic conservative construction, the picture of one who does not recognize that in this divinely ordered world there are certain inevitable evils which must be accepted for the stability and perfection of the whole. Harley uselessly wears himself out reacting against a world which he cannot change, which does not need to be changed, and which, in fact, he has no real idea of changing. In the one instance in which his endeavours achieve some result, in uniting the seduced Emily with her father, nothing but fresh oportunities for graphic misery arise. The father can only wish her dead, rather than dead to honour, and though Harley agrees that the world's notions of the case are hard, he can only counsel him to look to the hereafter (Mackenzie 1771: 73). Social attitudes can only be accepted, never combated, and if tran-scended, only in the prospect of divine mercy. Many of the novels of sensibility have a similar pattern. The subject of distress, invariably a woman, is subject to various modes of oppression, many of them arising from society, yet the author largely eschews social criticism to focus on the virtuous resignation of the Griselda-like heroine as she displays the Christian and specifically female virtue of passive fortitude. The order of society seems to be indentified with the order of nature as part of a Providential scheme which commands submission. One has to look to the novels of the 1780s and 1790s to find convincing examples of the man of social benevolence and the woman of active courage.

After the Americans and then the French had strongly proposed a doubt that British society was divinely ordered, the conflicts between individual and society were viewed more equally. The attitude towards the typical female victim-heroine of earlier literature changed. We find direct contradictions of the image, like Holcroft's Anna St Ives or Wollstonecraft's Maria, who refused to 'sentimentalize herself to stone' under her oppression (Wollstonecraft 1976: 154). We also find parodies, like Bage's Miss Campinet and Charlotte Smith's Geraldine. Godwin notes the ambiguous response now possible to previous works, here Rowe's *Fair Penitent*:

> The moral deduced from this admirable poem by one set of readers will be, the mischievous tendency of unlawful love, and the duty incumbent upon the softer sex to devote themselves in all things to the will of their fathers and husbands. Other readers may perhaps regard it as a powerful satire upon the institutions at present existing in society relative to the female sex, and the wretched consequences of that mode of thinking, by means of which, in woman, 'one false step entirely damns her fame'.
>
> (Godwin 1797: 136–7)

Many writers attacked the conservative principles on which the conventions of sentimental fiction were based. Godwin attacked the partial affections, those family loyalties which narrowed the range of benevolence and perpetuated inequality. Wollstonecraft attacked the specifically feminine interpretation of sentimental virtues like modesty, delicacy, passive fortitude and honour. Bage attacked all the shibboleths of sentimentalized femininity, and prescriptive familial, religious, and social reverence. Charlotte Smith parodied the conventions of the conservative sentimental novel, modelling her heroes and heroines on conventional figures only to involve them in the most unconventional activities.

The proponents of radical Sensibility, referring back to the tradition of Shaftesbury and Hutcheson, attacked not only Burke, but particularly Adam Smith, whose *Theory of Moral Sentiments* reached its sixth edition in 1790. Two of its crucial passages found their way into Coleridge's notebooks (Coburn 1957: 155), and Wordsworth identified Smith as a major antagonist in his letter to 'Christopher North'. Godwin and Mary Wollstonecraft took issue with Smith's definition of the 'impartial spectator' as the ultimate judge of one's actions, but appreciated the force of Smith's community of feeling to limit individuality.

A more general point of philosophical debate became a major flashpoint in the 1790s. Godwin commented in 1801 that persons not versed in the mysteries of controversy, may perhaps be at a loss to understand, why . . . the doctrine of 'universal philanthropy' should awaken in lawyers and divines, in reviewers and scribblers for the circulating libraries, such fierceness of invective, and such vehemence of reprobation.

(Godwin 1968: 331)

Perhaps Godwin's complaint was disingenuous, since in the early years of the decade he had hailed philosophy as no longer a spectator but an actor in national events. 'Universal philanthropy' was indeed one of the most bitterly attacked notions of the 1790s. It was claimed to subvert the loyalties to country, to the Church, and to family, which were seen as the bulwarks of national and even personal identity, and to dissolve the natural feelings which gave them authority in an arid rationalism and rootless cosmopolitanism. Robespierre's rhetoric of *sensibilité* gave such notions a sanguinary edge as he sought to impose egalitarian virtue by means of the guillotine (see Trahard 1936). Richard Price scandalized Burke by preaching that love of one's country is best shown by extending its liberties. Price was no revolutionary. He defended 'constitutional' rights and called for them to be made more complete by the toleration of Dissenters (Price 1789: 35–6). But he used the language of Sensibility to link Dissenters with an undefined mass of those excluded from their 'proper' place as citizens, and gestured towards France as a beacon to equal rights. The term 'patriot' became a notable site of conflict as radicals adopted Price's cosmopolitan sense. Price, like most writers, held that natural Sensibility should be regulated, but maintained that it was the narrow, partial affections which had to be regulated by the expansive conception of the good of the whole and a rational assessment of ways and means. The main development of conservative Sensibility had been to restrict a potentially unlimited capacity for sympathy to the exclusive bounds of country and family. One effect of the proscription of overt political debate in the 1790s was to displace its conflicts of principle into the sphere of personal and domestic conduct.

Charlotte Smith was one of the popular novelists of the 1790s who enforced a political interpretation of the traditional subordinations of domestic life. The surface of her novels seems conventional until one notices the devices of parody, irony, and structural parallelism which question traditional roles and expectations. Diana Bowstead (1986: 259) has pointed out the parallel in *Desmond* (1792) between the treatment of Geraldine by her husband and the oppression of the French under the *ancien régime*. She fails, however, to recognize Geraldine as a parody-heroine, carrying conventional behaviour to a ludicrous extreme, while at the same time engaging in activities which subvert traditional standards. Geraldine is a Griselda figure, a self-confessed martyr to most obligations of feminine propriety, especially in her wifely obedience to an unfeeling wastrel. Yet

Smith uses her to voice the most unequivocal approval of the Revolution, including an acceptance of the deaths involved in the first phase. Only at the end do we learn that this impossible paragon has arranged the lying-in of a 'fallen woman', who owes her condition to the man Geraldine later accepts as a husband. The technique doubly licenses transgression. The conventional reader might be drawn to sympathize with the tolerant humanity of transcendent virtue, the more liberal reader to reject her self-martyrdom as exorbitant. In *The Old Manor House* (1793) Smith uses a more elaborate parallel between the domestic situation of the Manor and the wider political world. The old Royalist, Mrs Raynal, is governed by her 'prime minister', Mrs Lennard, who keeps secret files on the nefarious doings of the other officers of the household. Smith's attacks on lawyers have often been considered a reflection of her own injustices at their hands, but she anticipates a later focus of radical criticism in showing the growing dominance of sinister financial and legal functionaries over the Manor. This development is mirrored in the rise of the bourgeois Woodford from the wine trade, to Parliament, and then to a more lucrative intimacy with government contracts and finance. Another interesting feature of the book is that if Scott took the name of Waverley from *Desmond*, he took more than a hint for his plot from *The Old Manor House*. The hero, Orlando Somerive, a member of an estranged branch of the family, has the same favoured position in the house of an old-fashioned zealot and, like Waverley, he undergoes disillusionment in warfare, here against the Americans.

The Banished Man (1794), which many saw as a retraction of radical views, is in fact a reaffirmation of faith in the original principles of the Revolution, and technically one of her most ambitious works. She takes a French emigré, D'Alonville, for a hero, and submits him to continuous irony in his aristocratic disdain, not only for the *sans-culottes*, but for everything to do with the Revolution. A parallel is drawn between the French emigrés and the British Denzil family, victims of Lord Aberdare's legal chicanery. The emigrés have been oppressed by men like Robespierre who turned the liberty promised by the new Constitution into anarchic terror, while the Denzils are oppressed by an aristocrat who has perverted the so-called liberty of the British Constitution and the supposed equity of British law. Charlotte Smith's use of the code of Sensibility is seen in the attack on the private affections and family pride. While D'Alonville attacks the Revolutionists' language of republican equality which dissolves the ties of blood and honour, the families of the enemies of Revolution are represented as oppressive and vengeful, and lack any family affection. His brother, a Revolutionary whom he scorns as a renegade, shows him exemplary friendship, saving him from execution and facilitating his escape from France. Charlotte Smith was well read in the literature of political and philosophical controversy, as her footnotes witness, but the subtlety with which she manipulates the techniques of the novel of Sensibility have yet to be fully acknowledged.

The writers of radical Sensibility are principally distinguished by their criticism of conservative Sensibility. In this difference within a common tradition lies the difficulty of classifying them. There is a long-standing view of Godwin and Mary Wollstonecraft as rationalistic critics of Sensibility. There is also a well-established criticism of their inconsistencies. Godwin is supposed to have subverted the entire structure of *Political Justice* (1793) by admitting the influence of the feelings; Mary Wollstonecraft is accused of sharing the sentimental basis of the attitudes which she condemns. I would not claim that they are free of confusions, but I believe that they had a consistent purpose within the framework of radical Sensibility. They both affirm the priority of individual feeling as the source of Revolutionary action, but feelings which are directed to the general good and actions which are sanctioned by reason.

Mark Philp (1986) asserts that the first edition of *Political Justice* is founded on the premises of Rational Dissent, specifically the doctrines of Richard Price. He maintains, however, that in subsequent editions, Godwin replaced the Rationalist framework with one based on the benevolist premises of 'British Moralists' (Philp 1986: 208). In 1814 Dugald Stewart made a more specific attribution when he identified Godwin's system as 'precisely the system of Hutcheson', with the mischievous addition of the obligation of justice to the promptings of the moral sense (1854: 599). The first volume of Stewart's work came out in 1794. The second, from which the quotation is taken, appeared in 1814. Godwin studied Hutcheson at Hoxton, and his proposal for a seminary at Epsom in 1783 uses the language and ideas which we associate with his work after *Political Justice*. He appeals to an 'intuitive principle' of morality, speaks of the imagination as the 'grand instrument of virtue', and praises 'that very elegant philosopher, Mr. Hutcheson' for demonstrating that 'self-love is not the source of all our passions, but that disinterested benevolence has its seat in the human heart' (Godwin 1966: 194–7). The epithet 'elegant' also suggests the influence of Shaftesbury.

The turn to Hutcheson was then a *re*turn, if indeed, Godwin fundamentally turned at all. Altogether, there is just too much stress, even in the first edition, on the 'great and inexpressible operations of reflection' (Godwin 1793: I, 58) to content a Hartleyan and too much stress on natural benevolence to content a Rational Moralist. In the revisions the Hutchesonian basis becomes much clearer. 'Virtue' in the first edition is regularly replaced by 'benevolence', a key point of identification, since Hutcheson was notorious for reducing the concept of virtue to the approval of benevolence. Even in 1793 virtue is defined as 'a desire to promote the benefit of intelligent beings in general, the quantity of virtue being as the quantity of desire' (1793: I, 254). Godwin's standard of justice is notoriously discriminating, judging the worth of individuals by their virtue. Yet here too, virtue is equivalent to benevolence, the capacity to spread happiness and enlightenment to others. In what Lamb called the 'famous fire cause, Archbishop Fénelon versus my mother' Godwin complained that people had misunderstood him to imply that the saving of Fénelon would proceed from calculation, whereas the saving of the mother would be precipitated by passion. No noble action, he maintained, can be performed without passion, and in other parts of *Political Justice* the reader is in no doubt that Godwin is praising the most ardent passion of benevolence in Roman heroes who sacrificed their lives for their country. The difficulty arises because in the Fénelon passage Godwin is attacking the partial affections which had been exaggerated into unthinking principles of action by conservative Sensibility. In his attack on family affections he is attacking the exclusivity and self-aggrandizement of the great aristocratic families who monopolized the wealth and power of Britain. The French abolition of aristocracy (or at least titles of nobility) was noted enthusiastically in red ink in his Diary for 19 June 1790. He went on to write several drafts of a Letter to Sheridan which focused his dissatisfaction with the constitutional wranglings of the 1780s and welcomed the progress of public opinion towards accepting the abolition of hereditary greatness. Passages from the Letter found their way into *Political Justice* and the attack on aristocracy was continued in his suggestion for the abolition of surnames.

Godwin was aware that he was assaulting feelings and principles which were deeply cherished by conservative Sensibility and celebrated in sentimental literature. He discriminated between feelings which were directed to the good of society, viewed as a society of equals, and feelings which were bred by inequality and dependence. Godwin blamed the unequal institutions of society for producing the bad passions of envy, jealousy and malice, but he also saw a similar generation of factitiously exaggerated 'amiable' passions which prevented the progress of society. He attacked gratitude, the slavish dependence which made men the objects of demeaning and ostentatious charity rather than fellow beings claiming a just right to the means of life. Gratitude, he comments, 'a principle which has so often been the theme of the moralist and the poet, is no part of either justice or virtue' (Godwin 1793: I, 84). He was not an isolated doctrinaire in his attacks on established forms of charity. Wollstonecraft and Wordsworth similarly criticized them as marks of inequality and oppression.

Godwin's passion for society was a passion for reforming it. In elaborating his scale of happiness from the labourer to the man of cultivation and benevolence, he wished to raise everyone to the highest state of human existence. Like Wollstonecraft, Coleridge and Williams, he took little pleasure in the nostalgic pictures of contented rustic life which charmed conservative sentimentalists. Yet it seems that in following the social passion of benefiting society, the individual must sedulously avoid society, fleeing the contamination of its regressive institutions. All progress comes from individual exploration, yet for progress to be introduced into society, mind must conspire with mind, and new ideas permeate the masses. Such disparate duties might be conceivable in the early 1790s, when like-minded society was readily to be found. But as reaction triumphed, the danger facing the exploring mind was isolation and impotence. The idea of a reformed society no longer found a reflection in widely shared aspirations but remained a shining vision in the mind and a weighty volume on the shelf.

The prospect of wandering in an ideal world was an ever-present possibility to Mary Wollstonecraft. In fact the idealization of the object of aspiration is for her ennobling, testifying to the true home of the soul in the hereafter, and essential for personal development. Without illusions fostered by the imagination and the passions, we would have no stimulus to any activity. On the face of it, this is a rather pessimistic philosophy, ill-adapted to a reforming crusade. The world, viewed objectively, is a fundamentally unsatisfying place. Superiority of mind 'leads to the creation of ideal beauty, when life, surveyed with a penetrating eye, appears a tragi-comedy, in which little can be seen to satisfy the heart without the help of fancy' (Wollstonecraft 1792: 309). The creation of an ideal realm might lead to an inability to do justice to the world of reality. This a fault of which she accuses Rousseau and Burke, and a similar criticism is made of those females not of a superior mind whose imaginations dwell in the dream-world of sentimental novels. The factor which legitimizes the workings of passion and imagination as revolutionary powers is the reason.

In the *Vindication of the Rights of Men* (1790) she sees the sacred 'feelings of the heart' as the 'sun of life', but in order for it to bring forth virtue it must 'impregnate' the reason (1790: 70). Emotions 'that reason deepens' are justly termed 'the feelings of humanity' (1790: 137). Imagination elevates these emotions: 'My passions pursue objects that the imagination enlarges, till they become only a sublime idea that shrinks from the enquiry of sense, and mocks the experimental philosophers who would confine this spiritual phlogiston in their material crucibles' (1790: 76–7). The trouble with Burke and Rousseau is that the working of the imagination dominates the work of the reason, especially in their view of woman. To both she applies the comment that their reflection inflames the imagination instead of enlightening the understanding. This feminist insight encourages Wollstonecraft in her adherence to reason in her criticism of Burke's Sensibility.

The guides of Burke's Sensibility, she argues, are not feelings or instincts but habits, and habits

> with which the reason of others shackled them . . . Affection for parents, reverence for superiors and antiquity, notions of honour, or that worldly self-interest that shrewdly shows them that honesty is

78

the best policy: all proceed from the reason for which they serve as substitutes; – but it is reason at second-hand.

(1790: 71–2)

Among these so-called instincts she includes the family affections, which 'may be included in the sordid calculations of blind self-love' (1790: 44). Yet she refers to 'natural' parental affection with respect when criticizing primogeniture: 'it is the spurious offspring of overweening pride – and not that first source of civilization, natural parental affection, that makes no difference between child and child, but what reason justifies by pointing out superior merit' (1790: 46). This is a typical example of the struggle between conservative and liberal/radical interpretations of the same terms. Both Burke and Wollstonecraft appeal to natural family feelings, but what is natural is defined within differing ideological contexts.

Wollstonecraft's *Vindication of the Rights of Woman* (1792) is a sustained attempt to redefine the terms of conservative Sensibility, such as delicacy, chastity, and modesty in ways which suggest equality, self-respect and independence, and in ways which are applicable to men as well as women. Real modesty, in her definition, can be attributed to the heroine of *La Nouvelle Héloise*, Christ, Milton and Washington! Sometimes the battle for the terms of sensibility can lead to downright confusion. In *Mary* (1788) she predominantly uses 'delicacy' in the accepted conservative sense of behaviour conforming to propriety. In a passage from *The Wrongs of Woman* (1798) the heroine comments on her rejection of the sympathetic overtures of other men when she was totally alienated from her husband and ascribes this to 'delicacy':

> My reserve was then the consequence of delicacy. Freedom of conduct has emancipated many women's minds; but my conduct has most rigidly been governed by my principles, till the improvement of my understanding has enabled me to discern the fallacy of prejudices at war with nature and reason.

(1976: 156)

'Delicacy' here is the same conservative principle, subsequently dissolved by reason. Later, however, when Maria is ready to consummate her relationship with Darnford and is pressurized to return to her husband, Darnford comments: 'In her case, to talk of duty, was a farce, excepting what was due to herself. Delicacy, as well as reason, forbade her ever to think of returning to her husband' (1976: 187). This is a delightfully iconoclastic use of the term. For conservative Sensibility, delicacy would demand the penitent return of a strayed wife. 'Delicacy' here has the radical sense of integrity to personal feelings. Yet we have to register the almost sacramental terms in which, a page later, Wollstonecraft describes Maria's sexual union with Darnford: 'As her husband she now received

79

him' (1976: 188). That delicacy which prescribes exclusive loyalty to a 'husband' is seen as the natural concomitant of a union based on feeling. Wollstonecraft looks forward to a society where marriage might be more sacred, instead of wishing to abolish it like Godwin. She is enmeshed in disputes within the terms of Sensibility, rather than wishing to break entirely with traditional social forms.

Despite her strictures on Rousseau, Wollstonecraft, like most writers of radical Sensibility, counted genius and imagination as allies in the moral reformation of society. The didactic purpose of the art of Sensibility was to develop and refine the social affections. Writers like Blair anticipated Wordsworth's interpretation of taste as an active expansion of the reader's sensibility. Taste and genius were closely linked, just as Shaftesbury's virtuoso shared the elevation of the art which he appreciated. This linking survived in the ideas of Shelley, though the ecstatic experience which he celebrated as the inspiration of the poet and the auditor was all too easily affected and parodied.

It is a common assumption, fostered by the anti-Jacobin writings of Edgeworth and Austen, that Sensibility, especially a sensibility expanded by poetry and music, and ready to engage in a love-relationship which transgresses social prohibitions, is inevitably self-indulgent and anti-social. It leads typically to tragedies like fainting on wet ground and contracting a fatal fever. If the protagonist has any redeeming features, such sensibility must be drastically curbed. Submission to the traditional roles and obligations of society must be imposed. Marianne Dashwood, her enthusiasm quenched, ends up mistress of a family and patroness of a community, integrated into the conservative patriarchal order and reconciled to the elderly Colonel Brandon, who is seen as the practical and realistic, if unexciting, destiny of fortunate women.

Mary Hays provides a comparable fiction which maintains a continuity between the 'excessive' Sensibility nourished by the imagination and the chastened Sensibility which finds its true end in social goals. In her story of Henrietta (1794) the heroine has a warm sensibility, cultivated by reading and music, a 'glowing imagination', and a 'warm animated mind'. She had even 'vainly sought to find a lover, and a friend resembling the portraits coloured by her vivid imagination' (Hays 1974: 105). Enter the answer to her dreams, Edwin, with 'a fancy equally lively, and a heart not less sensible and tender; with a form, and countenance distinguished for symmetry and manly beauty' (ibid.: 105). He is not a suitable match, yet, with no thought of marriage, they prolong their intimacy. They

> rambled over the hills, and the valleys; visited the lakes and the fells, the forests and the caverns. . . . While Henrietta employed herself with her needle, Edwin read to her; when she sung to her harpsi-

chord, he would hang over her with breathless attention: he chose the flowers, which she imitated in crayons.

(1974: 101, 108)

They 'forgot the dictates of duty and discretion' and were privately united. Edwin then died and Henrietta gave way to 'delirium and burning fever', followed by 'lassitude and melancholy'. For six years she 'indulged a luxury of tender melancholy' until it threatened mental alienation and death. Eventually she 'began to feel that she had been dignifying with the name of virtue, a criminal weakness', and realized that 'this world is a state of discipline, in which we are placed for duty, for usefulness, and for action' (ibid.: 112). So far the parallel is fairly close. Given a sensible sister, she might have abridged the six years. But the scene of her usefulness is not in the world of subservience and custom. She goes to London to join the march of intellect, the pursuit of 'moral and religious truth'. Attempts to distinguish between realism and wish-fulfilment in these treatments have to recognize that Mary Hays's story is essentially autobiographical. She became engaged in similar circumstances and was prostrated by her lover's death. After a period of despair amply documented by her published letters, she moved to London, continued to assert the nobility of Sensibility, and joined the Revolutionary literati. Radical Sensibility could provide just as much in the way of discipline and a sense of social usefulness as the conservative variety, and aimed at extensive benefits to society which were stigmatized as illusory by conservatives.

NOTE

1 John Mullan (1988) tends to confine the term to individual sensitivity; Janet Todd (1986) similarly sees any social idealism in the concept dissolving towards the end of the century. While she sees Godwin as incorporating some aspects of sentimentalism, she sharply differentiates his use of reason from the practice of sensibility. Wollstonecraft too is seen as 'newly anti-sentimental' (Todd 1986: 132) in her criticism of Burke.

BIBLIOGRAPHY

Bowstead, D. (1986) 'Charlotte Smith's *Desmond*: the epistolary novel as ideological argument', in M. A. Schofield and C. Macheski (eds) *Fetter'd or Free?*, Athens, Ohio University Press: 237–63.

Coburn, K. (ed.) (1957) *The Notebooks of Samuel Taylor Coleridge 1784–1804*, London, Routledge & Kegan Paul.

Godwin, W. (1793) *Political Justice*, 2 vols, London, Johnson.

—— (1797) *The Enquirer*, London, G. G. and J. Robinson.

—— (1966) *Four Early Pamphlets*, Gainesville, Florida, Scholars' Facsimiles and Reprints.

—— (1968) *Uncollected Writings*, Gainesville, Florida, Scholars' Facsimiles and Reprints.

Hays, M. (1974) *Letters and Essays Moral and Miscellaneous*, New York, Garland.

Hume, D. (1739/40) *A Treatise of Human Nature*, ed. L. A. Selby-Bigge and P. H. Nidditch, Oxford, Clarendon, 1978.

_____ (1888) *Hume's Enquiries*, ed. L. A. Selby-Bigge, Oxford, Clarendon.

Jones, C. (1989) 'Helen Maria Williams and radical Sensibility', *Prose Studies* 12(1): 3–24.

Kelly, G. (1989) *English Fiction of the Romantic Period 1789–1830*, London, Longman.

Mackenzie, H. (1771) *The Man of Feeling*, ed. B. Vickers, Oxford, Oxford University Press, 1987.

Mullan, J. (1989) *Sentiment and Sociability*, Oxford, Clarendon.

Philp, M. (1986) *Godwin's Political Justice*, London, Duckham.

Poovey, M. (1984) *The Proper Lady and the Woman Writer*, Chicago, University of Chicago Press.

Price, R. (1789) *A Discourse on the Love of Our Country*, London, T. Cadell.

Smith, A. (1759) *The Theory of Moral Sentiments*, ed. D. D. Raphael and A. L. Macfie, Oxford, Clarendon, 1976.

Smith, C. (1792) *Desmond*, 3 vols, London, G. G. and J. Robinson.

_____ (1794) *The Banished Man*, 4 vols, London, T. Cadell Jun. & W. Davies.

_____ (1969) *The Old Manor House*, ed. A. Ehrenpreis, London, Oxford University Press.

Stewart, D. (1854) *Elements of the Philosophy of the Human Mind*, ed. G. N. Wright, London.

Todd, J. (1986) *Sensibility: An Introduction*, London, Methuen.

Trahard, P. (1936) *La Sensibilité révolutionnaire*, Geneva, Slatkine Reprints, 1967.

Voitle, R. (1984) *The Third Earl of Shaftesbury*, Baton Rouge and London, Louisiana State University Press.

Williams, H. M. (1790) *Julia*, 2 vols, London, T. Cadell.

_____ (1792) *Letters from France*, Series 1, vols 1 and 2, London, T. Cadell, G. G. and J. Robinson.

_____ (1793) *Letters from France*, Series 1, vols 3 and 4, London, G. G. and J. Robinson.

_____ (1795) *Letters from France*, Series 2, 4 vols, London, G. G. and J. Robinson.

Wollstonecraft, M. (1790) *A Vindication of the Rights of Men*, London, J. Johnson.

_____ (1792) *A Vindication of the Rights of Woman*, ed. M. Kramnick, Harmondsworth, Penguin, 1975.

_____ (1976) *Mary* and *The Wrongs of Woman*, ed. G. Kelly, Oxford, Oxford University Press.

Wordsworth, W. (1979) *The Prelude 1799, 1805, 1850*, ed. J. Wordsworth, M. H. Abrams and S. Gill, New York, Norton.

7

Crabbe's regicide households

Gavin Edwards

The English Tory journal the *Anti-Jacobin*, founded in 1797, announced in its Prospectus that it would:

> oppose JACOBINISM in all its shapes, and in all its degrees, political and moral, public and private, whether it openly threatens the subversion of states, or gradually saps the foundations of domestic happiness.

> (Butler 1984: 216)

Of course the Jacobins were a French Revolutionary grouping: strictly speaking there were no Jacobins in England for the *Anti-Jacobin* to be anti. It was a catch-all term applied to every sort of radical and reformer by their conservative enemies; a name, as John Thelwall put it, 'fixed upon us as a stigma by our enemies' (Kelly 1976: 12).

George Crabbe did not fix the name 'Jacobin' on any of his characters. Nevertheless, the stories in verse which he wrote and published in the first two decades of the nineteenth century were very much a part of that 'war of ideas' between polarized sets of moral and political and aesthetic principles in which the *Anti-Jacobin* was prominently engaged. Crabbe's position in this conflict is both more nuanced and more ambivalent than the *Anti-Jacobin*'s; but his stories are nevertheless continuously and anxiously preoccupied with what the *Anti-Jacobin* calls 'moral' and 'private' Jacobinism, those attitudes of mind and forms of behaviour which 'sap the foundations of domestic happiness'.

Crabbe's major volume of stories in verse, the 1812 *Tales*,[1] in fact opens with a poem about the 'political' and 'public' Jacobinism which, according to the *Anti-Jacobin*, 'openly threatens the subversion of states'. This poem – 'The Dumb Orators; or, The Benefit of Society' – dramatizes the clash between Jacobins and anti-Jacobins in the encounters between the radical lecturer Hammond and the Tory Justice Bolt. Much of the action is clearly set in the period 1792–5, between the founding of the radical Corresponding Societies and the passing, in 1795, of the Seditious Meetings Act and the Treasonable Practices Act. Almost certainly, Crabbe's Hammond is partly based on John Thelwall who, after the closing of his London lecture rooms in the wake of the Seditious Meetings Act, undertook a dangerously eventful speaking tour of East Anglia, preaching reform in the fairly transparent guise of lectures on 'Roman History'. Crabbe's Hammond who, like Thelwall, finds himself stranded in Tory and Anglican territory gives

> Historic lectures, where he lov'd to mix
> His free plain hints on modern politics:
>
> (ll. 315–16)

None of the subsequent poems in the 1812 volume are so significantly specific in their historical reference or place their action in a historical period so distinctly prior to the time of their publication. Nevertheless, by placing 'The Dumb Orators' first in the volume Crabbe encourages his readers to notice that the subsequent tales, with their predominantly domestic preoccupations, can also be read politically. War with France, and fears of invasion, come and go in the background of these tales; in the foreground Crabbe explores the private, moral, domestic forms of disorder and subversion that worried the *Anti-Jacobin* so much. Crabbe makes the link between the public and the domestic in a number of ways, including by metaphor. In 'The Mother', for instance,

> All was domestic war; the Aunt rebell'd
> Against the sovereign will, and was expell'd . . .
>
> (ll. 233–4)

Of course analogies between the State and the household were not invented by Crabbe; nor is Crabbe's own interest in domestic politics a product only of the French Revolution and the subsequent war. The Revolution and the war gave a new relevance to ancient analogies, and shed new light on issues which had preoccupied Crabbe well before 1789. In the remainder of this essay I shall try to define the nature of Crabbe's longstanding interest in the politics of domestic life and the effect on that interest of the Revolution in France.

Traditional analogies between the life of the State and of its constituent households were patriarchal in character and tended to see the hierarchical relationships involved in a positive light.[2] But of course the power of masters and fathers and kings could be experienced as tryanny. When it was, people frequently reached for comparisons with slavery. Crabbe did so in *The Village* (1783) when he likened working people living in fertile parts of England to 'the slaves who dig the golden ore,/The wealth about them makes them doubly poor' (ll. 138–9). And two years before, in the course of a petitioning letter to Edmund Burke, he had referred to 'my slavery' in describing an episode in his own early life. 'My father', he wrote to Burke:

had a large family, a little Income and no Oeconomy: he kept me two years at a Country boarding School and then plac'd me with an apothecary [at Wickhambrook] who was poor and had little Business but the premium he demanded was small: I continued two years with this man, I read Romances and learned to Bleed; my Master was also a Farmer and I became useful to him in that his principal Occupation. There was indeed no other Distinction between the Boy at the Farm and myself but that he was happy in being an annual Servant and I was bound by Indentures: I do not mean Sir to trifle with you but it is by no means a small matter with me, how I stand in your opinion, and now when I speak of my mingled Follies & misfortunes I wish to say all I can consistently with Truth in Vindication of the former – I rebelled in my Servitude for it became grievous; my Father was informed of his Son's Idleness and Disobedience; he came and was severe in his Correction of them; I knew myself then injured & became obstinate & a second visit of my father put an End to my Slavery, he took me home with him, and with me two thirds of the money he had advanced; He then placed me on very easy Terms with a Man of large Business in a more reputable Line [John Page, a surgeon at Woodbridge], but I was never considered as a regular apprentice and was principally employ'd in putting up Prescriptions and compounding Medicines.

(Faulkner with Blair 1985: 9–10)

Crabbe stayed with surgeon Page at Woodbridge from 1771 to 1774. During that time he met his wife-to-be, Sarah Elmy. Sarah's widowed mother lived in Beccles but Sarah spent a considerable part of her teenage and early adulthood living in the household of her aunt and uncle Tovell at Ducking Hall, Parham, not far from Woodbridge. The Tovells were wealthy yeoman farmers.

Crabbe's letter to Burke and the biographical details it helps us to establish are illuminating in a number of respects. In the first place they show us Crabbe, well before 1789, using a political analogy – of slavery and rebellion – to talk about domestic life. In the second place they show him identifying his past self with the rebellious slave, and wishing to justify himself ('vindicate his follies') to Burke. Finally – and this is the most important point in the present context – we are reminded by Crabbe's letter and by Sarah Elmy's sojourn at Ducking Hall that when Crabbe or the *Anti-Jacobin* talk about 'domestic' life they probably have in mind the life of households rather than the life of what we would call families.

The Tovell household at Ducking Hall and the households referred to in the letter to Burke include a number of people apart from the immediate family. Notably, they include various kinds of young, unmarried, temporary residents: the niece on a very long-term visit, the apprentices, the 'farm boy' (whom Crabbe also refers to as an 'annual servant', that is a young person hired by the year and living – more or less like the apprentice – under the roof and the authority of the master).

In his poetry Crabbe continually returns to such people: young workers or dependent relatives living as more or less temporary members of families which are neither their families of origin nor the family they may expect to establish later by getting married. The institutions which these people helped to constitute would have been called families, though we would call them households (Snell 1985: 320–1).

Apprentices and husbandry or workshop servants were discouraged from marrying and would normally expect to establish independent households through marriage at the termination of their indentures or of their life as servants. George and Sarah Crabbe however started their married life as members of somebody else's household, the Duke of Rutland's household at Belvoir Castle where Crabbe, through the efforts of Edmund Burke on his behalf, had been appointed 'domestic chaplain' in 1782. Eventually Crabbe did become the head of his own household when he moved to nearby Stathern as curate, and in 1789 he took up the living of Muston, also in Leicestershire. But despite this new independence, both livings were close to the Belvoir estate and, as Marilyn Butler (1986: 3) has pointed out, 'throughout the time he held them, until 1814, it is clear from Crabbe's letters that he thought of himself as belonging to the Duke's service'.

In any case, the Crabbes did not live in their own household for long. Crabbe held onto the Muston living till 1814, but he and his family moved back to Suffolk in November 1792 and stayed there till 1802 when laws against absentee clergy forced him to return. The move back to Suffolk in 1792 was forced on the Crabbes by the death of old Mr Tovell, Sarah's uncle, who had appointed Crabbe co-executor of his will. The Crabbes lived at Ducking Hall from November 1792 until the end of October 1796 when they moved to the nearby parish and parsonage of Great Glemham. Crabbe later referred to Ducking Hall as 'that unfortunate house' and it is not hard to see why: there were resentments about the transfer of property, two Crabbe children were born and died within a year of their birth, and Sarah Crabbe was increasingly subject to what her husband referred to as 'those nervous Disorders which render Life so grievous to be borne'. But my reasons for focusing on this 'unfortunate house' is that Crabbe wrote a remarkable letter about it to his friend Edmund Cartwright Jnr, then in the First Regiment of the West Yorkshire militia stationed at Doncaster. The letter is dated 4 September 1793. The Crabbes had been living at Ducking Hall for ten months; but the letter also causes us to remember public events that had taken place during those ten months: the trial and execution of Louis XVI, the French declaration of war on Britain, the Terror, the execution of Marie Antoinette. Crabbe writes as follows:

In any other Situation than mine I should rejoice to have you in the same County with me, because I should hope you would soon be in the same House; but now I know not how to flatter myself with so agreeable a Prospect. – I am in this place my dear Sir, neither as a Tenant, an heir nor an Executor but in some measure, as all these. I am neither Master of the House, nor Guest. Mrs Crabbe neither Commands nor obeys: the Servants are neither ours nor any other persons. Mrs Tovell (the widow of our Uncle . . .) is in some degree Mistress & House keeper – In short This is nobody's House and Nobody governs, nobody obeys; nobody is satisfied, but everybody agrees that it is a miserable place & joins in hope that it will be better. . . . My little Boys wonder what strange Place they are arrived at: they were not accustomed to many things beyond mere decent Accommodations at Muston, but they had at least tolerable Attendance & something like a Habit of Government and Regularity in their House – Here everything & Everybody are huddled together. A confused Equality blends us all and even the Days of the week, (as if Sunday were an Usurper) are pass [sic] without Distinction. We dethrone order, but let not our Anarchy fright you (if you be near) from approaching us –

(Faulkner with Blair 1985: 53)

Crabbe pictures Duckling Hall as a miniature version of the French State plunged into revolutionary turmoil by the removal of its head. For the middle-aged Crabbe, fear of egalitarian disorder on the French model seems to have superseded fear of slavery on the imperial model. But the letter to Cartwright is interesting partly because it does not actually mention France. Crabbe can draw upon a way of talking about domestic life politically which is wholly conventional and English. His use of the word 'government' to talk about domestic order and authority is commonplace, scarcely a metaphor at all, any more than is Austen's talk of Sir Thomas Bertram's 'government' of Mansfield Park. But it is as if in the process of writing the letter this traditional language and recent events in France gradually draw attention to one another in Crabbe's mind, each giving a fresh significance to the other. The letter to Cartwright gradually turns into a kind of extended and partly humorous riddle to which the (increasingly obvious) answer is 'The Revolution in France'.

The conventional language insists that the house – in the sense of the household – is a kind of State and that the State is a kind of household. While this language may be described as patriarchal it is compatible with a variety of specific political positions. It is not necessarily monarchical. Commonwealth theory for instance was patriarchal, conceiving of the State as the assembly of heads of households. Nevertheless, in the most influential English version of these analogies between national and domestic life, fathers are linked to the king (who is father of his people) and both are linked to God the Father. This is important in the present context because the crucial event behind Crabbe's letter to Cartwright is the judicial execution of Louis XVI. Regicide – not just the killing of the king by a rival claimant but the judicial execution of the king by a republican State – is a very serious threat to patriarchal order, even if (as in seventeenth-century England) it is carried out by people who are themselves committed to patriarchal order. Regicide, as Michael Walzer (1974; 1–89) points out, threatens not just the king but kingship, and not just kingship but what sustains every level of patriarchal authority by enabling each to borrow prestige from the others. In addition French regicide is dangerous because it may revive more than old metaphors: it may revive the carefully buried memory of England's own regicide and revolution a century and a half before. Indeed, by not actually mentioning France in his letter Crabbe allows the reader's mind to go direct to seventeenth-century England, rather than contemporary France, for the answer to the riddle: the letter patently reverberates with its immediate historical context, but it could conceivably have been written ten years previously, with Charles I rather than Louis XVI in mind.

It is the surviving heirs of the English regicides who preoccupy Crabbe in his remarkable 1812 tale 'The Frank Courtship'. This is a story about patriarchal authority in a latter-day puritan household, 'a remnant of that crew,/Who, as their foes maintain, their Sovereign slew' (ll. 33–4). But just as the letter to Cartwright can draw our minds away from the Revolution in France to the seventeenth-century revolution in England so 'The Frank Courtship', whose ostensible subject is not English Jacobins but modern Cromwellians, has as a crucial unspoken context the Revolution in France and the danger, for this group of wholly unrevolutionary citizens, of any association with contemporary French regicide.

By comparison with the complexities of 'The Frank Courtship' the analogies – between State and household, France and Ducking Hall – in the 1793 letter to Cartwright seem quite straightforward. Crabbe implies that Ducking Hall and France are aberrations, deviations from the normal State and the normal household. The implied norm, so far as households are concerned, is a situation in which everybody knows their place and knows the title or combination of titles that defines their place: master or servant, master or guest, master or mistress, housekeeper, tenant and so on. These are the titles Crabbe mentions in his letter and, as the way I have listed them suggests, most of them fall into binary pairs; they reciprocally define one another. They are interdependent in the same way that the people they refer to are supposed to be interdependent. And one of the titles – 'master' – is the senior partner in most of the relationships. The master in this case had been Mr Tovell who was also a father and a husband. To be all three – a master, a husband, a father – was normal, but not essential. Households had a necessary and close relation to families (in our sense) though the two were not identical. In Tovell's case the master was the husband of the mistress, the father of some of the young people, and stood *in loco parentis* to the servants (or to some of them). These relationships to the master within the household are distinct from one another in many respects, but they should not be separated into the familial, the economic, and the political. In the wider analogy between household and State, heads of households are like kings but only one of them actually is a king, and kings – like heads of households – are not gods; they are, like the rest of us, God's servants. The normative household was based on a quite elaborate coordination of similarities and differences.

Crabbe was preoccupied throughout his life with the politics of the household. At Ducking hall, as at Mansfield Park, things start to get out of hand, to lose their cohesion and identity, when the head of the body politic has been removed. In his poetry Crabbe appears to focus as much on the aberrant individual within a household as on the aberrant household; nevertheless, the way in which he formulates the situation of these apparently anomalous individuals constantly reminds us of the letter to Cartwright. He lives at Ducking Hall, he writes, 'neither as Tenant, as Heir or Executor but in some measure as all of these . . . neither Master of the House, nor Guest'. The girls in 'The Widow's Tale' are 'Guests without welcome – Servants without pay' (l. 264). In the 'Confidant'. '*Anna*'s station frequent terrors wrought' because 'she was poor, – /Above a servant, but with service more' (ll. 15, 35–6). The heroine of 'Procrastination' can never get herself free of her aunt's household because 'Servant, and nurse, and comforter and friend/*Dinah* had still some duty to attend' (ll. 42–3). And it is worth remembering that Crabbe had previously – in the letter to Burke – identified himself as one of these anomalous figures, as a person of uncertain status within the household and within the hierarchy of social classes. Because his father could not afford to support him in a proper apprenticeship Crabbe feels that, at Wickhambrook, he was neither apprentice nor farm servant but something betwixt and between, living in the worst of both worlds, a kind of long-term indentured farm servant.[3] And then at Woodbridge he 'was never considered as a regular apprentice'.

The implication in all these fictional and non-fictional formulations is that we are dealing with deviants. Normally, we are to believe, people know what they are: they are apprentices, or servants, or masters, or housekeepers. However – and this is what makes Crabbe's poetry so fascinating and disturbing – the distinction he wishes to maintain between the deviant and the normal seems repeatedly to break down. His aberrant households, or his aberrant individuals within ostensibly normal households may not, we come to suspect, be aberrant at all.

If Dinah is 'Servant, and nurse, and comforter and friend' the assumption presumably is that Dinah and Crabbe and the reader know very well what these titles mean and what kinds of people they can properly be applied to: Dinah's problem is that the tasks expected of her and the attitudes displayed towards her are not consistently those appropriate to any one of these roles or titles. That might be one reason for not being sure whether you are a servant or a friend. But another reason – not perhaps wholly distinct from the former – might be that you are not sure what kind of person those titles are supposed to name; and if this kind of uncertainty arises then *everybody's* identity is put in question. This is what frequently happens with Crabbe, but it happens for the most part without his knowledge. A comparison of Crabbe's use of the word 'servant' in the 1781 letter to Burke and in the 1793 letter to Cartwright illustrates the point.

In the letter to Burke, Crabbe referred to the 'farm boy' at Wickham-brook as an 'annual servant'. This would be a young man hired by the year, living as part of the master's household and subject to the master's authority. By comparison with this boy, and with normal apprentices, Crabbe feels his status is unclear. But in the letter to Burke there is no lack of clarity in Crabbe's description of lack of clarity. In the letter to Cartwright however the situation is rather different because we cannot be sure what kinds of people Crabbe means to include in the category 'servant'. He probably has a wider range of people in mind than the people we would call 'domestic' servants (maids, cooks and so on) but we cannot be sure about this, or about who those other people would be. He may well mean to include husbandry servants (the 'annual servants' of the letter to Burke) though we cannot be certain. More crucially, he may even be referring, among other people employed by the Tovells, to agricultural day labourers. The reason for our uncertainty about Crabbe's meaning is not that he is being especially lazy in his usage but that there was, as Anna Kussmael (1981: 7) has shown, a pervasive uncertainty in the word's use, an uncertainty to which Crabbe's letter is not immune. As the name of a position in the social order, the word could be used in a narrow or a wide sense: to distinguish annual 'servants' from day 'labourers' or to refer to a wider range of employed persons, including day labourers. The two meanings could be found even within the same text; and I have argued elsewhere (Edwards 1990: 13–17, 109–17) that the vagueness in Crabbe's usage in 'The Parish Register' enables him to avoid facing up to crucial differences in the economic and sexual circumstances of annual servants and day labourers.

Master and servant are fundamental terms in the list Crabbe provides in his letter to Cartwright. A vagueness or shiftiness in the meaning of these terms therefore threatens the clarity of all of them. The disorder at Ducking Hall (and in France) no longer stands out clearly as a deviation from a norm. The nomenclature which defines the norm is itself confused. At the same time, and for some of the same reasons, the whole patriarchal analogy between household and State becomes problematic. The terms 'master' and 'servant' are fundamental binary terms which, as E. P. Thompson (1974: 382–4) points out, define a subordination of a general rather than a specifically economic or instrumental kind. A master, unlike a mere employer, openly aspires to control over the whole life of the servant and not just over his or her labour power. It is essentially for this reason that the household can plausibly be thought of as the basic unit of, and model for, the wider society: it was not so easy as it has subsequently been to believe that there is a distinct 'economic' or 'political' sphere which allows the family to be defined as, by contrast, a purely private domain.

Nobody knows their place in France, or at Ducking Hall. But perhaps nobody was very sure of their place anywhere in England, French Revolution or no French Revolution. Certainly many people could not know quite what it meant to be called a servant or who should most properly be called one. And of course it might equally be a matter of uncertainty and contention whether the person who employed you was your master or only your employer.

The master–servant is not the same as the father–son or father–daughter relationship. But is less clearly distinct from them than is the employer–employee relationship. Crabbe's most famous poem 'Peter Grimes' is an agonized exploration of the similarities and differences between the master–servant relationship and the father–son relationship. Are these relationships indistinguishable or absolutely distinct? Peter Grimes has a father who is also his master (and who is also called Peter Grimes). Peter's revolt against his father–master is a kind of domestic Jacobinism: after the old man's death Peter remembers his own attempts

> To Prove his Freedom and assert the Man;
> And when the Parent check'd his impious Rage,
> How he had curs'd the Tyranny of Age, –
> Nay, once had dealt the sacrilegous Blow
> On his bare Head and laid his Parent low:
>
> (ll. 23–7)

The struggle between father and son is represented as a battle between the divine right of father-masters and the right of young men to overthrow tyrants in the name of freedom. But the victorious revolutionary becomes the tyrant: Peter Grimes becomes a (brutal) master of apprentices, and as such a kind of father since he stands to his apprentices *in loco parentis*. In the 1781 letter to Burke, Crabbe had described his own father first siding with the tyrannical master and then removing his son from the master. Here, thirty years later, Crabbe is still trying to work out how to coordinate the differences and the similarities between fathers and masters, between a father who is also a master and a master who is a kind of father.

The household at Ducking Hall had no head, it was 'nobody's house'. In Crabbe's fictional households it is seldom really clear who is in charge. Crabbe is fascinated by the master–servant dialectic; he explores the power of servants and the servitude of masters, the fearful interchangeability of antagonists. This preoccupation is most clearly illustrated in the stories about people who believe – usually under the influence of political or religious freethinking – that they can break altogether free of relationships based on hierarchical dependence. The impossibility of proving one's freedom, of being 'a man' rather than a servant or a master, is a recurrent theme of Crabbe's tales. Freedom is impossible for Peter Grimes because he is dependent on his dependents for it, and subsequently becomes the victim of his victims. The socially mobile freethinking intellectuals who frequent the 1812 *Tales* all come to bad ends. The 'genius' Edward Shaw who

> unfix'd, unfixing look'd around,
> And no employment but in seeking found;
>
> (ll. 47–8)

eventually loses his wits. People like Edward, and Stephen in 'The Learned Boy', are unable or unwilling to adopt any available social role. They do not want to be farmers or clerks or doctors; they do not want to be either servants or masters; they want to be themselves, and their desires are dangerously contagious, 'unfix'd, unfixing'. In Crabbe's stories people who don't know what they want to be frequently want to be writers. John, the versifying son of the bailiff in 'The Patron', believes there is a position in his aristocratic patron's household called 'Poet'; but eventually 'the Poet found he was the Bailiff's son' (l. 165).

Characters in at least three of Crabbe's poems use an almost identical phrase to describe the kind of freedom to which they aspire. Hammond, the radical Orator in 'The Dumb Orators', describes.

> 'the free creatures in their woods and plains,
> Where without laws each happy monarch reigns,
> King of himself,' . . .
> Thus with licentious words the man went on,
> Proving that liberty of speech was gone;
> That all were slaves – nor had we better chance,
> For better times, than as allies to *France*.
>
> (ll. 201–3, 223–6)

Gwyn, the gentleman farmer in the poem of that name, wishes 'to prove that *he alone was king of him*' (l. 252). Crabbe fixes on these dethroning phrases because they always embody, unknown to the people who utter them, the paradox and self-delusion at the heart of the search for individual autonomy. People who want to be sovereign individuals do not want to be mastered and usually think they do not want to master. But this only means that they are subject to – dependent upon – others in ways of which they are not aware. Orator Hammond finds himself struck dumb when he is deprived of his normal supportive audience; Gwyn ends up as the puppet monarch in a household of parasitical and manipulative dependants.

Domestic tyranny, and domestic rebellion, could be said to arise when the differences between levels of patriarchal authority are erased by the similarities: when, for instance, a father acts all too much like a monarch and a god. But rebellion is not the only dangerous consequence of the abolition of such differences. If father and king – household and State – cannot be distinguished, serious consequences could also arise for sexual life and the kinship order. After all, if a king was literally father of his people, all sexual relationships would be incestuous. This may seem an outlandish notion, but such intolerable logical possibilities are, in my view, relevant to these poems in which domestic politics have as much to do with sexual as with social status.

It is perhaps not surprising however that this aspect of domestic politics normally remains an illusive and confused issue in Crabbe's poems; or that it is presented openly only in the very few cases where the problems are happily resolved. The story of Sybil Kindred in 'The Frank Courtship' (like the story of Richard Monday in 'The Parish Register') plays on the double meaning of the word 'sire' to highlight the issues involved:

> Grave *Jonas Kindred, Sybil Kindred*'s sire,
> Was six feet high, and look'd six inches higher;
> Erect, morose, determin'd, solemn, slow,
> Who knew the man could never cease to know;
> His faithful Spouse, when *Jonas* was not by,
> Had a firm presence and a steady eye;
> But with her husband dropp'd her look and tone,
> And *Jonas* rul'd unquestion'd and alone.
>
> (ll. 1–8)

They are religious sectarians,

> a remnant of that crew,
> Who, as their foes maintain, their Sovereign slew;
> An independent race, precise, correct,
> Who ever married in the kindred sect;
> No son or daughter of their order wed,
> A friend to *England*'s King who lost his head;
> *Cromwell* was still their Saint, and when they met,
> They mourn'd that Saints were not our Rulers yet.
>
> (ll. 33–40)

Jonas Kindred is a self-conscious patriarch, modelling himself on Abraham

93

and Cromwell. He is his daughter's 'sire' in the sense of her father, and also – so he believes and wishes her to believe – her absolute ruler, her 'sire' in that sense. The Kindred Family and the 'kindred sect' are almost co-extensive, separated only by the difference between the upper-case 'K' and the lower-case 'k'.[4] Sybil Kindred must almost – but not quite – marry one of her own kin. The climax of the poem is the wonderful battle of words, looks, and gestures between Sybil and the pious young man Josiah whom her father is determined she should marry. This long scene is a domesticated version of the civil war between roundhead and cavalier, English seventeenth-century history repeating itself as comedy. As a result of her remarkable encounter with Josiah, the girl Sybil – unlike the boy Peter Grimes – is able both to assert her freedom and obey her tyranical father. She agrees to marry Josiah, who – as his name tells us – is almost, but not quite, Jonas her sire.

NOTES

1 All quotations from Crabbe's poetry are taken from Dalrymple-Champneys and Pollard (1988).
2 In the present essay 'patriarchy' is taken to mean the rule of fathers rather than the rule of men.
3 In a letter to Eliza Bishop, dated 5 November 1786, Mary Wollstonecraft described her situation in the Kingsborough household as follows: 'I am treated like a gentlewoman – but I cannot easily forget my inferior station – and this something betwixt and between is rather awkward – it pushes me forward to notice – ' (Wardle 1979: 124).
4 The comments on 'The Frank Courtship' in these paragraphs condense a longer discussion (Edwards 1987, 1990: 197–215) which considers, *inter alia*, the possible link between decapitalization (the reduction of upper to lower case initial letters) and decapitation (regicide).

BIBLIOGRAPHY

Butler, M. (ed) (1984) *Burke, Paine, Godwin, and the Revolution Controversy*, Cambridge, Cambridge University Press.
—— (1986) 'Invariably cloudly and cheerlessly calm', *Times Literary Supplement*, 3 January: 3–4.
Dalrymple-Champneys, N. and Pollard, A. (eds) (1988) *George Crabbe: The Complete Poetical Works*, Oxford, Clarendon Press.
Edwards, G. (1987) 'Crabbe's so-called realism', *Essays in Criticism*, xxxvii: 303–20.
—— (1990) *George Crabbe's Poetry on Border Land*, Lewiston, Edwin Mellen Press.
Faulkner, T. C. with Blair, R. (eds) (1985) *Selected Letters and Journals of George Crabbe*, Oxford, Clarendon Press.
Kelly, G. (1976) *The English Jacobin Novel, 1780–1805*, Oxford, Clarendon Press.
Kussmael, A. (1981) *Servants in Husbandry in Early Modern England*, Cambridge, Cambridge University Press.
Snell, K. D. M. (1985) *Annals of the Labouring Poor: Social Change and Agrarian England, 1660–1900*, Cambridge, Cambridge University Press.

Thompson, E. P. (1974) 'Patrician society, plebian culture', *Journal of Social History*, 7: 382–402.

Walzer, M. (1974) *Regicide and Revolution: Speeches at the Trial of Louis XVI*, Cambridge, Cambridge University Press.

Wardle, R. M. (ed.) (1979), *The Collected Letters of Mary Wollstonecraft*, Ithaca, Cornell University Press.

8

From terror to terror: Dickens, Carlyle and cannibalism

Angus Easson

In a letter of news and gossip of 1 November 1854 to the Honourable Mrs Richard Watson, an old friend with whom he could be expansively relaxed, Dickens ranged widely over personal and public affairs: how he felt 'used up' after the labour of writing *Hard Times*, of his scorn for the humbug of the re-opened Crystal Palace, of his intended public readings of *A Christmas Carol*, of a desire to see victory against Russia in the Crimea even while he felt 'something like despair' as 'the old common smoke and blood-mist obscure the wrongs and sufferings of the people at home', of a holiday in Boulogne, of a book about whether other planets were inhabited. He averted also to the newly arrived report on the fate of Sir John Franklin's 1845 Arctic expedition in search of the North-west Passage. Dr John Rae of the Hudson's Bay Company had gleaned from Eskimos stories and objects that were the first certain indication that, as feared, the expedition had perished.[1] One point in particular in Rae's account struck Dickens and was to work within him:

> Dr. Rae's account of Franklin's unfortunate party is deeply interesting – but I think hasty in its acceptance of the details – particularly in the statement that they had eaten the dead bodies of their companions. Which I don't believe. Franklin on a former occasion was almost starved to death – had gone through all the pains of that sad end and lain down to die – and no such thought had presented itself to any of them. In famous cases of Shipwreck, it is very rare indeed that any person of any humanizing education or refinement, resorts to this dreadful means of prolonging life. In open boats, the coarsest and commonest men of the shipwrecked party have done such things; but I don't remember more than one instance in which an officer has overcome the loathing that the idea has inspired.[2]

Dickens never doubted Rae's integrity; yet the suggestion that a party of men, subject to the high moral discipline of a gentleman like Franklin, endorsed as Franklin must be by his previous record, could resort to cannibalism, triggered a series of shockwaves in Dickens that ripple out

96

into all kinds of enterprises of the 1850s and intersect with an array of other concerns. Dickens subsequently declared that the memory of the lost Arctic voyagers must be defended, since they could not defend themselves: 'Because they served their country well, and deserved well of her, and can ask, no more on this earth, for her justice or her loving-kindness; give them both, full measure.' (Dickens 1854b: 392).

Perhaps one reason why Dickens, apart from a commonly-shared and deep-seated repugnance for cannibalism, was stung into denying its occurrence so vehemently, to Mrs Watson and later, was the way in which both the fact and rumours of cannibalism had followed Franklin. There had undoubtedly been a cannibal episode during his expedition of 1819–22, when Franklin was in charge of an overland exploration of the Arctic shores of Canada. The expedition went badly wrong in the winter of 1821, through Franklin's inexperience, and ten men (one British officer and nine of the locally recruited Canadian 'voyageurs') died, from starvation and violence, one of the worst records in Arctic exploration until the disaster of Franklin's 1845 North-west Passage venture, when all 129 men were lost. In October 1821, Franklin had divided his party, pushing on to seek help and leaving behind Dr John Richardson with charge of two officers, Hood and Hepburn. Dickens, in his letter to Mrs Watson, focuses on Franklin's group (whose situation was indeed desperate), but consequently seems to elide Richardson from the narrative. An Iroquois Indian, Michel Teroahaute, who had gone off independently, returned to Richardson's group and then produced what he claimed was wolf's meat. Richardson and Hepburn ate it, though they quickly became convinced it was flesh from one of two other Canadians, separated from the party, who had either died or else been murdered by Michel. Subsequently, after Michel had killed Hood, Richardson himself shot Michel, believing he and Hepburn were in turn to be destroyed, once Michel discovered the route that Franklin had taken. The episode, given by Richardson in a revised version of his confidential account to the Admiralty (the original has not been traced in the naval archives), was published in Franklin's *Narrative* (1823) and is quite explicit about the cannibalism: Richardson there states he 'became convinced from circumstances' that the so-called wolf's meat 'must have been a portion of the body of Belanger or Perrault'.[3] Whether or not Richardson suspected the meat when he was offered it or only afterwards, there is no doubt he ate it: but he had not proposed that anyone be killed to procure it, nor did he eat of it again. The published account also makes clear that there had been a breakdown of discipline amongst the expedition's complement, under the stress of adverse conditions. The breakdown is yet clearer in Richardson's journal (Richardson 1984), to which of course Dickens had no access. Yet it is still worth comment that Dickens, who was familiar with Franklin's narrative and extracted at length from it in his vindication of Franklin, did not see the account overall as calling in question Franklin's discipline and leadership.[4]

Certainly cannibalism seemed to attach itself to Franklin: it was there in the 1819–22 narrative (Franklin 1823), it was in Rae's evidence, and it was alive in the popular mind. In September 1852, two years before Rae's report, the Rev. William Harness (a friend of Dickens and a friend also of Franklin's first wife) noted in his diary that a cannibalistic episode in the book 'of Franklin's first voyage' had been suppressed at proof stage. Harness had it from Miss Mitford to whom it had in turn been told: not the most authentic witness, of course, but it is the fact of the rumour, not the fact itself, that is interesting.[5] Harness's version indeed implied murder to provide food. Rae had not suggested that anyone had deliberately been killed to provide sustenance and Dickens's initial reaction, powerful as it is, was to the sole fact of eating human flesh: the idea of murder, of taking life to sustain life, is a thread that only subsequently became twisted into the yarn.[6]

Dickens's immediate response was two articles called 'The lost Arctic voyagers' in his weekly journal, *Household Words*. In these, while accepting the essential contents of Rae's account, he challenged the likelihood of cannibalism, calling in question the evidence of the Eskimos and citing from Franklin's own earlier travels and from accounts of shipwrecks and distress analogous evidence that where proper discipline was maintained, cannibalism neither happened nor was the idea entertained. Dickens also published Rae's response, in two parts, making four lead articles in all, a remarkable series unprecedented and unrepeated on any single topic in *Household Words*.[7]

If in all this, Dickens seems slightly naive in his admiration for the qualities of the Englishman (the darker references in 'The lost Arctic voyagers' to the nature of non-Europeans point forward to his disturbingly easy support of Governor Eyre of Jamaica), he had made his case and seemingly could let the matter rest. But the idea and act of cannibalism, as those four lead articles in *Household Words* suggests, produced a deep revulsion that linked itself, also, with ideas of moral and public breakdown to produce a complex that continued working within him and interacting with other events, public and personal, of the mid to late 1850s.

In late 1854 and the first half of 1855 pressures were building up for Dickens. The summer and early autumn of 1854 had seen England devastated by Asiatic cholera, areas of London cordoned off, the social services unprepared, the Government's only notable act being its dismissal of the distinguished social reformer Edwin Chadwick from the Board of Health. Dickens himself, quite apart from his concern for hygiene and social welfare, had had a nasty shock when, holidaying in Boulogne, his daughter Mamie was taken ill with cholera: though, fortunately, it proved to be not the deadly Asiatic, but the milder English variety. In the Crimea, where

98

the English and French had landed near Sebastopol in September, the campaign turned into a siege, despite a false report of the city's capture that came with news of the Battle of the Alma. As the winter progressed it became increasingly clear that an English army was being destroyed outside Sebastopol, not by the enemy but by English maladministration. So moved was Dickens that he not only raged in letters and journalism against the Government, whether led by Aberdeen or after February 1855 by Palmerston; not only supported Austen Henry Layard, the parliamentary spearhead of criticism; but also joined the Administrative Reform Society and spoke to great applause at one of its meetings, at the Theatre Royal, Drury Lane.[8] At a more personal level, the dissatisfaction in his marriage that led to separation in 1857 began to be hinted at, while the restlessness associated with the onset of ideas for a new novel, although a familiar creative symptom, was another strain, especially since the work was to be *Little Dorrit*, the writing of which began amid and was to represent his anger at the betrayal of British soldiers, officers and men, by their leaders. *Little Dorrit*, for all the apparent safety of its 1820s setting, is simultaneously a novel of the present crisis of 1855. The novel's first episode, with its opening in France, with its quarantined travellers, and with its Sunday bells in London sounding as though the plague were in the city, offered signs demanding little effort for the contemporary reader to decode. It is a novel aware also of the possibility of the collapse of social order.

At this time and increasingly as the autumn of 1854 turned into the spring and summer of 1855, Dickens was haunted, perhaps even while he was fascinated, by the fear of Revolution. His declared mentor Thomas Carlyle had warned of its possibility. For Carlyle the Revolution in France, begun in 1789, was not yet complete (1830 and 1848 both showed that), while England's revolution might be yet to come. Revolutions were costly and they were best avoided, Carlyle had declared:[9] yet if society were so much a sham, were so dead to all real life, revolution might be better than the crust that bound in and denied any new growth. Even in October 1854 Dickens could not resist painting for Angela Burdett Coutts an apocalyptic vision of the people rising up, if their proper needs by way of social utilities – pure water; wholesome air; good housing – were not given them, especially as they advanced through knowledge and an understanding of their own political power:

> It is more than ever necessary to keep their need of social Reforms before them at this time, for I clearly see that the War will be made an Administrative excuse for all sorts of shortcomings, and that nothing will have been done when the cholera comes again. Let it come twice again, severely, – the people advancing all the while in the knowledge that, humanly speaking, it is . . . a preventable disease

– and you will see such a shake in this country as never was seen on Earth since Sampson pulled the Temple down upon his head.

(26 October 1854)

By April 1855 Dickens was writing to Layard, encouraging him in his Parliamentary enterprises, noting too that there 'is nothing in the present time at once so galling and so alarming to me as the alienation of the people from their own public affairs'. Dickens added:

> I have no difficulty in understanding it. They have had so little to do with the Game through all these years of Parliamentary Reform, that they have sullenly laid down their cards and taken to looking on. The Players who are left at the table do not see beyond it – conceive that gain and loss and all the interest of the play are in their hands – and will never be wiser until they and the table and the lights and the money are all overturned together. And I believe the discontent to be so much the worse for smouldering instead of blazing openly, that it is extremely like the general mind of France before the breaking out of the first Revolution, and is in danger of being turned by any one of a thousand accidents . . . [into] such a Devil of a conflagration as has never been beheld since.

(10 April 1855)

One should not discount the sense almost of glee that Dickens has in such John Martinesque word-painting. Still, the shams (a favourite term of Carlyle's) were in power in England, as shams overwhelmingly had been before the first French Revolution, shams, Carlyle insisted, who permeated the whole fabric of French society. As the Elected of France moved in procession to the opening session of the Estates General, says Carlyle, in his great history, *The French Revolution*, 'in that immeasurable Confusion and Corruption . . . there is . . . this one salient-point of a New Life discernible: the deep fixed Determination to have done with Shams' (Carlyle 1837: I, 156). Dickens might well see the parallels between France then and England now. Such shams included the Barnacles of *Little Dorrit*, who with the Circumlocution Office have perfected 'How Not To Do It': – not even 'How to do it wrongly'; that at least would mean doing something – but how to avoid doing anything at all. Such shams may be even one step worse than the quacks of Carlyle's pre-Revolutionary France, on whom he cries 'Woe!' What produced the Revolution? 'Friends! It was every scoundrel that had lived, and quacklike pretended to be doing, and been only eating and *mis*doing, in all provinces of life' (Carlyle 1837: I, 61). *Little Dorrit* may be set in the 1820s; its imagery, though, echoes an older and deeper past even as the novel also mirrors the present. The children that haunt Covent Garden will bring a new fall of the Temple upon the Philistines, a new Revolution like that of France: as the criminal rats metaphorically gnaw the foundations in Venice, as the ruins of Rome proclaim a fallen state, so the arches of Covent Garden cry out,

> where the miserable children in rags, slunk and hid, fed on offal, huddled together for warmth, and were hunted about (look to the rats young and old, all ye Barnacles, for before God they are eating away our foundations, and will bring the roofs on our heads!)[10]

As Carlyle stressed, inertia will prevail as long as it may, since 'it is singular how long the rotten will hold together, provided you do not handle it roughly'; a rind forms, enclosing systems of habit. Yet the rind once breaking, the 'fountains of the great deep boil forth . . . instead of a green flowery world there is a waste wild-weltering chaos – which has again, with tumult and struggle, to *make* itself into a world' (Carlyle 1837: I, 39–40). Dickens might well take a clew from Carlyle to understand the maze of these latter-days, just as Carlyle himself in 1837 saw a meaning for the present day in that first French Revolution of which he was historian, a Revolution which as meaning and as Revolution, was still alive in his day. Carlyle saw the first French Revolution as necessary and Dickens thought a revolution might not be avoidable: at least revolutions were ways, like the Apocalypse, to uncover the rind and in breaking up the waters of the deep to bring about 'new heaven, new earth'.

How then do these two concerns come together? There is, on the one hand, Dickens's impending sense that the social order was threatened, that men, advancing to understanding but denied power, would under the intolerable wrongs of Do Nothingism turn to anarchy and break up the whole fabric of society, even to violent destruction. There is, on the other hand, the idea and fact of cannibalism, which so preoccupied Dickens in November and December 1854 and becomes an underburden to a significant part of his activities in the later 1850s. The breakdown in social order that Dickens feared, yet prophesied with a kind of justificatory delight, had its metaphorical parallel in that breakdown of moral order which leads to cannibalism. That metaphor of breakdown and flesh-eating (and the fact upon which the metaphor is ordered) is found again and again in Carlyle's account of the French Revolution, that great event to which Dickens, in writing to Layard in April 1855, cast back his mind as a parallel for the present and so a warning of the future. We need have little doubt that it was to Carlyle's version that Dickens was referring: in summer 1851, he claimed, in serious jest, to be reading *The French Revolution*, 'that wonderful work', 'for the 500th time' and in the 'Preface' to *A Tale of Two Cities*, while hoping 'to add something to the popular and picturesque means of understanding that terrible time' of the French Revolution, Dickens was sure that no one could 'hope to add anything to the philosophy' of Carlyle's book.

The great central image of devouring was of course to hand both for

Carlyle and Dickens (and they both seized upon it) in the Appetite of Shakespeare's Ulysses, that 'universal wolf', which seconded with will and power, 'Must make perforce an universal prey,/And last eat up himself.'[11] The horror is peculiarly intensified when the act proves not to give life, the supposed purpose of such vileness, but to destroy even the destroyer. For Carlyle, the French Revolution was a devouring force, engendered in literal hunger, by (as he notes ironically in another context) 'the very operation of the gastric juices' (Carlyle 1837: I, 297). This hunger becomes in turn a driving metaphor, as society is devoured and finally the Revolution, like Ulysses's Appetite, eats up itself: 'The Revolutionary Tribunal, after all it has devoured, has now only, as Anarchic things do, to devour itself' (Carlyle 1837: II, 434). In the process and before that ultimate cannibal egoistic satiety, literal and metaphorical acts of eating and drinking permeate the work, ferociously passing over into the eating of flesh and the drinking of blood. Carlyle saw revolution as crucially linking the failure of the social and the personal order: if society and self are so far gone that the only way to regeneration is through revolution, then we may have to begin, as the pre-Revolutionary state of France makes Carlyle early declare, with a 'Primitive Fact', and the 'lowest, least blessed fact one knows of, on which necessitous mortals have ever based themselves, seems to be the primitive one of Cannibalism: That *I* can devour *Thee*' (Carlyle 1837: I, 57). Dickens, with his 500 readings of Carlyle's 'wonderful book', would have read those words often enough and responded to Carlyle's rhetorical demand: 'What if such Primitive Fact were precisely the one we had (with our improved methods) to revert to, and begin anew from!' (Carlyle 1837: I, 57). Carlyle's metaphors, indeed, go beyond the eating of dead flesh to sustain life, to the slaughter of the living: Thyestes' banquet is such a compounded cannibalism, and there is a nice ambiguity in the charge against Berthier that he devoured the 'substance' of the people.

England's discontent, Dickens thought in April 1855, was 'extremely like the general mind of France before ... the first Revolution'. Hunger is notoriously the base of Marie Antoinette's supposed witticism of cake (though neither Carlyle nor Dickens mentions it), and Foulon, who had declared 'The people may eat grass' (Carlyle 1837: I, 117), being found alive, was hanged and his head, the mouth stuffed with grass, carried on a pike; his son-in-law, Berthier, brought to Paris, is hung with placards that are his indictment: they include 'He devoured the substance of the People' and 'He drank the blood of the widow and orphan'. His head too was soon on a pike and the dismemberment went further: his heart was on another (Carlyle 1837: I, 216–7, 217 n. 1). It is one of the few episodes of violence against individuals that Dickens in writing *A Tale of Two Cities* takes in any detail from Carlyle and he ironically contrasts the suppers of those who played their part in dismembering the mockers of the hungry, as the people of Saint Antoine go to meals which are 'innocent of meat', even while there is a sense almost of repletion as 'Fathers and mothers who had had their full share in the worst of the day, played gently with their meagre children.' (Dickens 1859: 274–6). The very fact of hunger means that both Carlyle and Dickens are drawn by sympathy to the hungry, as the parents' tenderness in Dickens's postlude persuades the reader: these people have not lost love of children and indeed have gained nothing except a savage satisfaction in what they have savagely done. Yet the waters of the deep are broken up and the savagery of the ordinary man revealed. It is not the least part of Carlyle's terrible insight into Primitive Fact that cannibalism is an egotistical act of *me* against *you* ('That *I* can devour *Thee*'), as I with all my confidence in my civilization and my essentially good ideas and feelings and instincts descend to eating you, selfishly to preserve my own life (and in the process lose it too, eaten in turn until the welter of anarchy eats out itself).

There are literal episodes of cannibalism in Carlyle's *French Revolution*. Of these, one of the most vivid facts of cannibalism is the more curious and the more significant because it is not egotistical but self-sacrificing. During the September Massacres, as the prisoners are dragged forth, summarily judged, and slaughtered, a few are acquitted, fragments of the 'wild virtues' which 'turn up in this shaking asunder of man's existence'. The daughter of M. de Sombreuil declares her father is not an aristocrat: 'I will swear it, and testify it, and in all ways prove it'. She is asked if she will drink aristocrats' blood. 'The man lifts blood (if universal Rumour can be credited); the poor maiden does drink. "This Sombreuil is innocent, then!" Yes, indeed' (Carlyle 1837: II, 152–3). Dickens makes no mention of this episode, yet it combines the horror of blood-drinking with all the self-sacrificing virtue of a daughter saving her father.[12] More marginal as regards the act of cannibalism, yet still of note, are the wigs made from the hair of the executed, worn 'not without mockery; of a rather cannibal sort', linked to the tannery for human skins at Meudon, where from the guillotined 'perfectly good wash-leather was made'. Carlyle laments over this most detestable of terrestial cannibalism, 'Alas . . . is man's civilization only a wrappage, through which the savage nature of him can still burst . . .?' (Carlyle 1837: II, 376). Such questions Dickens asked himself, if he had not before, in 1854 and 1855.

Since the French Revolution in Carlyle's account stems from hunger, in a society that reduces all value to faith 'merely in the Everlasting Nothing and man's Digestive Power' (Carlyle 1837: I, 342), and since that hunger devours society, the rhetoric of the Primitive Fact recurs frequently: blood flows, 'the aliment of new madness'; at the Feast of Pikes, the more men swear Brotherhood in bumpers, so the more surely the Lapith feast, that began as a wedding and ended in drunken carnage, will 'lead to Cannibalism'; while in a moment that is uncertainly image or fact, the Mayor of Chartres, 'like to be eaten himself' as the grain supply fails, cries to the

Convention for help (Carlyle 1837: I, 201, 373; II, 202). France is so possessed by hunger and by drunkenness that we cannot be sure whether the mayor might literally supply the place of grain in these people's diet.

The Lapith feast is echoed by other classical allusions. The repetitive cluster of references to a Thyestes banquet by the Regiment de Flandre, which proves not to be 'the *ultimate* act of communion', except in its fatality to the officers who eat their own death, as Thyestes ate his by the flesh of his children (Carlyle 1837: I, 256–7; and also 258, 290), is intertwined with the march of the women of Paris on Versailles, demanding bread. These Maenads, as Carlyle calls them, echo the followers of Bacchus who tore living animals to pieces and devoured them, echo also Agave who tore and devoured her son Pentheus. Communion draws together: drunkenness and cannibalism drive on to violence and death. The larger image constantly presses of universal collapse, of anarchy that has (paradoxically) organized itself and is both destructive and self-destructive (Carlyle 1837: II, 360; repeated II, 383), an image that is classically enforced by Saturn devouring his children: 'The Revolution, then, is verily devouring its own children?' (Carlyle 1837: II, 383). The prediction latent (but rhetorically deliberate on Carlyle's part) in the Primitive Fact, the progress and conclusion of Revolution which vindicates that prediction and that Fact, is of slaughter and flesh-eating, along with the destruction of the most valued social and most sacred familial ties. That the prediction was becoming fact was recognized by the Girondist Vergniaud, whom Carlyle calls as an enforcing witness, that Vergniaud who presided at a last supper in prison with his friends and flung selflessly away the poison that might have spared him the guillotine but which was only enough for himself, not enough to share with his friends (Carlyle 1837: II, 327). Vergniaud had observed that 'The Revolution, like Saturn, is devouring its own children' (Carlyle 1837: II, 329). And once the Revolutionary tribunal has eaten up the others, it remains only to eat up itself. Carlyle's Primitive Fact is accomplished. 'That *I* can devour *Thee*' is both repulsive and fascinating, the threat of such cannibalism the more compelling to the imagination because it is seated not outside but within the self, within *myself*. The terrible fact, as Carlyle recognizes, is not that others may be compelled to eat me (when at least my will need not consent to the act, however personally inconvenient the business may be), but rather that I may be brought to the Fact of being myself a cannibal. It is potentially a fact in all of us, as Carlyle also suggests, if we but admit, as it has been written – what scriptures are these? Carlyle's own, in *Sartor Resartus*, it turns out – that every man 'holds confined within him a *mad*-man' (Carlyle 1837: II, 462; and I, 40). The image of cannibalism binds together society and self. It is a fear, dark, primitive in Carlyle's term, still powerful to us, when the possibility of it is once admitted, the circumstances imagined or become a circumambient reality, that may go far to help in understanding why

104

Dickens was so provoked by the allegation that Franklin and men under his command had descended into this anarchy. Perhaps the extremity had been reached; perhaps the madman had broken forth; yet if there, why not also in English society and why not also in Dickens himself? Such a descent seemed possible, if not in himself (and yet what might pressure do?), yet in the mood of the people; and provided with that fear, feeling those pressures upon himself and those that he believed operating upon society, Dickens explores, in a number of works and areas of activity in the mid to late 1850s, the links between order and cannibalism: sometimes overtly, sometimes covertly as in the child-rats that gnaw at the foundations in *Little Dorrit*, as despised as Sampson in his weakness, yet as capable as he of giving 'such a shake in this country' as when the Temple came down on Philistines and Israelite together.

Cannibalism or at least its 'phantom' appears in Dickens's contribution to *The Wreck of the Golden Mary*, the 1856 Christmas number of *Household Words*. In an open boat amongst the survivors of the *Golden Mary* is a child, Lucy, who dies and is committed to the deep. The narrator, whose fear of cannibalism is prompted by memories of shipwreck narratives, though certain that 'instances in which human beings in the last distress have fed upon each other are exceedingly few, and have very seldom indeed (if ever) occurred when the people in distress . . . have been accustomed to moderate forbearance', determines to bring the idea out into the open, lest the others, dwelling upon it secretly, might magnify the idea 'until it got to have an awful attraction about it'. He does this obliquely by an account of Captain Bligh adrift after the mutiny, one of the very examples Dickens had used in 'The lost Arctic voyagers'. His fellow sufferers respond with such revulsion to the notion that the narrator is convinced that 'there was no danger, and that this phantom, at any rate, did not haunt us'. Suffering on land rather than by sea is the subject of *The Peril of Certain English Prisoners*, the Christmas 1857 number of *Household Words*, and cannibalism does not appear, but steadfast endurance and readiness to obey authority for the common good are reminiscences of Franklin's commanding influence, of the disciplined endurance of the Crimean army, and of the goodness of the human heart, all bulwarks erected by Dickens against anarchy. There is a necessary slight frisson when we come to the name of the naval captain who commands the party that sets out in pursuit of the pirates: Captain George Carton. Dickens did not commonly re-use names, so his employment of what is more famous as Sidney Carton's surname in *A Tale of Two Cities* gives a resonance to the *English Prisoners*.

Another area of activity in these years was Dickens's involvement in theatricals, especially important being the collaborations with Wilkie Collins. The 1855 success of *The Lighthouse* in turn prompted the production in 1857 at Tavistock House and later on tour of *The Frozen Deep*. This play, in which Dickens followed up his strong dramatic performance in

The Lighthouse as Aaron Gurnock by the overwhelmingly powerful portrayal of Richard Wardour, was a collaboration with Collins even in the writing, and the rather ludicrous melodrama was clearly sustained by Dickens's production and performance.[13] Both play and performance were important to Dickens for a number of reasons: professional actresses were employed for the public performances outside Tavistock House, amongst them Ellen Ternan, with whom Dickens formed an association, (see Slater 1983, ch. 10, Tomalin 1990, esp. chs 6, 7) and Dickens himself tells how the idea of *A Tale of Two Cities* came to him while acting in *The Frozen Deep*. The melodrama's emotional triangle is an obvious patterning for Darnay, Lucie and Carton in the novel.[14] *The Frozen Deep* (I treat it as essentially a collaborative text, as much Dickens's work as Collins's) returns us to Sir John Franklin. Its second and third acts are set in the Arctic regions and on the coast of Newfoundland respectively. The main emotional charge is sexual, since the explorers Aldersley and Wardour discover in conversation that they are the accepted and the rejected suitor of Clara. Will Wardour abandon Aldersley in the icy wastes and declare he is dead – or will he save him, restoring him to the woman they both love?

The answer may be obvious: Wardour does indeed preserve Aldersley, even at the cost of his own life, carrying Aldersley in (when ugly suspicions have arisen) and safely depositing him before Clara in the Newfoundland cavern to which most of the cast, including the heroine and a Scotch nurse with second sight, have come. Yet if the all-male endurance of Franklin is wanting here, the finer quality of Wardour emerges under extreme conditions and cruel temptation. The Primitive Fact, 'That *I* can devour *Thee*', is challenged, since if I can devour thee, so also I can give my life to sustain thy life, just as de Sombreuil's daughter had made a sacrifice to save the life of her father. Cannibalism is egotistical: it sustains me. Sacrifice is an eating as well, offered, most obviously in the Christian myth, in feasting ('Take ye and eat, for this is my body') and in giving up of life. Such idealism purifies, even while it seems to replicate, the horrors of cannibalism.[15] As already noted, in the end, the anarchic devouring of revolutionary cannibalism ends not even in saving oneself alive: the Universal wolf eats up me as well. But sacrifice may preserve the life of others: it is communal and beneficent, it may not save one, for the moment, but it may duly save many. So at the end of *A Tale of Two Cities* it is not Darnay and Lucie who are imagined at the place of execution in Carton's vision, but rather Lucie's child and his son, bearing Carton's name. Lucie's grandson serves to bring the story to the present day, a reminder of a revolution which is not yet complete in France and might still come in England; but equally important, Carton, by his sacrifice, sustains not one but many, even as he sustained the seamstress that rode with him.

Whether or not Dickens had Carlyle's 'Primitive Fact' formula in mind (it can hardly be doubted: there are those 500 readings of Carlyle's history), the equation of I and Thee is enforced in *A Tale of Two Cities* by the mirror likeness of Darnay and Carton. The likeness is of course a plot necessity, in the 'minor' salvation of Darnay at the treason trial (when Carton 'gives' his likeness in exchange for Darney's life) and in the 'major' salvation at the end. Yet the likeness enforces how Carton might have committed a cannibal-like act: have stood aside in his jealousy, so that Darnay was devoured. Such an act would have been self-destruction. Carton could not have made himself better by it nor could he hope by it to win Lucie. In self-sacrifice he gives himself life, both in his physical mirror, which is Darnay, fulfilled in love and paternity, and in his future reincarnated mirror, the grandson bearing his name. Dickens reverses the Primitive Fact by turning, perhaps too easily, yet with some rhetorical force, to the Sublime Fact, uttered by an unidentified voice as Carton steps to the guillotine: 'I am the Resurrection and the Life'. The new Fact is 'That I can save Thee'; and Carton's act is scripturally repeated and approved by the voice of God. So Sidney Carton is saved alive, in memory and in the futurity of the child. He has found those qualities of an Englishman, of whom Franklin was a model, of one trained in and finally acknowledging 'moderate forbearance', that are Dickens's riposte to cannibalism.

Revolutions are expensive, Carlyle declared; to be avoided if possible. Regeneration is what is called for, Faith to withstand, to amend, to begin by amending oneself. In choosing to set his story, inspired by Franklin out of *The Frozen Deep*, in two cities amidst the image of Revolutionary Terror, Dickens necessarily turned to Carlyle. He was intimate with *The French Revolution*; Carlyle further sent him a 'cartload' of books to aid his researches (Sanders 1988a, 1988b: 3–7). What we may note is how Dickens gives us remarkably little direct detail of the violence. He seems rather to rework Carlyle than to use him directly. The deaths of Foulon and Berthier are in the novel, to stand for so much else. It is as though Carlyle could not be beaten at his own game: yet it is also the shift from the panoramic stage of Carlyle to the more intimate melodrama of fictive individuals. The reader's knowledge of terror is assumed, the image has been so stamped on his imagination by Carlyle, and is enforced by suggestion. Like Mr Jarvis Lorry, the reader knows only too well the purpose of that grindstone set up in the Paris courtyard overlooked by Tellson's Bank. If Mr Lorry preserves Lucie from the sight, we know not only what is directly below that window but also whence come the men and women who sharpen their implements and what business they are about. Dickens does not need to pass de Sombreuil's daughter before us: the image is in Carlyle and in the reader's vision, so that the novel is in some sense a collaboration with Carlyle's history. Lucie's ignorance which within the story's setting is also innocence is no longer possible to the novel's readers because the September Massacres have become history, both in the past and in Carlyle: though Carlyle's widespread use of the present tense ensures that within his narrative, history is also a living present, not just the antiquarian dead bones of Dryasdust.

And as Dickens, assuming this knowledge, offers an alternative choice of events (many, of course, his own fictional invention), so also he tends to prefer cannibalism as blood-drinking rather than Carlyle's primary act of flesh-eating. True, the hunger of Jacques 3 should not be discounted, a craving which if at first is for neither food nor drink, transforms Jacques into a 'life-thirsting, cannibal-looking' juryman, who ends an Ogre and an epicure of flesh (Dickens 1859: 205, 390, 444). Yet blood is strong: Manette's account, meant as a witness against injustice, is written in the Doctor's blood and is strong against the life of his own flesh and blood. From the spilled wine at the beginning, through the stained bacchantic slaughter of September, to Carton's own death, the image and the actuality of blood and drink are mingled. As the women count his death – Twenty-Three – so the crowd swells forward in a mass, 'like one great heave of water' (Dickens 1859: 464). They are both the deep that has burst forth to overwhelm the earth, yet also, at least potentially, the cleansing flood, the precursor of the new heaven, new earth of Carton's prophetic vision that is the novel's coda. Blood is to be washed away.

The two terrors of my title are the Terror of the French Revolution and its image in *A Tale of Two Cities*. Dickens received a version of the Terror from Carlyle's history and was prompted to seize upon one of its primary metaphors through the wish to do justice to the memory of Sir John Franklin. The path that he consequently set out on leads him, as a strand of his psycho-biography and of his imaginative creation in the 1850s, from the terror of the Arctic wastes to the figure of justice in the grown child of Darnay and Lucie, become 'the foremost of judges and honoured of men' (Dickens 1859: 465), a clew in this labyrinth being the cannibalism that I have taken here. That Terror, in its act and image as cannibalism, was a creative stimulus for the best part of half a decade: its metamorphoses emphasize how Dickens sought, if sometimes naively, to proclaim the goodness of human nature in the face of pressures that led him to see the possibility of his own collapse; how also Dickens made good his discipleship of Carlyle, and how Dickens was touched by certain facts that shoot their painful stimulus deep into him and are productive of Revolutionary images powerful in British culture.

NOTES

1 Dr John Rae (1813–93), explorer, worked for the Hudson's Bay Company and had already taken part in expeditions (1848–9 and 1851) in seach of Franklin's lost enterprise; while on a surveying mission in 1854 he had obtained from Eskimos information about Franklin's fate and identifiable objects. Rae wrote a report to the Admiralty (dated 29 July 1854); this, along with other material, was published in *The Times*, 23 October 1854, where Dickens read it. Rae's

official report, dated 1 September but not completed until October 1854, was read at the Hudson's Bay Company's Committee meeting, 13 November, and passed to the Admiralty, 1 December. Only in 1859 was it established that Franklin had died 11 June 1847. See Rae 1953, Wright 1959, Beattie and Geiger 1987.

2 This, along with the other Dickens letters quoted here, is in Dickens 1992; for Franklin's and Dickens's responses, see particularly the letters to Mrs Watson, 1 November 1854, and to W. H. Wills, 20 November 1854.

3 Franklin 1823: 451; see also p. 51 for a reference to cannibalism amongst the Indians. For an assessment of the episode and the disappearance of Richardson's original account, see Richardson 1984: 217–19.

4 Richardson 1984: 208–9; Franklin 1823: 417. Rae himself was much more sceptical (or realistic) both about the nature of Franklin's crews in 1845 and about what men will do under extreme pressure. He noted in his response to Dickens's arguments against his suggestions of cannibalism that while 'Much stress is laid on the moral character and the admirable discipline of the crews . . . their conduct at the very last British port they entered was not such as to make those who knew it, consider them very deserving' of Dickens's 'high eulogism' (Rae 1854b: 458).

5 'George Whitaker told Miss *M.* that, in the proofs of Franklin's first voyage, it was related, that during the time of their great want, the Ship's Crew *killed & eat* the Negro, – The Page, in which this fact was recorded was cancelled. – That certainly the Negro is never heard of after the account of the famine. – ' (2 September 1852, MS Mrs Elsie Duncan-Jones). Since Franklin's first published expedition (the *Narrative* of 1823) was by land (as was his second) and since no negro is mentioned, the rumour is puzzling. None the less, it shows that rumour was afloat only two years before Dickens's fierce reaction to the linking of Franklin with cannibalism.

6 Rae did not claim in 1854 that he had personal proof that Franklin's men had resorted to cannibalism; he reported what he had been told by the Eskimos. But he also insisted that his interpreter was an expert linguist, that Eskimos did tell the truth, and that the accounts were detailed and circumstantial. Support for his account and the Eskimos' veracity comes from remains found in 1981, which seemed to indicate that the last survivors kept going, as late as July or August 1848, by eating their dead companions (Beattie and Geiger 1987: ch. 5).

7 Dickens wrote 'The lost Arctic voyagers' [I] (Dickens 1854a) and [II] (Dickens 1854b); Rae's response was printed as 'The lost Arctic voyagers' [III] (with a tail-note by Dickens) (Rae 1854a) and 'Dr. Rae's report' (Rae 1854b). Dickens also published Rae's official report, dated 1 September 1854: 'Sir John Franklin and his crews' (Rae 1855).

8 Dickens 1992 provides Dickens's responses and the background annotation to these details; for the meeting at Drury Lane, see particularly Dickens 1960: 197–208.

9 Carlyle 1839: II, 192, 210. Dickens had publicly affirmed his admiration for Carlyle in 1854 by the dedication of *Hard Times*.

10 *Little Dorrit* Bk I, ch. 14. For the background of *Little Dorrit*, see Butt and Tillotson 1957: ch. 9, and Easson 1991.

11 *Troilus and Cressida*, I. iii. 121–4; see Kenneth Palmer's note in the Arden edition (1982), including his reference to Kenneth Muir's note on *King Lear*, IV. ii. 49–50. For a revolutionary parallel, see 'Robespierre guillotining the executioner' in Schama 1989: 850.

12 The episode's fame, apart from Carlyle, is witnessed by an anonymous painting, *Le Dévouement héroique de Mademoiselle de Sombreuil* in the Musée Carnavalet, Paris: a detail is the cover illustration for the 1988 edition of Dickens 1859. In another vein, Dickens has Miss Snevellici in *Nicholas Nickleby* recite 'The Blood-Drinker's Burial' (ch. 14), a performance Mrs Crummles had bequeathed to her, having given it over herself as too tremendous for the audience's feelings (ch. 25).

13 *The Frozen Deep* failed in professional performance: see Robert Louis Brannan's account of the play and productions in Brannan 1966.

14 The 'Preface' to *A Tale of Two Cities* makes the link, though acecdotally rather than causally; see Andrew Sanders's introduction (Dickens 1859) for a recent consideration of the relationship between play and novel; see also Sanders 1988b: 1–3.

15 Though how difficult even the idealism can be is suggested by those disciples who walked no longer with Jesus after he declared life could only come by eating his flesh and drinking his blood (John, 6); even as idealism it is not a simple question of the difference between the literal and the metaphorical: Mlle de Sombreuil's idealism demanded literal blood drinking, while the doctrine of transubstantiation makes real the flesh and the blood under the elements of bread and wine.

BIBLIOGRAPHY

Beattie, O. and Geiger, J. (1987) *Frozen in Time: The Fate of the Franklin Expedition*, London, Bloomsbury.

Brannan, R. L. (1966) *Under the Management of Mr. Charles Dickens: His Production of 'The Frozen Deep'*, Ithaca, New York, Cornell University Press.

Butt, J. and Tillotson, K. (1957) *Dickens at Work*, London, Methuen.

Carlyle, T. (1837) *The French Revolution*, ed. K. J. Fielding and David Sorensen, Oxford, Oxford University Press, 1989.

—— (1839) 'Chartism', in his *Essays*, 2 vols, London, Dent, 1950: II, 165–238.

Dickens, C. (1854a) 'The lost Arctic voyagers' [I], *Household Words* X(2 December): 361–5.

—— (1854b) 'The lost Arctic voyagers' [II], *Household Words* X(9 December): 385–93.

—— (1859) *A Tale of Two Cities*, ed. Andrew Sanders, Oxford, Oxford University Press, 1988.

—— (1960) *Speeches of Charles Dickens*, ed. K. J. Fielding, Oxford, Clarendon Press.

—— (1992) *The Letters of Charles Dickens, Vol. VII (1853–1855)*, ed. Kathleen Tillotson, Graham Storey and Angus Easson, Oxford, Clarendon Press.

Easson, A. (1991) 'A novel scarcely historical? Time and history in Dickens's *Little Dorrit*', in Angus Easson (ed.) *History and the Novel* (Essays and Studies): 27–40.

Franklin, J. (1823) *Narrative of a Journey to the Shores of the Polar Sea in the Years 1819, 20, 21, and 22*, London, John Murray.

Rae, J. (1854a) 'The lost Arctic voyagers' [III], *Household Words* X(23 December): 433–7.

—— (1854b) 'Dr. Rae's report', *Household Words* X(30 December): 457–9.

—— (1855a) 'Sir John Franklin and his crews' *Household Words* XI (3 February): 12–20.

—— (1953) 'John Rae's correspondence with the Hudson's Bay Company', ed. E. E. Rich and A. M. Johnson, *Hudson's Bay Record Society* XVI.

Richardson, J. (1984) *Arctic Ordeal: The Journey of John Richardson Surgeon-Naturalist with Franklin 1820–1822*, ed. C. Stuart Houston, Kingston, McGill – Queen's University Press.

Sanders, A. (1988a) 'Cartloads of books: some sources for *A Tale of Two Cities*', in Joanne Shattock (ed.) *Dickens and Other Victorians*, Basingstoke, Macmillan: 37–52.

—— (1988b) *The Companion Guide to A Tale of Two Cities*, London, Unwin.

Schama, S. (1989) *Citizens: A Chronicle of the French Revolution*, London, Viking.

Slater, M. (1983) *Dickens and Women*, London, Dent.

Tomalin, C. (1990) *The Invisible Woman: The Story of Nelly Ternan and Charles Dickens*, London, Viking.

Wright, N. (1959) *The Quest for Franklin*, London, Heinemann.

9

'My own mind is my own church': Blake, Paine and the French Revolution

David Bindman

Blake's sympathy for and engagement with the French Revolution have long been recognized, and his political radicalism in the 1790s was the subject of David's Erdman's classic *Blake: Prophet Against Empire* (1956). Erdman's book has carried such authority that the subject has rarely been addressed since, except on the basis of Erdman's conclusions. He argued persuasively that all the evidence points to 'a stronger affinity [on Blake's part] for the artisan radicalism of the Constitutional and Corresponding Societies than for the more Whiggish radicalism of such younger men as Wordsworth and Coleridge',[1] and though there are some problems in that formulation, I do not propose to challenge the distinction between artisan and Whiggish radicalism that Erdman makes, nor Blake's adherence to the former. Blake was not, in fact, a member of either of the societies mentioned above, but the radicalism represented by Wordsworth and Coleridge, and by William Godwin and Mary Wollstonecraft, was problematic for him in its emphasis on the role of reason and nature in the renovation of society (Essick 1991). This incompatibility of artisan and Whiggish radicalism, in the sense that Erdman uses the terms, can be seen as well as anywhere in the contrasting positions of Blake and Paine: the latter clearly belongs to the rational and sceptical tradition of Locke and Voltaire (Ayer 1988: 17–20), for which Blake frequently declared his abhorrence. Yet – and this is the nub of the essay that follows – Blake on a number of occasions expressed extravagant admiration for Paine, comparing him on one occasion to Jesus and claiming him to be a 'worker of miracles'.[2]

I want to consider this apparent paradox in the light of the development of Blake's attitudes towards the French Revolution in the years 1791–8, concentrating on a small number of texts and designs from within that period.[3] The mass of new material brought forth by the commemoration of the bicentenary of the French Revolution in 1989 has made even more evident the rapidity and depth of political change, and response to that change in Britain, in the Revolutionary years. The widespread belief in 1789–91 that the French Revolution would lead on inexorably to universal benevolence was by the summer of 1792 scarcely tenable even by the most optimistic of British radicals. The imposition of a constitution on the French monarchy in the years 1789–90 could recall to British observers the 'Glorious Revolution' of 1688, and appear even to conservatives to be a legitimate curtailment of 'despotic' royal power: as the monarchy came under increasing threat in those years the English Revolution of the seventeenth century emerged as an appropriate precedent for the events in France (Bindman 1989, esp. cat. nos. 49, 64). The state of war between England and France which arose in late 1792 and the 'Terror' of 1793–4 created a situation in France which appeared, in England at least, to go beyond English precedent. Though most 'Whiggish' radicals withdrew all sympathy from the infant French Republic, the questions raised for English radicals by the events of *l'an II* did not, as is so often assumed, always lead to disillusionment or a panicky flight into conservatism. The brief rule of the Committee of Public Safety could be explained away variously as an inheritance from the Inquisition,[4] a temporary detour from the relentless progress of improvement (Wollstonecraft 1795: 127), or a sign that the French, unlike the English with their ancient traditions of liberty, were unfitted by their history to carry out a successful revolution.[5]

BLAKE'S BASTILLE

The obvious starting point for a discussion of Blake's attitudes towards the Revolution is the letterpress volume *The French Revolution* dated 1791, 'a poem in seven books' of which only the first is known in a single copy in the Huntington Library (Keynes 1976: 134–7).[6] The reasons for its failure to be published are not known. Though the publisher Joseph Johnson, after publishing Paine's *Rights of Man* in March 1791, had become alarmed enough to hand the book over to another publisher, it seems unlikely that he would have thought *The French Revolution* too hot to handle at such an early date in the progress of the Revolution. In late 1792 such a work might have appeared to be potentially seditious but even at the end of 1791 its viewpoint was barely unconventional let alone threatening.[7] In essence *The French Revolution* is a 'Bastille' poem, belonging to a well-established genre, encompassing dramas, operas (Beethoven's *Fidelio* being the best-known example), and even paintings, produced mainly, though not exclusively, in the years immediately following the prison's destruction.[8] The Bastille genre depends upon an absolute contrast between 'despotism', represented by a luridly imaginative picture of the Bastille as a place of hideous cruelty towards the innocent, and a vision of 'liberty' in which man may reach joy and perfection after his release from the prison. Blake's Bastille has seven towers each of which contains an exemplary prisoner condemned to rot for a righteous challenge to the political or religious hegemony of the French State. As has often been noted the Bastille was, by eighteenth-century standards, a relatively benign institution by July

1789 (Godechot 1970), but as Paine himself observed, 'The downfal[1] of it included the idea of the downfal[1] of Despotism; and this compounded image was become as figuratively united as Bunyan's Doubting Castle and Giant Despair' (Paine 1792: I, 15).

The idea of the Bastille as a place of terror has a history in both French and English writing of the eighteenth century and it was a commonplace even in England to refer to a place of unjust confinement as a 'Bastile' (Bindman 1989: 37–8). But the extremity of the horror in Blake's account goes beyond most of its literary or artistic sources. The role of the Bastille in Blake's poem as the cruel heart of the *ancien régime* is expressed in the prison's disturbed response to the meeting of the Estates-General in May–June 1789, and in the vulpine form of the Governor Delaunay pacing the walls. The main part of the text consists of a debate at the Estates-General between the forces of reaction and the proponents of revolution. A warlike defence of rank and ancient chivalry is given by the fictitious Dukes of Burgundy and Bourbon, supported by the fearful Archbishop of Paris who invokes heaven to urge the crushing of the people. On the other side are Lafayette, the protector of the people, the Duke of Orleans 'generous as mountains' who advocates brotherhood and equality, and Sieyes who offers a brief glimpse of a post-Revolutionary future, when the oppression of war, priesthood and rank shall be thrown off:

> Then the valleys of France shall cry to the soldier: Throw down
> thy sword and musket,
> And run and embrace the meek peasant.
>
> (*The French Revolution* 1791: K: 144)

In Sieyes's speech the vision of liberty presented is of a single continuous action in which the people rise up, and in casting off their oppressors awake from 'the dark night of feudalism' (Erdman 1956: 165). When that is achieved and 'Nobles have put off the red robe of terror, the crown of oppression', then the arts will be liberated, shepherds freed from fear, 'The mild peaceable nations be open'd to heav'n, and men walk with their fathers in bliss' (K: 145). The post-revolutionary state is, then, a pastoral paradise which follows the removal of the chains of the old order and is also a return to the 'original' happy state before their imposition. Such optimism and the belief that the irresistible logic of revolution would imminently conquer Britain is characteristic of the exultant radicalism of the years 1789–91, and can be found also in Richard Price's famous address to the Revolution Society of 4 November 1789, which sparked off Burke's reply in *Reflection on the Revolution in France* (1790). In his peroration Price invites 'friends of freedom' to 'Behold kingdoms . . . starting from sleep, breaking their fetters, and claiming justice from their oppressors! Behold, the light you have struck out, after setting AMERICA free, reflected to FRANCE, and there kindled into a blaze that lays despotism in ashes, and warms and illuminates EUROPE!' (Butler 1984: 32). In Paine's *Rights of Man*, Part I, which Blake may just have read before writing some or all of *The French Revolution*, the throwing off of the shackles of despotism is, simultaneously, the assumption of the renewed state of liberty. There is, however, an important difference: in *The French Revolution* the state of liberty is historically unspecific (at least as far as the poem goes), but for Paine and Price it is identifiable with the creation of the new American Republic, which by throwing off its British oppressors, had entered into a state of democratic grace (Paine 1792: 17–19).

If Paine's idea of the post-revolutionary state in *Rights of Man* is close to, and possibly influential upon, Blake's conception in *The French Revolution*, then we might also see the reactionary Duke of Burgundy's speech as a sublime parody of Burke's defence of aristocracy in *Reflections on the Revolution in France*, which Blake must certainly have read before writing his poem.[9] Some of Burgundy's rhetoric is undeniably Burkean ('the ancient forests of chivalry'),[10] and his speech can readily be read as an hysterical response on behalf of the old order to the threat of revolution. Burgundy does not answer the argument of revolution, but pours forth a series of high-flown and warlike images, which recall Paine's criticism of the 'horrid pictures' in Burke's text.[11]

BURKE, PAINE AND THE REVOLUTION CONTROVERSY

Blake's illuminated prophecy *America*, announced as available for purchase in October 1793 (K: 207), ostensibly deals with the events of the American Revolution, but I want to argue that the debates between Orc and Urizen are, like *The French Revolution*, also conducted in terms of the Burke–Paine controversy. With the hindsight given by the French Revolution, the American Revolution was, if one were a Painite, the opening of a redemptive process which might culminate in universal revolution. If one were a Burkean, on the other hand, it was nothing less than a plague which threatened to engulf the world. In *America* plate 6, the American Revolution is presented as the consequence of the release of the youthful Orc, or energy, from the chains which have bound him from the earliest history of man. He embodies revolution as a primary and violently sexual impulse of mankind, which only at the end of the eighteenth century is able to break out of its age-old captivity (Paley 1970: 73f.).

The pivotal action of *America* is to be found in a highly-charged confrontation between Orc, now broken free (plate 9.1), and the aged figure of Albion's Angel, representing, among other things, the old and corrupt order in Britain (plate 9.2). Orc first addresses Albion's Angel with a beautiful vision of the new revolutionary order, describing the release of a prisoner from a 'Bastille', where

Thus wept the Angel voice & as he wept the terrible blasts
Of trumpets, blew a loud alarm across the Atlantic deep.
No trumpets answer; no reply of clarions or of fifes,
Silent the Colonies remain and refuse the loud alarm.

On those vast shady hills between America & Albions shore;
Now barr'd out by the Atlantic sea: call'd Atlantean hills;
Because from their bright summits you may pass to the Golden world
An ancient palace, archetype of mighty Emperies,
Rears its immortal pinnacles, built in the forest of God
By Ariston the king of beauty for his stolen bride.

Here on their magic seats the thirteen Angels sat perturb'd
For clouds from the Atlantic hover oer the solemn roof.

9.1 William Blake, 'Thus wept the Angel voice', from *America a Prophecy*, 1793, relief etching, London, British Museum.

The terror answerd: I am Orc, wreath'd round the accursed tree:
The times are ended; shadows pass the morning gins to break;
The fiery joy, that Urizen perverted to ten commands,
What night he led the starry hosts thro' the wide wilderness;
That stony law I stamp to dust: and scatter religion abroad
To the four winds as a torn book, & none shall gather the leaves;
But they shall rot on desart sands, & consume in bottomless deeps;
To make the desarts blossom, & the deeps shrink to their fountains,
And to renew the fiery joy, and burst the stony roof.
That pale religious letchery, seeking Virginity,
May find it in a harlot, and in coarse-clad honesty
The undefil'd tho' ravish'd in her cradle night and morn:
For every thing that lives is holy, life delights in life;
Because the soul of sweet delight can never be defil'd.
Fires inwrap the earthly globe, yet man is not consumd;
Amidst the lustful fires he walks: his feet become like brass,
His knees and thighs like silver, & his breast and head like gold

9.2 William Blake, 'The terror answerd', from *America a Prophecy*, 1793, relief
etching, London, British Museum.

the inchained soul, [has been] shut up in darkness and in
  sighing
Whose face has never seen a smile in thirty weary years
(*America* plate 6, K: 198)

Like Sterne's Captive and the mythical Comte de Lorges (Bindman 1989:
38–42) the prisoner has been imprisoned indefinitely, and could only hope
for release through revolution. Orc ends his first address to Albion's Angel
by reaffirming the dream of 1789: the revolution in destroying despotism
has already been completed: 'For Empire is no more, and now the Lion
& Wolf shall cease' (*America* plate 6, K: 198).

But the beautiful dream of liberty is received not by a fraternal embrace,
but by the Burkean voice of Albion's Angel who instantly (and correctly)
sees revolution to be a threat not only to his political power but to the
whole theological basis of the old order in Europe:

Blasphemous Demon, Antichrist, hater of Dignities,
Lover of Wild Rebellion, and transgressor of God's Law,
Why dost thou come to Angel's eyes in this terrific form?
(*America* plate 7, K: 198)

Burke's characterization, in the *Reflections* and later writings, of the French
Revolution as a monstrous birth, a 'Promethean aberration' (Gengembre
1989: 921), is clearly reflected in the language of Albion's Angel's response.
Burke, though he had supported the Americans in 1776, was the first to
present the French Revolution as an unprecedented transgression of the
natural order, threatening the very existence of religion and civilization.
For Burke in his French Revolutionary writings the abolition of rank was
a form of blasphemy, and Albion's Angel's initial reply to Orc, quoted
above, is surely intended also as a parody of Burke's apocalyptic language.

Albion's Angel acts, as Burke may be said to have done, as the warlike
voice of the British *ancien régime*. In reply to Albion's Angel's description
of him as a 'Blasphemous Demon'. Orc proclaims the end of the *ancien
régime* and of the rule of 'the stony law' of Moses, prophesying a new age
when man shall be armoured against the fires which 'inwrap the earthly
globe'. But Orc finds that this prospect of revolution and the end of
oppression does not, by an irresistible vision of human felicity, bring about
universal brotherhood; on the contrary it causes the forces of reaction to
sound their war-trumpets and bring out armies to crush 'the rebel form
[that] rent the ancient Heavens' (*America* plate 9, K: 199). Blake, therefore,
is now assuming that the vision of 1789 which underpinned *The French
Revolution* and Paine's *Rights of Man* is no longer adequate to the situation
of 1793; the old order is bound to reject the fraternal embrace of revolution
and seek to destroy it by proclaiming it to be blasphemy.

The armies called up by Albion's Angel are not military but ideological,

In thunders ends the voice. Then Albions Angel wrathful burnt
Beside the Stone of Night; and like the Eternal Lions howl
In famine & war, replyd. Art thou not Orc, who serpent-form'd
Stands at the gate of Enitharmon to devour her children;
Blasphemous Demon, Antichrist, hater of Dignities;
Lover of wild rebellion, and transgresser of Gods Law;
Why dost thou come to Angels eyes in this terrific form?

9.3 William Blake, 'In thunders ends the voice', from *America a Prophecy*, 1793,
relief etching, London, British Museum.

RIGHTS OF MAN   SEDITION

PAIN SIN and THE DEVIL

TRES JUNCTI IN UNO.

1793.

INTERCEPTED CORRESPONDENCE,

FROM

SATAN to CITIZEN PAINE;

Wherein is discovered a secret Friendship between Honest *Thomas and a* Crowned Head, *in spite of his avowed principles of Opposition to all Monarchy.*

Beloved Thomas,

THY Interest and mine is so nearly allied, that I cannot forbear giving thee a few *more* gentle hints with respect to thy conduct above stairs.—Firstly and principally, beware of that beast, John Bull; for John will think for himself, and has burnt both thee and thy book so repeatedly, that Hell absolutely swarms with thy Effigies, Thomas.—*He* is withal so bigotted to his Constitution and his King, (by the bye George and I were never friends) that all our schemes are frustrated by what he calls Loyalty, therefore as thou valuest thy neck, avoid England, left happily we meet before thy term be expired, or our business half compleated —Indeed he has treated all our Emissaries so uncivilly, that they have been obliged to decamp bag and baggage (at least those who possessed any) and steal a march into other Countries more adapted to Innovation and less scrupulous about the means, fearful, no doubt, that as they professed to give *Liberty*, John might take Liberties with them. The encouragement, however, that they meet with in France, amply compensates for their defection in England; yet though the Convention has almost made a Desert of my lower Domains, I had my fears left they should be affected with *Humanity*, and disgrace their leader, 'till I saw thy name, *then* indeed Thomas, my fears vanished, and I looked upon the business as done ;—so keep them to it, my dear Fellow, keep them *to it*. You know Thomas from the beginning I never liked subordination, and have ever since been sowing the glorious seeds of Dissention and Rebellion among mankind ; and that too under various masks, and in as varied situations. From the fascinating Covert of the Wily Snake, to the Threadbare Night Cap of French Liberty.—From the fall of Man to the Fate of France ;—But of that hereafter. Thou hast doubtless met with our mutual Friend, Belezebub, whom I dispatched on Earth to second thy Projects, and aid our Machinations—He is easily distinguished by a certain puritanical *Priestly* Deportment ;—as no deception is (generally speaking)

so successful as that practised under the appearance of sanctity, we thought him secure of success, but by throwing off the mask too soon, he set John Bull upon his guard, and so frustrated all our intended operations ;—*He,* of *course,* will soon be with *us* again. Now in France, give a man his Champagne, his Fiddle, and his Wench, and the Devil (excuse the Egotism) may take the Hindmost : nay, I have led the whole Country a Dance for three years to the tune of *Ca-ira*; but those English Boors, this proud, self opionated people, are so devoutly given to trust their own senses, that there is no drawing them into the noose without allowing them to pry into Consequences—and that will never do, Thomas ! And then there's this King that they talk so much about, and that *thou* took'st so much pains to prove was but a *Man,* and that a *Man* was but a *Man,* make the most of him—thou wast right, I applaud thee—What are abilities ? what are faculties ?—all the prejudices of education.—What is it to the people that he is an excellent father, 'a generous husband, or a *good man* ? Then in consulting the good of his subjects he selfishly considers his own inclinations, and by encouraging arts or sciences, trade or commerce, why he rides his own hobby-horse, and yet, forsooth, this is call'd encreasing the credit of the nation!—Oh ! for a little equality ! Oh, Thomas, were the world reduced to thy level we should have rare doings below——But these people are impracticable and I fear we must leave them to their own inclinations.

Excuse this renewal of advice, my dear Thomas—follow it, and take heed till we meet, which in the common course of things (should no untimely accident occur) cannot be long, when you will find in me your *warmest* and most congenial associate.

SATAN.

We have *lost* our Cause in the Courts of Justice, Thomas, but we have *gained* an *Advocate.*

Published by J. AITKIN, Castle Street, Leicester Fields.

Price TWO-PENCE each, or TWELVE SHILLINGS and SIX-PENCE per Hundred.

9.4 Anon., *Pain Sin and The Devil, c.* 1792, etching, London, British Museum.

for the defence of the old order in England in 1793 was primarily in the hands of Burke's sympathizers in the Crown and Anchor Society, which from November 1792 flooded the country with propaganda associating even moderate reform with the atrocities, real and imagined, committed in the name of the French Revolution (Bindman 1989: 117–22). The inconclusive outcome of *America*, with Albion's Angel still in power in the form of an icy Northern god, may refer to the fact that the Crown and Anchor campaign did indeed damp the fire of revolution in England and place its ultimate outcome in doubt. At the heart of the Crown and Anchor and other loyalist campaigns drawing on Burke, was a sustained attempt to inscribe on the consciousness of the nation an image of revolution utterly alien to the ideal of brotherhood proclaimed by Paine. This conflict of image may be alluded to in the pastoral scene, accompanying, on plate 7 of *America*, Albion's Angel's denunciation of Orc as a 'Blasphemous Demon' (plate 9.3). It shows a kind of paradise in which two youthful figures sleep next to a large sheep. Whatever other meanings this image may contain it contrasts tellingly in mood with the sublimity of Albion's Angel's denunciation; both express mutually irreconcilable perceptions of the nature of revolution.

If the Burkean nature of Albion's Angel can be contemplated then we can also consider, as Morton Paley has already suggested, some kind of identification of Orc with Paine himself.[12] The idea of Paine as a 'Blasphemous Demon', sent by Satan to further his design for the destruction of Christianity and political stability, was a commonplace of popular loyalist propaganda of 1792–3 (Bindman 1989: 108f.). To take one example from many, a broadside published by J. Aitkin, probably at the end of 1792, entitled *Pain Sin and the Devil* (George 1938: no. 8152) (plate 9.4), purports to be a letter from Satan to 'Citizen Paine' congratulating him on his success in France and commiserating with his difficulties in the very difficult task of subverting John Bull and making a revolutionary of him. Paine's role is to carry out Satan's age-old mission in the present time:

> You know Thomas from the very beginning I never liked subordination, and have ever since been sowing the glorious seeds of dissension and Rebellion among mankind; and that too under various masks, and in as varied situations. From the fascinating Covert of the Wily Snake, to the Threadbare Night Cap of French Liberty. From the fall of Man to the Fate of France.
>
> (George 1938: no. 8152)

Paine's business is seen to have been as much to do with France as with England, and his flight to France and election as a deputy in late 1792 is taken to be a guarantee that France will not abandon equality: 'I had my fears lest they [the Convention] should be affected with *Humanity*, and disgrace their leader [i.e. Satan], 'til I saw thy name, *then* indeed Thomas, my fears vanished, and I looked upon the business as done; – so keep them to it, my dear Fellow, keep them *to it*'. Another example of such popular anti-Paine propaganda is a money token circulated widely in 1793 with the inscription 'The Wrongs of Man' and the date 21 January 1793 on the verso, and a hanging man inscribed 'The End of Pain' on the recto: even the execution of Louis XVI is attributed to the contagion of Paine's ideas (Bindman 1989: no. 54a).

The idea of Paine as a demonic spirit moving from country to country setting each one ablaze has a certain logic if one also brings into account Paine's role in the American Revolution. The publication of Paine's pamphlet *Common Sense* in 1776 played a major part in the American colonists' decision to seek full independence from Britain, and Blake in the *Annotations to Bishop Watson* of 1798 may be alluding to its effect in his account of Paine as a modern 'worker of miracles': 'Is it a greater miracle to feed five thousand men with five loafs than to overthrow all the armies of Europe with a small pamphlet?' (K: 391).

The question of Blake's attitude towards Paine and of the progress of the French Revolution brings one back again to the problem of Blake's hostility to deism and rationalism. From what we know of Blake's attitudes we can reasonably infer that he would have had reservations about the military expansionism and rational ethic of the Girondin government, which remained tenuously in power in France until June 1793. Nor would he have felt at ease with Robespierre's 'Republic of Virtue', and especially not with the deistic cult of *l'Etre suprême*. On the other hand there is some evidence in Blake's writings of this time of *sans-culotte* attitudes towards 'aristocrats' and especially towards the French Royal Family, whose fate seems to have left him unmoved, though it excited widespread sympathy in England. The much scratched-out doggerel poem in the *Notebook*, probably dating from late 1792 or early 1793, beginning 'Let the Brothels of Paris be opened',[13] refers satirically to Burke's extravagant account of Marie Antoinette in the *Reflections*, and the first line itself may be a response to Burke's claim that the Revolution had unleashed the forces of male sexual desire (Kramnick 1977: 156). The poem is hostile not only to Louis XVI and Marie Antoinette, but is also scathing in its characterization of the constitutionalist Lafayette, whose attempts to affect a rapprochement between the French monarchy and the Revolution are derided by Blake as the moral weakness which leads to greater crimes. In an oblique reference to the suggestion made frequently in Paris street literature and caricature that Lafayette had enjoyed a passionate affair with Marie Antoinette, Blake depicts him as submitting to the female principle represented by the harlot Queen of France:

> Fayette, Fayette, thou'rt bought & sold,
> And sold is thy happy morrow;

Thou gavest the tears of Pity away
In exchange for the tears of sorrow.
(K: 186)

The king and queen of France are revealed as, under the aegis of 'old Nobodaddy aloft', releasing Pestilence and Famine upon their rebellious people, while Lafayette fatally pities the royal couple as they lay 'In tears & iron bound', abandoning his nation in treacherous flight. The engraving of *Lucifer and the Pope in Hell* of 1793–4 (Essick 1983: X, 1A; Bindman 1989: 70–1 and cat. no. 164), (plate 9.5) is also passionately anti-monarchical though not necessarily tied to specific events. It illustrates a passage from the Book of Isaiah, which prophesies that all kings and tyrants will end up in Hell, and the king's jowly visage recalls, probably deliberately, both Louis XVI and George III.

Blake, we may surmise, would have been more upset by the rationalism of the French Revolution than its violence, which could be seen as fulfilling the prophecy of the Book of Revelation that the material world would end in destruction. Hence Paine's role as a revolutionary destroying angel would have had a part in a Blakean teleology despite his own 'Urizenic' beliefs. Blake's fullest comments on Paine are to be found in the pencil annotations to Bishop Watson's *An Apology for The Bible in a Series of Letters Addressed to Thomas Paine*, a book first published in 1796 as a response to the second part of Paine's *The Age of Reason*, published the previous year (Erdman 1956: 301–2). Both parts of the *The Age of Reason* had caused offence to the clergy. Part I assailed 'the three principal means that have been employed in all ages, and perhaps in all countries, to impose upon mankind ... mystery, miracle and prophecy' (Paine 1795: Part I, 91), while the second part contains a sustained assault on the truth of the Bible and a firm denial of Revelation. Blake's annotations are dated 1798, a year in which, Blake assures us, 'To defend the Bible in this year 1798 would cost a man his life' for 'The Beast & the Whore rule without control' (K: 383).

Blake, like Bishop Watson, accepts the validity of the Bible as revelation, none the less there can be no doubt whatever that his sympathies are with Paine. It is not that he *agrees* with Paine's dismissive account of the Bible as a fable, but that Paine, unlike the Bishop, is not part of the political-ecclesiastical power structure of the old order. Blake claims that Watson, like Burke, well-known as a liberal before the French Revolution and, as it happens, a close friend of Blake's future patron and tormentor William Hayley (Bishop 1951: 199 and *passim*), was in an inherently false position by virtue of his office. Watson's defence of the Church of England makes him, to use the categories of *Marriage of Heaven and Hell*, an 'Angel' who is challenged by Paine's 'Devil': thus the Bishop must find himself defending 'Antichrist' whom Blake had claimed to be synonymous with the Catholic/

123

9.5 William Blake, *Lucifer and the Pope in Hell*, 1793–4, line engraving, London, British Museum.

Anglican tradition. The overtly rational and deistic basis of Paine's attack on the Bible, on the other hand, presents Blake with a problem that cannot be so easily dismissed; it is inconceivable that Blake could have accepted Paine's positivistic complaint of the historical implausibility of the Bible.

To cope with the awkwardness presented by this position Blake first claims that Paine attacks not the Christian message but 'The Perversions of Christ's words & acts . . . & also the perversions of the Bible', arguing that 'Paine has not attacked Christianity. Watson has defended Antichrist' (K: 383). It is true that Paine is careful to exalt that 'virtuous and amiable man' Jesus Christ, who 'preached most excellent morality and the equality of man', but there is no mistaking the tone of Voltairean scepticism which pervades *The Age of Reason,* and which provoked so many apoplectic responses from clergymen. Could Blake really have read Paine's derisive claim that the Book of Revelation was 'a book of riddles that requires a revelation to explain it' (Paine 1795: I, 58) without blenching, given his bitter hostility towards the 'mockery' practised by Voltaire and Rousseau? Certainly in the Annotations to Bishop Watson's *Apology* Blake notes the material nature of Paine's Christianity ('the Bishop never saw the Everlasting Gospel any more than Tom Paine' (K. 394)), but he counters this with the claim that Watson has not dared to consider Paine's arguments: 'One, for instance, which is that the books of the bible were never believ'd willingly by any nation & that none but designing Villains ever pretended to believe . . . this he has shewn with great force, which calls upon his Opponent loudly for an answer' (K: 390).

Paine then redeems himself by arguing 'with great force' and this is brought out strongly in Blake's angry comment on Watson's appeal to 'the judgement of learned and impartial men'. Paine is 'either a Devil or an Inspired man. Men who give themselves to their Energetic genius in the manner that Paine does are no Examiners. If they are not determinedly wrong they must be right or the Bible is false' (K: 386). Paine as an energetic spirit is more likely to reach the truth than the 'Serpentine dissimulation' of Bishop Watson, and though in Blake's eyes he may be wrong in arguing 'That the Bible is all a State Trick', or 'that all Commentators on the Bible are Dishonest Designing Knaves', he is redeemed by his passion, certainty and commitment. If one applies Blake's view of the Paine–Watson dispute to the relative situations of England and France in 1798 then England can be seen to be firmly in the grip of State tyranny and State religion: 'The Beast and Whore rule without control', while France had at least broken with the older system of State religion symbolized by the Bastille, despite a series of attempts to reimpose it in a covert form, not least by Robespierre himself.

THE FORMATION OF THE OLD ORDER

Robespierre's ability to impose State religion on a country that had so dramatically thrown off despotism brought into question not only the future of revolution but also its past. If *America* is concerned principally with the ability of the old order to resist the benign force of revolution, then *Europe* and the other 1794 books can be seen to contain an agonized examination of the means by which the old order was able to keep mankind in its thrall. If we distill from *Europe* the story of how, in modern times, man had reached the dire condition which made a revolution inevitable, we are left with the following scheme: the Catholic Church, as heir to the pagan world, came into being by usurping the spiritual authority of Jesus Christ following his Incarnation. On the basis of this usurped authority the Church, and its successor the Church of England, was able to reimpose an essentially heathen society based on repression and pagan ceremonial in the name of religion. The name of Jesus was thus attached to a series of false and repressive beliefs, as is revealed by Enitharmon:

> Go! tell the Human race that Woman's love is Sin;
> That an Eternal life awaits the worms of sixty winters
> In an allegorical abode where existence hath never come.
>
> (*Europe*, plate 5, K: 240)

This phase of repression lasts until the current age of revolution, which arises not only from the external force represented by Orc, but from its internal contradictions: Albion's Angel is 'smitten with his own plagues'.

The process of 'veiling', by which the Christian message is distorted by ceremonial is perhaps best expressed in the visual images on plates 5 and 10 (plates 9.6 and 9.7), which reveal the hideous reality of war and deception which lies behind the rituals of Catholicism and of the Church of England. In plate 10 the ass-eared bat-winged Pope appears to the eye of the artist as a false idol. The two plates appear, therefore, to reflect upon the relationship between power and religion under the influence of Paine's account of the origins of the established order in England in *Rights of Man* Part I. According to Paine bad governments may be based on either superstition or power, but in the case of Britain the rule of the sword which 'assumed the name of sceptre', initiated by William the Conqueror, eventually availed itself of the power of superstition, uniting 'fraud to force'. The first consequence was the idol of Divine Right which 'in imitation of the Pope, who affects to be spiritual and temporal, and in contradiction to the Founder of the Christian religion, twisted itself afterwards into an idol of another shape, called *Church* and *State*' (Paine 1792: I, 33). For Blake and for Paine, then, papal power and the power of the English king and Church are synonymous and equally idolatrous. Blake's image of the bat-winged Pope may be seen to be, therefore, a representation

9.6 William Blake, 'Now comes the night', from *Europe a Prophecy*, 1794, relief etching, Glasgow, University of Glasgow.

9.7 William Blake, 'Albion's Angel rose', from *Europe a Prophecy*, 1794, relief etching, Glasgow, University of Glasgow.

of what Paine calls 'the mule-animal' caused by the union of Church and State in Britain.

In *The Age of Reason*, dated in the 'Preface' 27 January 1794, Paine returned to the attack on state churches, but with a rueful attack on Robespierre's cult of *l'Etre Suprême*. Paine makes the emphatic claim that all national churches have been 'set up to terrify and enslave mankind, and monopolise power and profit' (Paine 1795: I, 50). Yet he denies being an atheist, and sees in the present time, the height of the Terror, the danger of the destruction not only of false systems but also of wider morality (a view that would have been sympathetic to Robespierre!): he was encouraged to write, he claims, 'lest in the general wreck of superstition, of false systems of government and false theology, we lose sight of morality, of humanity and of the theology that is true'. By 'religion', then, Paine means Natural Religion, but also the exercise of individual conscience without any reference to institutional religion: 'My own mind is my own church' (Paine 1795: I, 50).

If Blake and Paine agreed on the centrality of individual conscience and on the nature of the old order, which thrived on war, oppression and mass poverty, there is none the less an insistent apocalyptic note in Blake's vision of the past as well as the future: in *Europe* physical oppression is everywhere related to the issue of divine judgement and divine intervention in the form of the evils of War, Famine and Pestilence which had been released upon the English Nation. For Paine, on the other hand, the old order was a function of irrationality. The imposition of rational principles was the key to the post-revolutionary world; for Blake the triumph of rationalism represented the last gasp of the old order itself.

MAN'S ORIGINS AND REVOLUTION

Blake's enquiry into the origins of ecclesiastical repression presented in the prophetic book *Europe* belongs with a larger enquiry into the earliest history of man contained in the other Illuminated books of 1794 and 1795. These, with the exception of *Songs of Experience*, are all concerned with the period from the Creation to the Mosaic Dispensation. Can this return to origins be connected with Blake's response to the course of the French Revolution in those years? Certainly eighteenth-century radical thought was grounded in a theory of man's origins, for ideas of natural right necessarily presupposed a particular conception of man's original state. In Paine's words, 'Why then not trace the rights of man to the creation of man?' (Paine 1792: I, 29). For Paine, and also for Thomas Spence his more radical follower, government in the modern sense was an oppressive imposition upon the original happy state of man (Dickinson 1982). If the French Revolution had indeed lost its way, and no one could have been more conscious of this than Paine, writing Part I of *The Age of Reason* in a Paris prison under imminent threat of the guillotine,[14] then the situation required an urgent answer to the question of whether man's original nature might prevent him from ever casting out despotism, obliging him to repeat an eternal cycle of liberation and repression. Paine in *The Age of Reason*, therefore, neither renounces revolution nor seeks to justify its current course, but instead returns to the question of god and man.

The Age of Reason certainly derives some of its theological scepticism from the starkly rational view of religion presented by the French Revolutionary scholar Count Volney in *Les Ruines ou Méditations sur les révolutions des empires*, first published in 1791. A translation appeared the following year in England under the imprint of Joseph Johnson with the title *The Ruins: or a Survey of the Revolution of Empires* (Volney 1795), and the book, often in an abridged form, eventually achieved a popularity in England comparable to *Rights of Man* itself. Volney's denial of even the very existence of Jesus, the book's ruthless reduction of all aspects of Christianity to 'superstition' and its provocative comparison of Christianity's irrationality with that of Muhammedanism,[15] gave the work an honoured place in loyalist demonology as the very essence of French 'atheism'. Blake's response to Volney is not recorded, but, despite some obvious objections, he might have been sympathetic to the view that the evils which beset the modern world, tyranny, rank, war and exploitation, did not represent the state of man's primal origins. Volney claimed that 'Untaught man knew neither servitude nor tyranny' (Volney 1795: 31–2), just as for Blake the Ancient Britons were 'naked civilized men' who were 'overwhelmed by brutal arms' (K: 577). Aristocracy, kingship and religion are all seen as part of a pattern emerging in the earliest history of man by which the strong usurped power and then developed means of justifying their possession of it. One can see parallels between Volney's vision of the rise of religion and Blake's picture of its imposition in the prophecy *Europe*. According to Volney, 'In the secrecy of temples, and behind the veil of altars, they have made the God speak and act; have delivered oracles, worked pretended miracles, ordered sacrifices, imposed offerings, prescribed endowments; and, under the name of *theocracy* and *religion*, the state has been tormented by the passions of priests' (Volney 1795: 37). As in *Europe* the people were forced into a state of depression and despair which they attributed to superior and invisible powers, creating a god or gods in their own image: 'because they had tyrants upon earth, they supposed there to be tyrants in heaven; and superstition came in aid to aggravate the disasters of nations' (Volney 1795: 42–3). They are left only with a 'gloomy and misanthropic system of religion, which painted the gods malignant and envious like human despots'; hence they saw life 'as a fatiguing journey' and sought refuge in visions of paradise. For Volney, as for Paine, the antidote was to be found in nature and reason, from whose triumph would follow political equality.

The man-created gods of Volney and Paine may also have contributed to Blake's account of Urizen in *The First Book of Urizen*. He is presented as a kind of parody of a Hebraic deity, giving form to a despairing picture of the universe based on 'One King, One God, One Law' (K: 224). But unlike Volney and Paine, Blake seeks to locate the tyrant's original existence in a period before the creation of man's material form on earth. The creation of Orc or revolution is coterminous with Urizen's emergence into a recognizable form, and institutional religion comes into existence as a consequence of Urizen's imposition of material laws upon the cities of men. Urizen's world is symbolized by instruments of measurement: line and plummet, dividing rule, scales and weights, a brazen quadrant, and golden compasses (K: 233); he remains the antitype of Orc who has the ability to give life and awaken the dead. There can be little doubt that Urizen's obsession with measurement and his baleful effect upon humanity with his 'dark & cold' web of religion is meant to suggest not only the Jehovah of the Old Testament and the tyranny of the *ancien régime*, but also the way in which the French Revolution had itself perverted the true message of revolution into the worship of Reason.

W. J. T. Mitchell has drawn an analogy between the rationalism of Urizen's universe and Condorcet's mathematical schemes for revolutionary France,[16] while Essick has seen it as a critique of the rationalism of the Johnson circle (Essick 1991), but it is worth noting not only that Orc remains separate from Urizen, but that Fuzon, who appears only at the end of *The Book of Urizen* and in *The Book of Ahania* of 1795, takes on, as Morton Paley has pointed out (Paley 1970: 81f.) the role of a Robespierre-like revolutionary, and like Moses whom he most resembles, 'succumbs to the Urizen principle', and the false path of rational rather than spiritual revolution.

The Thermidorean regime, which followed the fall of Robespierre in July 1794, and the Directory which governed France from late 1795 until Bonaparte's *coup d'état* in 1799, were less obviously despotic than the 'Republic of Virtue' they replaced, but they would not have persuaded Blake that the Revolution had returned to the true Spirit. If Robespierre was a false Moses who failed to lead his children out of Egypt, then the Directory only confirmed their captivity to reason. The Theophilanthropy or nature-religion of the Directory[17] would hardly have appeared to be an improvement on the cult of *l'Etre suprême*. On the other hand the failings of the French State did not improve matters in an England which remained without energy even to contemplate melting the icy grip of Urizen.

None of the foregoing argument implies that Blake renounced the idea of revolution before the end of the century, or had developed in the course of the 1790s a cyclical view whereby revolution inevitably takes the place of what it opposes, though one should not, perhaps, assume that Blake was any more consistent than anyone else in those years. Blake's position may be summarized as follows: France had, as a consequence of the

Revolution, achieved a society which had destroyed despotism and old corruption to place Reason on the throne. In England, on the other hand, with the Treason Trials of 1794 and the 'Gagging Acts' of late 1795, the old order of 'King and Priest' had reasserted itself with murderous ferocity. By attacking Paine and suppressing radicalism the rulers of England demonstrated their pharisaical vengefulness: 'Christ died as an Unbeliever & if the Bishops had their will so would Paine' (K: 387).

If, as Blake implies, Paine's political defiance of the old order redeemed his adherence to false religion, then it suggests that Blake was more of a Painite in the 1790s than is usually assumed. Indeed, despite Paine's demonic reputation, it is arguable that Blake was in a political sense actually more uncompromisingly revolutionary than Paine. Paine as late as February 1792 had dedicated the second part of *Rights of Man* to Lafayette, though the latter was already an object of execration to the Montagnards, who, like Blake some months later, scorned his efforts to find a place in the Revolution for the French monarchy. Paine also voted against the execution of Louis XVI, and although Blake has left no opinion on the decision, he showed himself implacably opposed to kingship at all times in the 1790s, and unflinching at the prospect of political violence. We can see in Blake's attitudes towards Paine and other revolutionaries not only an admiration for their energy and social vision, but also a hope that they might be led away from the materialist basis of their philosophy. By 1798 such a hope was obviously forlorn: from 1793 onwards Whiggish radicals increasingly either withdrew from public life or joined the loyalist enemy; revolutionary energy, such as it was in Britain, passed to the plebeian sympathizers of the French Revolution (Goodwin 1979: 359f.). Blake might have had much sympathy for their 'sans-culottism', but as an engraver and artist his livelihood was still dependent on such Whiggish radicals as Henry Fuseli and Joseph Johnson, from whom he was increasingly distanced politically. By 1798, as the *Annotations to Watson* make clear, Blake was more isolated than he had ever been, in a country from which so many fiery spirits like Paine had fled or had been rendered harmless.

NOTES

1 Erdman 1956: 162. Essick (1991) remarks that 'the very thoroughness of Erdman's book has tended to preclude others from venturing into its territory'. There is perhaps a problem in the way Erdman puts under the same heading the Society for Constitutional Information, which had Whiggish tendencies, and the London Corresponding Society which more clearly represented an artisan culture.

2 Keynes 1957: 391 Hereafter references to Blake's writings from Keynes 1957 will be abbreviated to K.

3 I have where possible chosen different texts from Robert Essick, who kindly lent me the manuscript of his article, before publication, (Essick 1991).

4 'The intolerant spirit of Church persecutions had transferred itself into politics; the tribunal-styled revolutionary supplied the place of an inquisition; and the guillotine of the stake' (Paine 1795: II, 100).

5 'Seeing how deep the fibres of mischief have shot, I sometimes ask, with a doubting accent, Whether a nation can go back to the purity of manners which has hitherto been maintained unsullied only by the keen air of poverty, when, emasculated by pleasure, the luxuries of prosperity are become the wants of nature' (Wollstonecraft: 1793: 123).

6 K. 134–7. Erdman (1956: 152) suggests that it was written some time after February 1790, but there is no reason to suppose it was written any earlier than early to mid-1791, i.e. after the publication of Burke's *Reflections* and Part I of Paine's *Rights of Man*.

7 For more obviously dangerous works published by Johnson at this time, see Tyson (1979: 127–8).

8 Mrs George (1938: no. 7558) mentions an early English example of the genre, the opera *Island of St. Marquerite* by the Hon. John St. John, performed at Drury Lane on 13 November 1789, in which the Temple of Liberty rises from the ruins of the Bastille.

9 For the question of the dating of *The French Revolution* relative to *Rights of Man* see note 6 above.

10 The precise phrase does not appear in the *Reflections*, but the association of ancient trees with chivalry and rank is frequently hinted at in the book.

11 Paine 1792: 13. Essick (1991) also finds analogies between Burke's language and *The Book of Urizen*.

12 'One aspect of Orc's "thick-flaming, thought-creating fires" is the writings of Thomas Paine' (Paley 1970: 77). Note also that Paine is one of the Americans who 'Meet on the coast, glowing with Blood From Albion's fiery Prince' on plate 3 of *America* (K: 197).

13 K: 185. For a detailed account of the poem see Erdman 1956: 183–8.

14 For Paine's account of the circumstances see 'Preface' to the *Age of Reason* (Paine 1795: II, 100–2).

15 See for example Simpson (1793). Joseph Priestley (1797: 5) also complained that the book treated 'the history of Jesus Christ as a mere fable'.

16 In a paper presented at a Blake conference in Toronto, 1982.

17 Theophilanthropy was the final attempt by a Revolutionary government after the cult of *l'Etre Suprême* to find a theological substitute for Christianity in the form of Deism. It flourished in the years 1797–9, but was fatally associated with the Jacobins. Paine was an enthusiastic Theophilanthropist (see Ayer 1988: 156–8).

BIBLIOGRAPHY

Ayer, A. J. (1988) *Thomas Paine*, New York, Atheneum.

Bindman, D. (1989) *Shadow of the Guillotine: Britain and the French Revolution*, London, British Museum.

Bishop, M. [Pseud. Stoner, O.] (1951), *Blake's Hayley: the Life Works and Friendships of William Hayley*, London, Victor Gollancz.

Burke, E. (1790), *Reflections on the Revolution in France*, London, J. Debrett.

Butler, M. (ed.) (1984), *Burke, Paine, Godwin, and the Revolution Controversy*, Cambridge, Cambridge University Press.

Dickinson, H. T. (ed.) (1982) *The Political Works of Thomas Spence*, Newcastle-Upon-Tyne, Avero.

Erdman, D. (1956) *Blake: Prophet Against Empire*, rev. edn, Princeton, Princeton University Press, 1969.

Essick, R. N. (1983) *The Separate Plates of William Blake: A Catalogue*, Princeton, Princeton University Press.

—— (1991) 'William Blake, Thomas Paine and the biblical Revolution', Studies in Romanticism 30(2): 189–212.

Furet, F. and Ozouf, M. (1989) *A Critical Dictionary of the French Revolution*, Cambridge, Mass., Belknap Press of Harvard University.

Gengembre, G. (1989) 'Burke', in Furet and Ozouf (1989).

George, M. D. (1938) *Catalogue of the Personal and Political Satires Preserved in the Department of Prints and Drawings in the British Museum*, vol. VI, London, British Museum.

Godechot, J. (1970) *The Taking of the Bastille, July 14, 1789* trans. Jean Stewart, London, Faber & Faber.

Goodwin, A. (1979) *The Friends of Liberty: The English Democratic Movement in the Age of the French Revolution*, London, Hutchinson.

Keynes, G (ed.) (1957) *The Complete Writings of William Blake with Variant Readings*, London, Oxford University Press, and subsequent edns.

Kraminck, I. (1977) *The Rage of Edmund Burke: Portrait of an Ambivalent Conservative*, New York, Basic Books.

Paine, T. (1792) *The Rights of Man*, 9th edn, London.

Paine, T. (1795) *Age of Reason*, London.

Paley, M. (1970) *Energy and the Imagination: A Study of the Development of Blake's Thought*, Oxford, Clarendon Press.

Priestley, J. (1797) *Letters to Mr Volney, Occasioned by a Work of his Entitled Ruins, and by his letter to the Author*, Philadelphia.

Simpson, Rev. D. (1793) *An essay on the authenticity of the New Testament: designed as an answer to Evanson's Dissonance and Volney's Ruins*, Macclesfield.

Todd, J. M. (ed.) (1977) *A Wollstonecraft Anthology*, Bloomington, Indiana University Press.

Tyson, G. P. (1979) *Joseph Johnson: A Liberal Publisher*, Iowa City, University of Iowa Press.

Volney, Count (1795) *The Ruins: or A Survey of the Revolution of Empires* (1833).

Wollstonecraft, M. (1793), *Letter on the Present Character of the French Nation*, in Todd (1977).

—— (1795), *An Historical and Moral View of the Origin and Progress of the French Revolution*, in Todd (1977).

133

10

'David's Brickdust' and the rise of the British school

William Vaughan

The specific relationship between the French Revolution and British culture that I am going to discuss in this essay was a reactive one. That is, it is about an antipathy, rather than an attraction. It deals with the disapproval felt by influential British artists of the work of the leading French painter of the Revolutionary period – namely Jacques-Louis David (whose most celebrated painting, *The Oath of the Horatii* (1784) (plate 10.1) was habitually interpreted as encapsulating the mood of the Revolution) – and their determination not to do likewise.

The phrase 'David's Brickdust' that I have used as part of the title can serve as an indication of the strength of feeling and the length that it lasted. It comes from the diary of that tragic figure, the failed history painter Benjamin Robert Haydon (Pope 1963: V, 27).

The comment was written in 1841, more than half a century after the 1789 Revolution, at a time when Haydon had the mortification of seeing the opportunity that he had waited for all his life – that of being able to do large historical murals – slip away from him as the job of decorating the new Houses of Parliament was passed from him to a younger generation who had trained in or shown an interest in contemporary German mural painting. Such blatant favouring of a foreign manner put Haydon in mind of an earlier threat to British art. He writes. 'We escaped the contagion of David's brickdust which infected the continent, and the frescoes at Munich are but a branch of the same Upas tree' (Pope 1963: V, 27).

Haydon was a youth at the time of the Napoleonic Wars. His comment suggests that he regarded it as a mercy that political circumstances had held in check the influence of David's work in this country. The reference to 'brickdust' is presumably a dig at what he would have regarded as the crude colouring of David's work. It fits into a long British tradition of accusing the French of artifice, and shows how Haydon believed that – even if less skilled – he is at least nearer to nature than his Gallic counterpart. This might seem to be largely a formal objection, but there is as well a suggestion of moral censure – brought out by references to contagion and disease. Such references are common amongst British artists working

134

10.1 Jacques-Louis David, *The Oath of the Horatii*, 1784, oil on canvas, Paris, Musée du Louvre.

in the period between 1789 and 1848. In the 1830s, for example Constable wrote when having seen some of David's pictures in a British collection. 'I have seen David's pictures. They are indeed loathsome . . . David seems to have formed his mind in three sources – the *scaffold*, the *hospital, and a bawdy house*' (Taylor 1973: 227).

Such remarks – in which images of disease, sexual licence and execution are brought together – reveal the strong current underlying this antipathy. For while the censure is often expressed in visual terms, the real objection to David was of course his reputation as a leading participant in the French Revolutionary movement. He was the artist who had sided with the Jacobins and who had been prominent in the designing of Revolutionary fêtes. Worst of all, he had been a regicide. What seems to have angered the British art establishment was not just that David had taken part in such activities, but that he had put his art at the service of a political action. Such debasing of his high calling, they implied, had left it necessarily tainted.

At the centre of the objection to David, therefore, we find an interplay of moral and aesthetic issues. First, he had betrayed his calling as an artist by being 'actively' engaged in politics. Second, the politics he espoused were corrupt and had affected his sensibilities as an artist.

If it had been simply a matter of objecting to this basis, then perhaps the censure would have been no more than a passing matter. But there was much more at stake. For this period is precisely the one in which British artists were making a claim for themselves in the field of 'High' Art. David, as the leader of what was undoubtedly the most powerful and best organized art production system in Europe – namely that of the French Academy – represented a threat to the nascent British School that seemed every bit as real (with a suitable reduction of scale, of course) as the political threat represented to the British way of life by the French Revolution itself.

During the course of this essay I wish to explore the nature of that defensive reaction against David and to suggest ways in which it may actually have had a formative effect on the development of artistic practice in Britain during the period.

As a first stage in this, I want to outline the aspirations of artists in Britain immediately prior to this time. 'High' Art had been given a new impetus, of course, by the founding of the Royal Academy in 1768 and the subsequent tone adopted by its first president, Sir Joshua Reynolds, in the celebrated *Discourses* that he had delivered to the academy students each year. As John Barrell has recently suggested (Barrell 1986: 69–90) Reynolds sought in his *Discourses* to propagate an image of art as having a public role to play in the spread of virtue, and the reinforcement of the 'enlightened' rule by the patrician class. Reynolds also argued that it was important to foster art to improve the country's international standing:

It will be no small addition to the glory which this nation has already acquired from having given birth to eminent men in every part of science, if it should be enabled to produce, in consequence of this institution, a School of English Artists. The estimation in which we stand in respect to our neighbours, will be in proportion to the degree in which we excel or are inferior to them in the acquisition of intellectual excellence.

(Wark 1959: 169)

Reynolds saw the acquisition of a high-minded school of art as a matter of national prestige. Furthermore, considering the rivalry current in 1780 (the date when this *Discourse* was delivered), it is hard to imagine that he had anyone else in mind in his reference to 'our neighbours' than the French. But he does not specify the type or style of this art. This is largely because there can, in his eyes, only be one type of great art; namely that which follows in the footsteps of the old masters. He is an eclectic, who sees the duty of the moderns as being the crystallization of the excellence of the past. His nationalism is that familiar eighteenth-century variety that has been characterized as 'civic' nationalism, one that promotes the glory of a country in terms of universal values.

It is typical of this identification with 'universal' values that Reynolds should, in his own history paintings, attempt to exemplify an art that was dissociated from detailed partisanship. *The Infant Hercules*[1] represented his greatest opportunity to demonstrate this point in that he was given *carte blanche* in 1786 by his patroness, the Empress Catherine of Russia, to choose whatever subject he wished. Despite encouragement by his friends to select a theme that might have relevance for the relationship between Russia and Britain (such as, for example, Peter the Great working in the dockyard at Deptford) he fell back on pure allegory, using an image that could only in the most abstract way allude to the idea of Russia as a country of giant strength recently born and at the outset of a heroic career. Neither in its style nor its subject does it convey any sense of immediacy. There could hardly be a greater contrast between this work and the sense of urgency with which David invested his *Oath of the Horatii*, a picture, incidentally, that was painted at almost the same time.

Both in his later history paintings, and in the arguments in his *Discourses*, then, Reynolds promoted the concept of art as a 'pure' national asset – something like the gold reserve, perhaps. It was an asset because of its universal *quality*, not because of any local characteristics it possessed or any particular argument that it was framing.

But there were others who were prepared already to see a national art in terms of 'ethnic' values – values that emerged specifically out of the history and character of a people and their practices. In the visual field such types of arguments can be found first in the writings of Winckelmann.

137

Winckelmann had argued in his *History of Ancient Art* (1764) that the excellence of Ancient Greek art was a product of the 'liberty' prevalent during that period – a liberty expressed both in the promotion of democratic political institutions and from the habit of the free display of the naked body. A similar line of reasoning had led him to reflect that England could never produce a great school of art because the mists and bad climate rendered nude display improbable and the perception of perfect form difficult. Such an argument was contemptuously dismissed by the Anglo-Irish history painter James Barry in 1775 (Barry 1775: 248). Barry rejected Winckelmann's climatic argument, but he takes up the German critic's association of social conditions with the type of art produced. He makes use of this in a sophistcated manner, seeing art as being related to the political and educational institutions that are constructed within a country. Barry also talked of history painting as being the key to excellence, saying that it will provide 'tests by which the national character will be tried in after ages' (Barry 1775: 248).

Barry's writing provides us with an example of the association of art with the British 'national character' that was to be used so powerfully in the Romantic period.

There is a related point of great importance. This is that, with the change from 'quality' to 'character', artistic excellence is seen as being geographical rather than hierarchical. For Reynolds, art is essentially class-based. It is to appeal to men of learning and leisure. Only those whose station in life enabled them to become 'cultivated' could appreciate it. For Barry artistic quality grew out of the nature of the people and was not primarily the product of connoisseurship. On the contrary it was the emanation of a community and was intended to address the country as a whole, rather than just a privileged class.

It might be asked in what ways Barry sought to exemplify such national character. To some extent he did this iconographically – as in his picture *King Lear Weeping over the Dead Body of Cordelia* (1786–8),[2] which has Stonehenge prominently in the background. But more generally he did it by attempting a more primitive style – something that might seem to hark back to the earliest stages of society.

Just at the time when this egalitarian vision was being born, the traditional argument was receiving a new impetus. In practical terms this was given an urgency by the outbreak of the French Revolution, whose bloody outcome put in question the notion of a people who could naturally and simply inherit their birthright.

Burke's celebrated *Reflections on the Revolution in France* of 1790 has a relevance here. For Burke set out to prove that the egalitarianism that lay at the basis of the Revolutionary movement was not based on any system of natural feeling or natural justice. His opening argument – which was that the French Revolution was not the successor of political upheavals in

Britain – was important because of the way that it distinguished between the two developments in terms of type. Essentially he saw British political developments as being *natural*, those that grew out of a due respect for law and tradition, which only altered what was strictly necessary (as in the case of the slight modification of the principle of inheritance involved in the 'Glorious Revolution' of 1688). They were therefore quite distinct from the *tabula rasa* method, based on appeals to principles of pure reason that were currently being applied in France. Burke argued that the attempt to impose a 'rational' solution in France had led to the straying from nature. 'you think you are combatting prejudice, but you are at war with nature' (quoted in Hill 1975: 315).

This straying from nature not only leads to chaos and collapse – as Burke felt he was witnessing in the events in France. It also dehumanized its perpetrators, for they themselves found themselves having to suppress their natural feelings as the unnatural political situation developed:

> The worst of these politics of revolution is this: they temper and harden the breast, in order to prepare it for the desperate strokes which are sometimes used in extreme occasions. But as these occasions may never arrive, the mind receives a gratuitous taint; and the moral sentiments suffer not a little, when no political purpose is served by the depravation. This sort of people are so taken up with their theories about the rights of man, that they have totally forgotten his nature. Without opening one new avenue to the understanding, they have succeeded in stopping up those that lead to the heart. They have perverted in themselves, and in those that attend to them, all the well placed sympathies of the human breast.
>
> (Hill 1975: 331)

I have quoted Burke because of the centrality of his publication. The fundamental argument – that of the distinction between 'natural' development and 'unnatural' revolution and of the detrimental effect of the latter process on the humanity of those who propagate the latter – was widely dispersed. It had its impact on the debate about the visual arts as elsewhere.

In particular, the argument affected the debate about the nature of history painting. The image of history painting that Reynolds had promoted in his lectures was reformist in the sense that it promoted a return to 'classical' values. But it was not revolutionary. It did not suggest an overturning of the European tradition to return to the *tabula rasa* of Greek art. It included a discussion of the High Renaissance and – more importantly – combined the colouristic and naturalistic excellencies of Venetians and the Dutch with the rigorous *disegno* of the Romans and the idealism of the Greeks. It was broad and patrician in the Burkean sense. In his lectures Reynolds steps back from the 'extremism' of the most recent

139

reformers – holds Winckelmann and Mengs at arm's length. For the most part such a position was developed before the French Revolution. Reynolds died in 1791 but his last *Discourse* – the fifteenth – was delivered on 10 December 1790, just a few months after the appearance of Burke's *Reflections*. Reynolds who was a friend of Burke (and would in any case have known his views) was further aware that this was the last discourse that he would be giving. He therefore deliberately made it valedictory and undertook in it to review his activities. He stressed the way that his teaching had emphasized the high manner by appeal to tradition, and had avoided any 'new' or 'erroneous' doctrine:

> In reviewing my *Discourses*, it is no small satisfaction to be assured that I have, in no part of them, lent my assistance to foster *newly-hatched, unfledged* opinions . . . I have pursued a plain and *honest method*; I have taken up the art simply as I found it exemplified in the practice of the most approved Painters.
>
> (Wark 1959: 269)

Reynolds is at pains to make clear that his classicism is the classicism of tradition and not the dangerous new-fangled ideas of the Neo-classical extremists. Significantly he quotes as an example of the fate that befalls those who follow the new untried extremism that of 'a student of the French academy' who he was acquainted with in Rome and who 'appeared to me to possess all the qualities requisite to make a great Artist, if he had suffered his taste and feelings . . . to have fair play' (Wark 1959: 270).

Reynolds mentioned no names – perhaps he did not in fact have one particular French painter in mind – but the importance was a generic one, and would underline to his listeners, little more than a year after the outbreak of the French Revolution, the unsoundness of French culture in its current radical and unnatural state. Another important point to bear in mind is that Reynolds does not question the ability of his French acquaintance. It is the failure to train this ability with the percepts of tradition that has led to the artist's downfall.

During the 1790s, with the growing revulsion to events in France, Reynolds's 'traditional' classicism remained a bastion within the Royal Academy and the new president, Benjamin West saw himself as carrying on the tradition. This is striking, both because of West's American background and retained sympathy with the politics of the land of his birth, and because of his own early adventures in the more extreme forms of Neo-Classicism.

There is no doubting the vigour and originality of West in his early years. Such pictures as *Non Dolet: Paetus and Arria* show an early adherence to spartan Neo-classicism with a severe, frieze-like picture in which a Roman wife exhorts her husband to do the honourable thing and kill himself by giving him a personal example.[3] In this work, West was showing himself to be very much 'in the movement', working in the manner of avant-garde artists in Rome at the time. In his celebrated *The Death of General Wolfe*, painted four years later, he struck out on his own.[4] In this work West managed to demonstrate the possibility of producing heroic history painting in modern dress – a feat that gained him his European reputation and the undying admiration of David.

But West was a compromised figure by the 1790s. He had abandoned his radical work – both the extreme severity of his early classicism and the modernity of his *Death of General Wolfe* – in favour of a more painterly style. In later pictures – for example his *Cupid and Psyche* (1808) he attempted to follow the Reynoldsian eclecticism and combine Grecian line with Venetian richness – thereby cancelling out both.[5] Furthermore, in the place of a respect for subject there is an abstracted formalism providing visual effect for its own sake. Visual effect for its own sake was never West's forte and, quite frankly, he lacked the technique for it.

Looking at such a change might lead us to conclude that Reynolds's influence – far from promoting a school of British history painting – had in fact extinguished it. This impression is strengthened when one considers how many other artists – such as Copley, Fuseli, Barry, Wright, Penny and Mortimer – had been producing innovative historical works in the 1770s, and how their work had subsequently declined or become marginalized. Nor can the work of those trained by Reynolds or at the Academy – such as Northcote, Westall or Shee – be said to have offered much of a replacement.

Taking the broader historical view, it may well be that the 'generality' promoted by Reynolds undermined a promising and original school. Yet we must remember that this was not the view of people at the time. There was much confidence in British history painting, enough for it to be a commercial success. This was exemplified by Alderman Boydell, who from 1786 onwards set up his gallery of Shakespearian subjects executed by British artists, and recouped his investment by selling prints of paintings. The prints sold well on the Continent – particularly in Germany. So British history painters could boast at this time of having a truly international reputation. Some – like Gillray in a notoriously vicious cartoon which has Boydell sacrificing to the gods of lucre – might see this as an unholy alliance between high-mindedness and lucre.[6] But others saw it as a victory for a liberal society against the totalitarianism of the French.

As I have already mentioned, this development left some of the former 'stars' of the British historical school in an isolated position. The most prominent of these was James Barry. His *magnum opus* at the Society of Arts (1777–84) remained largely unattended – although it was enthusiastically admired by Blake. Eventually, in 1799, he was expelled from the Royal Academy (where he had been Professor of Painting since 1782). His dismissal has usually been explained as a consequence of his irascible personality. Certainly he had by this time started to criticize his fellow Academicians publicly, but political opinions had their place as well. As Pressly made clear in his recent life of Barry, citing Farington's Diary entry of 22 March 1799 as evidence, one of the reasons advanced for his expulsion was that:

> this being a Royal Academy it was sufficient ground for suspension
> or removal to prove that a Member avowed democratical opinions,
> – which Barry had done saying a *Republic* was the proper Government
> for Art to flourish under, – That He has highly commended *David*,
> & Mrs Wolstoncraft & commended their principles.
>
> (Pressly 1981:180, n.24)

It is far from irrelevant that this view (recorded by Farington) was apparently expressed by Sir Francis Bourgeois, a painter of mediocre talent who owed his status to the fact that he had been appointed, in 1794, landscape painter to George III. Barry was at this time a man of mounting republican sympathy. True to his early adherence to Winckelmann, he believed that the finest art flourished in conditions of political 'liberty' – a liberty to be found in the republican worlds of Periclean Athens and of early Rome. In the 1790s Barry felt Britain was straying further and further away from such a concept of liberty. He claimed that England had grown corrupt through its opposition to America and suppression of Ireland and that this corruption was evidence in the 'impurity' of its art. Something similar was being asserted at the time by Blake. Interestingly both Barry and Blake were at this time advocates of clarity and outline. Blake was too peripheral a figure for anyone to bother about seriously at this time. But Barry, being a professor at the Academy, was in a very different position. The expulsion was necessary to distance the Academy from his views.

But interestingly it was also a means of the Academicians distancing themselves from the style of his art. It is striking that the 'purity' of Barry's art subsequently becomes a matter of censure and an indication of 'unnaturalness'. When in France three years later, Fuseli remarked that David's *The Intervention of the Sabine Women* (1799) (plate 10.2) 'was something like Barry's art' (Garlick and Macintyre 1979: 1826). Previously he and other British Academicians had censured David's *Sabines* for its unnaturalness. This taint remains too in the writings of Constable, where he speaks of the 'iron-bound outline and brazen lights of his pictures in the Adelphi' (Leslie 1843: 274).

I realize that I am on the verge of propagating an association between a 'hard-edge' primitivistic style and political radicalism that has frequently been rejected as naive and overstated. So let me make some qualifications. First, I would like to point out that I am recording an association that was prevalent amongst academicians in England in the 1790s, not trying

142

10.2 Jacques-Louis David, *The Intervention of the Sabine Women*, 1799, oil on canvas, Paris, Musée du Louvre.

to make a general claim for Neo-classicism as a style. The British academicians, I am arguing, associated the 'traditional' classicism of Reynolds
with British developmental attitudes and 'extreme' classicism with political
radicalism. Both Blake and Barry, on the other hand, saw artistic purity
as a cleansing of form that would lead back to the primeval world obscured
by corruption and privilege.

There is also another objection that can be made. For amongst the
academicians there was one who seemed to be in the forefront of Neo-
classical extremism.

This was, of course, the sculptor John Flaxman, who was producing his
visually radical *Outlines*; the first being those to *Homer* and to *Dante* that
were published in Rome in 1793. As well as being an honoured academician, Flaxman was also conservative in his own political views.

To answer this, I must go on to my second qualification. The second
qualification I would like to make is slightly more technical. This really
follows from the first point, because it is to do with the matter of *decorum*.
For Reynolds had always emphasized the matter of appropriateness,
making it clear that there was a hierarchy of genres and of styles. He was
also acutely aware of the distinction between different artistic practices. In
his last discourse he was talking about painting – as he most frequently
did. Elsewhere – notably in his tenth *Discourse* (1780) – he made a distinction between painting and sculpture. Sculpture in Reynolds's view, being
a more restricted art, was capable of greater purity and attention to
fundamentals. It could concentrate on line and form with an exclusiveness
not given to painting. In his drawing and sculpture Flaxman was exploring
the particular requirements of sculpture. Indeed, Flaxman made it perfectly
clear that he had intended his *Outlines* to be studies for friezes. He appears
to have been quite baffled by the success that they had on the Continent,
and even went so far as to say that he wished that the critics that had
praised them had better things to exercise their critical faculties on. While
the *Outlines* had been hailed on the Continent already by the mid-1790s,
they were at this time scarcely known in England. It was not until 1806
– four years after the Paris visit – that they first began to appear in an
English edition. It is noticeable in this case that it is on the Continent
that Flaxman is influential amongst painters, not in this country. It is
David and Ingres who adapt his designs to the art, not West or Northcote.
Ironically, David's *Sabines* – the work that Fuseli considered to be so like
Barry's – is one of those that shows such a debt.

The reservations that the British academicians had about the art of
David can be seen in greater detail in the rare moments of contact between
them. The most celebrated of these is that afforded by the visit to France
in 1802 following the Treaty of Amiens. For the British it gave a rare
opportunity to travel to the Continent. The leading figures of the Academy

went over in a spirit of great confidence – none more so than the president, Benjamin West, who took the opportunity to display the sketch for his *magnum opus* the *Death on a Pale Horse* at the French Salon (plate 10.3.).

We can gain considerable insight into this visit from the diary of the Academician Joseph Farington (who – as Sir Lawrence Gowing so perceptively observed a few years ago – 'wrote down everyone's opinion in the hope of forming his own'). Farington records on 1 September 1802: 'Opie thinks that the French artists are conscious of their inferiority to the English . . . West said today that the French paint statues' (Garlick and Mackintyre 1979: 1820). One can only assume that Opie had not actually discussed the matter with any French artists – or that if he had done so, his command of their language was inadequate. West's quip about them 'painting statues' can be related to the distinction between the aesthetic rules of painting and sculpture that enabled Flaxman and West to pursue their separate goals.

Farington's own views on the art of David are relentless in their censure. The *Sabines* was on view in the Louvre and Farington inspected it for 'more than an hour' in the company of Fuseli and Opie. He took great care with it, because he had been told that it was the principal ornament of the modern French school. His judgement on it was likely to be a judgement on the school as a whole;

> The Composition is laboured & Artificial; the Colouring without union, – and it can scarcely be said to have any Chiaro-Oscuro . . . I never saw a Composition in which the art of arranging was less concealed; every figure seems *placed* in its situation, and one in particular, a Woman holding a Child over her head, stands on a pedestal, & has so much the appearance of a Statue that it is difficult to consider it otherways.
>
> (Garlick and Mackintyre 1979: 1825)

The emphasis on artifice is the most dominant strain here. Painting has betrayed its true nature by becoming too much like sculpture. Colouring and chiaroscura have been ignored. The composition is artificial and contrived. There is also a suggestion of heartlessness in the hardness of effect. The turning of forms into statues also turns them into something hard and inhuman.

There is no little irony in the fact that while Farington and West were railing against the 'statue-like' hardness of David's *Sabines* the very sculptor who had inspired the design was standing in their midst, for Flaxman was of their company in this journey to Paris. There is no record of whether Flaxman recognized in the *Sabines* an echo of his *Iliad* design. However, even if he did, one feels that he would have been likely to disapprove, given his adherence to the Reynoldsian distinction between the properties of painting and sculpture.

10.3 Benjamin West, *Death on a Pale Horse*, 1787, oil on paper sketch, Philadelphia, Philadelphia Museum of Art (gift of Theodora Kimball Hubbard in memory of Fiske Kimball).

The other frequently used analogy with 'metallic' effect does much the same thing. Elsewhere Farington makes clear that David's republicanism is extreme and a result of his 'bad character' (Garlick and Mackintyre 1979: 1863).

An interesting further example is his record of the *Horatii*, which he saw on his visit in 1802. In the Sketch in his book he increases the frieze-like appearance of the work by reducing its top. He also makes the articulation mechanical and brutal by giving it four arches in the background rather than three, thus suggesting an unawareness that is simply not there in the picture (Garlick and Mackintyre 1979: 1862).

Farington makes these remarks essentially in visual terms. But – as the observations on the character of David makes clear – he also sees these as indicative of the moral character of the French nation. Just as the French nation had come to its moral knees by appealing to the mob, so had French art by going for striking effects that directly appeal in the market place. For Farington acknowledges that David's art strikes the eye and holds the attention. At first glance it might appear that this is a good thing, yet, whereas Farington believes in the humanzing effect of the art, he does not believe that this can work through direct appeal to the populace. Taste has to be nurtured, as Reynolds made clear. Real taste comes from careful study and judgement and is related to those other virtures to be found amongst the propertied and monied classes. One of the striking features of the British Royal Academy from its inception was its emphasis on exclusiveness. It had been at great pains to separate its exhibitions from vulgar shows and curiosities. It did this, quite deliberately, by restricting entry – servants in livery, for example were not admitted. It also charged an entry fee. The original purpose behind charging an entry fee was to keep out undesirables (Hutchinson 1986: 67). Only later was it discovered that this could also become an important source of revenue. When visiting the French Salon Farington smugly notes that such discrimination did not exist there;

> No money is paid for admission, and many low people got in among others. Indeed, if I had been to judge what sort of People Paris is inhabited by from those who I found there, I should have supposed that there was scarcely a Man with the appearance of a Gentleman in the City.

(Garlick and Mackintyre 1979: 1821)

That Farington has a low opinion of popular taste is made clear in another instance when he is visiting the collections of old masters in the Louvre. Here he notes that the populace go past the great Italian masters and dwell instead on a scene showing a gory execution by the Flemish painter Gerard David the *Justice of Cambyses* (1498) which formed part of the Musée Napoléon.

While being censorious of French art as a whole, Farington did admit that it had certain qualities. For example, the one composition of David's that he did like was the *Death of Socrates* (1787) (Garlick and Mackintyre 1979: 1861).[7] This appears to have been because it reminded him of Poussin, and also, I suspect, because it represented a philosphical subject, with heroic stoicism taking the place of the violent action indicated in the *Oath of the Horatii*. There was also general approval amongst the British artists of Gerard and Guerin who had both mediated Davidian harshness with subtler effects of light.

There was also a grudging recognition of the technical superiority of the French – particularly in the field of drawing. For the melancholy fact that Britain did not put its history painters through the rigorous education of the French and did not give them the same opportunities, did have its implications. Perhaps the most nervous moment for the British was the reception of West's work. West had all going before him, he was the hero of the *Death of General Wolfe* and it has been largely stated that his visit to Paris in 1802 was triumphant, with him being fêted by David. However West was no longer the painter of Wolfe, and had left his artistic radicalism well behind him. The lesson that he had to teach the French in 1802 was, if anything, 'return to the old masters'. By all accounts the reception was mixed and West did not get the expected medal at the Salon for his work. According to Shee, David praised West's work highly, but another artist overheard him calling the *Death on a Pale Horse* a 'caricature of Rubens' (Garlick and Mackintyre 1979: 1882). There seems no reason why these two reports should conflict. David felt a genuine debt to West for *Wolfe* – which had helped him make his own history painting address radical issues during the Revolutionary period. No doubt he saw the diplomatic advantage of not censuring the old American hero in public. But at the same time 'caricature of Rubens' is a fairly accurate account of what *Death on a Pale Horse* is, and one familiar with the *Marie de' Medici* cycle must have been all too aware of the painful shortcomings of West's attempts at colour and chiaroscuro.

West's mixed reception should perhaps have sounded a warning note, but in fact British bullishness about their history painting continued throughout the Napoleonic period. The 'artifice' of David gave them a buffer against the technical mastery of the French and led them to suppose that they were the sole upholders of the great traditions of historical – and by implication – democratic art.

During this period the stock of British history painting remained high. This can be seen in the sumptuous publication by John Britton, *The Fine Arts of The English School*, published in 1812. As the introduction of this work stated, this was intended to be the first of a series of collections of engravings that would celebrate the achievements of English painters in a way that similar foreign productions celebrated the old masters and the modern French School. Presumably the author had in mind in particular Normand's publication *Vies et oeuvres des peintres les plus célèbres* (Paris 1803–17), which included modern French history painters alongside the old masters. A visual point was perhaps made here in the fact that the French publication reproduced works in outline throughout, whereas the British publication used detailed tonal work. The French reduction of the aesthetic of pictures to a linear pattern was thus implicity censured.

The commentaries in Britton's collection were by different authors and there was no attempt at the definition of an English school, but to judge by the works reproduced, it was very much conceived of as 'school of Reynolds'. Of the thirteen paintings reproduced six were portraits, five history paintings, and two landscapes. Four of the portraits were by Reynolds himself and one was by Romney. The history paintings were by Reynolds, pupils and associates – Westall, Romney, Howard, Northcote and Benjamin West. There was no reference to genre painting, animal painting, conversation pieces or – most significant of all – to Hogarth.

While Britton refrained from definitions of the English school, its pre-eminence was being celebrated in other places. Two years earlier, in a supplement to John Gould's *Biographical Dictionary* (1810) a survey of the great European schools had made clear that the English School was now pre-eminent, largely because of its adherence to the principles of Reynolds:

> In the works of Northcote and Lawrence we hail the continuance of an English school and the happy application of those classical precepts which its founder, Sir Joshua Reynolds delivered with so much dignity and effect; and while the artists of this country are influenced by such rules, their improvement must be unrivalled, as by such a local advantage they will reach a degree of perfection to which the other modern schools of painting in Europe will in vain attempt to aspire.
>
> (Gould 1810: 29)

At the same time, this book contained the following damning account of the French:

> In speaking in general terms of this school, it appears to have no peculiar character; and it can only be distinguished by its aptitude to imitate easily any impression; and it may be added, speaking still in general terms, that it unites in a moderate degree the different parts of the art, without excelling in any one of them
>
> (Gould 1810: 19)

Gould seems to be hinting in this assessment that the French have skill, but lack judgement and character; something that David's career seemed also to have underlined. He himself clearly thought that Sir Joshua had given British artists the necessary sense of judgement. Elsewhere it was argued that the character of British art was deeply rooted in the nature of the indigenous culture and society. The author who wrote the accompanying text to Northcote's *Duke of Argyle Asleep* in Britton's collection praised the artist for having painted the work, as he puts it 'in English': 'For it appears to me that it is not by relinquishing, but by diligently cultivating and refining the national tendencies, that the original character is finally established in schools of art (Britton 1812: 17). The commentator is not altogether explicit on what this character is, but it seems to have focused largely upon the psychology of interpretation of the story which he felt 'accorded with the ability and the character of a philosphical nation' (Britton 1812: 17).

The reference to England as a 'philosphical nation' might seem a trifle myopic in an age when Kant and Hegel were pre-eminent. But the reference is clearly back to the Lockean tradition of the eighteenth century. And it accords once again with the apposition of the pondered classicism of Burke and Reynolds to radical extremism of the continentals.

Even after the Napoleonic Wars this high opinion of English art remained: 'It is not a little curious' wrote James Elmes in his *Biographical Dictionary of the Fine Arts* in 1826 'that at the time when painting was verging towards a state of hopeless decline all over the continent of Europe, it should have revived and that to no small purpose, in these islands, the inhabitants of which had been frequently taunted by foreigners as unable to execute a fine painting' (Elmes 1826: 24).

However, while confidence about British art remained high, there had been a significant shift in its characterization. After 1815, with the removal of David to Brussels and the emergence of other clear leaders in the French School, it was no longer possible to see this as a 'tainted' form of art. Furthermore the later painters had already followed those tendencies already discerned by the British Academicians in the work of Guerin and Gerard and brought back greater painterliness and colour, perhaps too much so. However the British could never defend their record in history painting as being the mastery of the probity of line. The defenders of Reynoldsian history painting became fewer and fewer in the 1820s. Instead it was the naturalistic tendency to be observed in British genre and landscape that ruled the day. Interestingly the argument about 'national character' travelled with it. Now it was the Hogarthian tradition that was seen as an integral part of British culture – a tendency that was linked unashamedly with the protestant tradition by many observers. In his *History of Sculpture, Painting and Architecture* in 1829 J. S. Memes wrote:

The Reformation, by restoring to the human mind the uncontrolled exercise of its own faculties, by unlocking the barriers by which the will and the powers of free enquiry had been imprisoned, has stamped upon every British institution, as upon every British talent, the worth and manliness of independent character. Our fine arts, though the last to feel, do at length experience this happy influence.

(Memes 1829: 209)

Once again this splendid, highly individual achievement, is contrasted with the characterlessness of the French: 'though academies have been formed, and government protection long and liberally afforded, it would yet be difficult exactly to describe in what the characteristics of the national style of art in France consist.' (Memes 1829: 190). Once again, too, David is seen as the 'heartless' man, who has destroyed himself by his own proclivities: 'Without doubt, however, David was a man of genius, and when he errs it is more through defect of system than of talent; but the former being his own creation, he stands responsible for its faults.' (Memes 1829: 201).

A very similar view was expressed by Cunningham in his seminal history of British art which began to appear in the same year. Perhaps it is relevant that both Memes and Cunningham were Scots coming from a strong Presbyterian background. While both Memes and Cunningham saw Hogarth as the progenitor of this 'protestant' independent art, it was their fellow Scot and contemporary David Wilkie who was the hero of the movement. His celebration of 'nature' and Britishness can be seen in his picture of *Chelsea Pensioners Reading the Gazette of the Battle of Waterloo* (1819) (Plate 10.4) – a picture, it might be argued, that proclaims the aesthetic as well as the military defeat of the French.

Significantly David – while not playing a major role – is still the bogey-man, the antipode of independent naturalism. This is clear from the savage attacks made on him by Constable which have already been alluded to. Apart from commenting on how David's art had been formed from the scaffold, hospital and a bawdy house, he also played once more on its heartlessness. In 1836 in his lectures he talked of David's 'Stern and heartless petrification of men and women – with trees, rocks, tables and chairs all equally bound to the ground by a relentless outline, and destitute of chiaroscuro, the soul and medium of art' (Leslie 1843: 242). The egalitarian nature of David's 'relentless' outline, reducing all forms to a similarity is typical, as well as the association of chiaroscuro – the management of light and shade with true sensibility and feeling. Yet in one sense Constable's naturalism is different from that hailed by Memes and Cunningham. It does not replace the 'vulgarity' of French egalitarianism with the 'vulgarity' of Hogarth and Wilkie's bourgeois genre painting. His naturalism is still mediated with the principles of Reynolds.

At the same time Constable was working on the picture that can be seen as the summation of his ideals. This is *The Cenotaph* (1836) which

10.4 David Wilkie, *Chelsea Pensioners Reading the Gazette of the Battle of Waterloo*, 1819, oil on canvas, London, Victoria and Albert Museum, Wellington Museum, Apsley House.

depicts a monument to Sir Joshua Reynolds set in a parkland scene.[8] It is as though the precepts of the first President of the Royal Academy were being shown here to be in perfect harmony with nature. Both trees and monument are given a sense of reflection and humaneness by the rich, overshadowing chiaroscuro. The tradition of Reynolds, Constable is claiming, is as central for serious landscape painting as it is for history.

Constable might feel in 1836 that it was still necessary to attack David in the fiercest tones – as did Haydon a few years later. But for the younger generation of British artists there seemed no such need. For them, it seemed that the French themselves had freed themselves from the influence of the regicide through their own Romanticism. This was the opinion of Thackeray in his *Paris Sketchbook* of 1840 'Of the great pictures of David, the defunct' he reports smugly when visiting the Louvre 'we need not say much' (Thackery 1885: 50). He then goes on to lampoon them for their nudity, talking of the absurdity of the passion for it in the Davidian school, and of the utter failure of this school to achieve the 'sublime' that they sought.

Thackeray – like Farington before him – also misrepresents the *Horatii*, supposing that it is Romulus who is taking their oath, and not their father. He includes a diagrammatic representation to mock their stiffness (plate 10.5), commenting:

'Romulus' is the exact action of a telegraph; and the Horatii are all in the position of the lunge. Is this the sublime? Mr. Angelo, of Bond street, might admire the attitude; his namesake, Michael, I don't think would.

(Thackeray 1885: 50)

Now the whole issue had become a matter for jokes about fencing masters. The issue of David was well and truly dead.

However, this is not quite the end of the matter. For it may be that David's example was having a formative – if *reactive* – effect on British landscape painting at a much earlier date. One of the artists who travelled to France following the Peace of Amiens in 1802 was Turner. Turner's first objective was to visit the Alps, where he obtained a new source for his scenes of sublime mountainous places. After this, Turner went to Paris, where he spent much time exploring the old masters in the Musée Napoléon and some looking at the modern French. His greater intimacy with the works of Poussin and Titian undoubtedly augmented his growing ambition to succeed as a painter of 'historical' landscape. But he also seems to have absorbed something of the modern French historical painter's sense of relevance.

One of the pictures that he saw was the heroic image by David of Napoelon crossing the Alps at the outset of his Italian campaign (plate 10.6). As it is clear from the inscription in the snow at the feet of his

153

Robin Hood twangs his bow, and the heathen gods fly, howling. *Montjoie Saint Dénis !* down goes Ajax under the mace of Dunois ; and yonder are Leonidas and Romulus begging their lives of Rob Roy Macgregor. Classicism is dead. Sir John Froissart has taken Dr. Lemprière by the nose, and reigns sovereign.

Of the great pictures of David, the defunct, we need not, then, say much. Romulus is a mighty fine young fellow, no doubt ; and if he has come out to battle stark naked (except a very handsome helmet), it is because the costume became him, and shows off his figure to advantage. But was there ever anything so absurd as this passion for the nude, which was followed by all the painters of the Davidian epoch? And how are we to suppose yonder straddle to be the true characteristic of the heroic and the sublime? Romulus stretches his legs as far as ever nature will allow ; the Horatii, in receiving their swords, think proper to stretch their legs too, and to thrust forward their arms thus,—

Romulus.   The Horatii.

Romulus's is the exact action of a telegraph ; and the Horatii are all in the position of the lunge. Is this the sublime? Mr. Angelo, of Bond Street, might admire the attitude ; his namesake, Michael, I don't think would.

The little picture of " Paris and Helen," one of the master's earliest, I believe, is likewise one of his best : the details are exquisitely painted. Helen looks needlessly sheepish, and Paris has a most odious ogle ; but the limbs of the male figure are beautifully designed, and have not the green tone which you see in the later pictures of the master. What is the meaning of this

10.5 William Makepeace Thackeray, *David's 'Oath of the Horatii'*, illustration to *Paris Sketchbook* (1840).

rearing horse, Napoelon is cast by David as the successor to other great military leaders who had crossed the Alps – notably Charlemagne and Hannibal. Turner's knowledge of this picture is attested to in a literal sense by the inclusion of the motif in his representation of Napoleon in *The Battle of Marengo* an illustration to Rogers's *Italy* (1831) (Gage 1987: 199). This demonstrates how the image stuck in Turner's mind.

Some years ago, John Gage suggested that Turner's sight of this picture may have set off a train of thought that reached fruition in his own landscape version of a military leader crossing the Alps – the large historical picture of *Snow Storm: Hannibal and His Army Crossing the Alps* (1812) (Plate 10.7). Thematically the picture – which shows Hannibal being harassed by the elements as he goes to his eventual downfall – might provide an ironic commentary on the career of Napoleon in the final stages of the First Empire.

Even if this is not literally the case, the picture seems to offer at every stage a response to the French historical tradition. In scale, design and achievement it sets landscape painting on an equal footing with historical subject painting. In doing so, it also provides an opposed view of the relationship of man to nature. David's picture is about a human's control of his own destiny. Nature is being mastered through a supreme heroic act. Turner's picture suggests by contrast that even the greatest human will get nowhere if he or she contravenes the laws of nature. Yet he also sees the struggle as heroic, and tragic.

In their different ways – Turner through irony and Constable through affirmation – the greatest British landscape painters of the period emphasized the role of nature in the affairs of man. However, I feel I might be straining credibility if I ended by proclaiming David to be the true and unacknowledged father of British landscape painting. But there might be some mileage in trying to see him as its wicked uncle. For he is at the same time a stimulus and a warning. He had dared to confront the academic system, while retaining its high idealism. He had, it is true, fallen foul of nature, but who were in a better position than landscape painters to put that right? And where else (apart from in the marginalized works of Blake) could they find that sense of relevance and heroic urgency that gave significance and fascination to their projects?

NOTES

1. Joshua Reynolds, *The Infant Hercules*, The Royal Academy, 1788, oil on canvas, St Petersburg, The Hermitage; reproduced in *Reynolds*, London, The Royal Academy, 1987: cat. 140, plate 15.
2 James Barry, *King Lear Weeping over the Dead Body of Cordelia*, 1786–8, oil on canvas, London, Tate Gallery (Pressly 1981: 234–5). Barry's first version of this work (now lost) was exhibited in 1774 (Pressly 1981: 55–6).

10.6 Jacques-Louis David, *Napoleon at St. Bernard*, 1800, oil on canvas, Rueil-Malmaison, Musée du Malmaison.

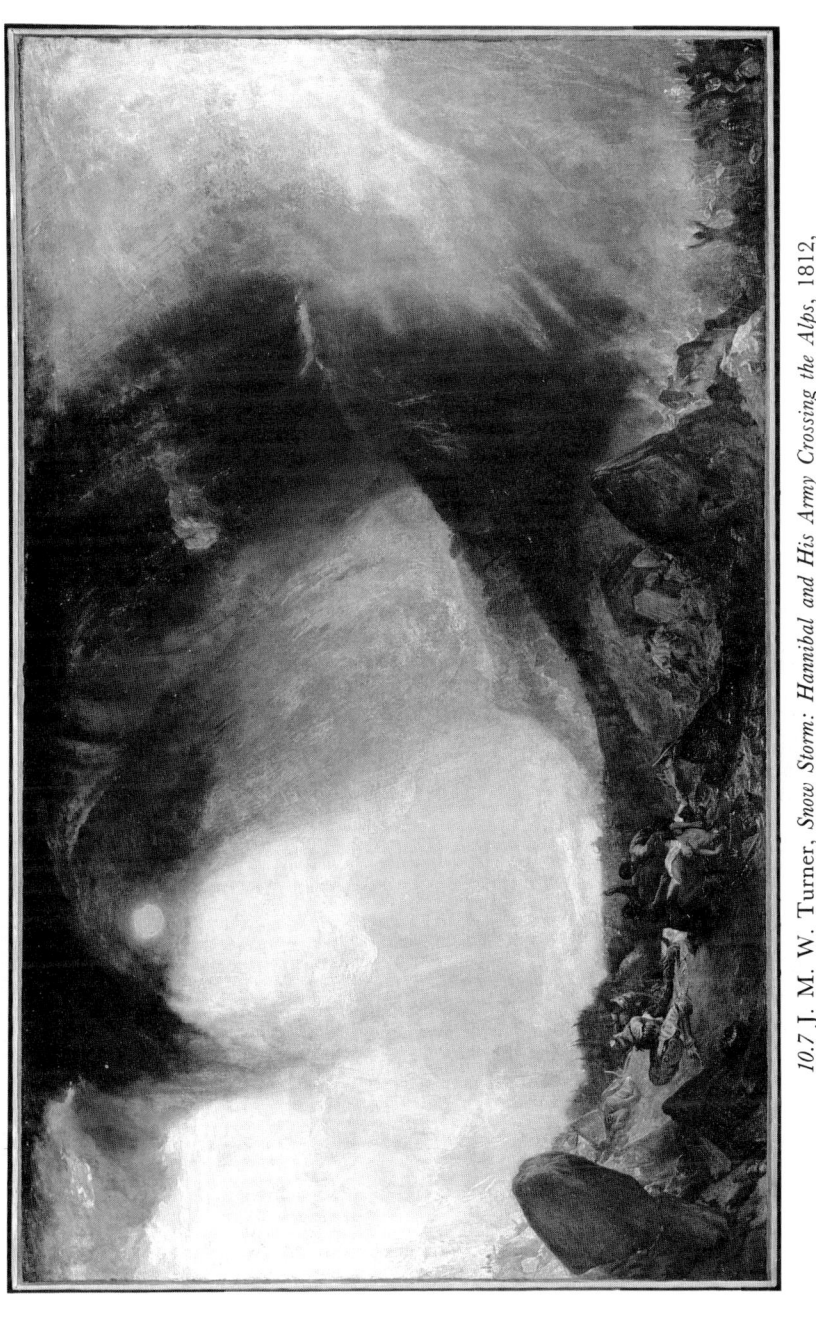

10.7 J. M. W. Turner, *Snow Storm: Hannibal and His Army Crossing the Alps*, 1812, oil on canvas, London, Tate Gallery.

3 Benjamin West, *Non Dolet: Paetus and Arria*, 1766, New Haven, Yale Centre for British Art.
4 Benjamin West, *The Death of General Wolfe*, 1770 (Royal Academy 1771). Ottawa, National Gallery of Canada.
5 Benjamin West, *Cupid and Psyche*, 1808, oil on canvas, Washington D.C., Corcoran Gallery of Art.
6 James Gillray, *Shakespeare Sacrificed; – or – The Offering to Avarice*, 1789, hand-coloured etching and aquatint (reproduced Pressly 1981: 142 [96]).
7 Jacques-Louis David, *The Death of Socrates*, 1787, oil on canvas, New York, Metropolitan Museum. When exhibited at the Paris Salon in 1787 it was studied by Reynolds (see *The Age of Neo-Classicism* London, The Royal Academy, Arts Council of Great Britain, 1972: 42).
8 John Constable, *The Cenotaph*, 1836, oil on canvas, London, National Gallery.

BIBLIOGRAPHY

Barrell, J. (1986) *The Political Theory of Painting from Reynolds to Hazlitt*, New Haven and London, Yale University Press.
Barry, J. (1775) *Inquiry into the Real and Imaginary Obstructions to the Acquisition of the Arts in England*, London, T. Becket.
Britton, J. (1812) *The Fine Arts of The English School*, London, Longman & Co.
Burke, E. (1790) *Reflections on the Revolution in France*, London, J. Debrett; repr. in Hill 1975: 277–359.
Elmes, J. (1826), *Biographical Dictionary of the Fine Arts*, London, Thomas Tegg.
Gage, J. (1987), *J. M. W. Turner 'A Wonderful Range of Mind'*, New Haven and London, Yale University Press.
Garlick, K. and Mackintyre A. (1979) *The Diary of Joseph Farington*, vol. V, New Haven and London, Yale University Press.
Gould, J,. (1810) *Biographical Dictionary of Painters, Sculptors, Engravers and Architects*, London, Priestley & Wheale.
Hill, B. W. (ed.) (1975), *Edmund Burke on Government, Politics and Society*, London, Harvester Press.
Hutchinson, S. C. (1986) *The History of the Royal Academy*, 2nd edn. London, Robert Royce.
Leslie, C. R. (1843) *Memoirs of the Life of John Constable*, ed. J. Mayne, London, Phaidon.
Memes, J. S. (1829) *History of Sculpture, Painting and Architecture*, from *Constable's Miscellany*, 89 vols, vol. 39. Archibald Constable & Co., London, Hurst, Robinson & Co., 1826–35.
Pope, W. B. (ed.) (1963) *The Diary of Benjamin Robert Haydon*, 5 vols. Cambridge, Mass.
Pressly, W. L. (1981) *The Life and Art of James Barry*, New Haven and London, Yale University Press.
Taylor, B. (1973), *Constable: Paintings, Drawings and Watercolours*, London, Phaidon.
Thackeray, W. M. (1885) (pseud. 'Mr. Titmarsh'), *The Paris Sketchbook*, (original pub., 1840) London, George Routledge & Sons, 1885.
Wark, R. (ed.) (1959) *The Discourses of Sir Joshua Reynolds*, San Marino, California, Huntingdon Library; rev. edn, New Haven and London, Yale University Press, 1981.

11

Spectacular fears and popular arts: a view from the nineteenth century

Claudine Mitchell

August 1885: the French press predicts a severe competition between the Musée Grévin and its London equivalent, Madame Tussaud's, over the acquisition of a bath-tub. Admittedly it was no ordinary object but the very bath-tub in which Jean-Paul Marat had been stabbed to death by Charlotte Corday on 13 July 1793. Patriotism helping, the object in question became the possession of the Musée Grévin who advertised, a year later, the opening of a new 'true to life' scene in its Galerie de la Révolution.

That Marat's murder should be singled out as a key event of the French Revolution in the history written in wax for the people seems to me crucial to the interpetation of the Revolution during the nineteenth century.

Was the interest invested in the event due to its sensational aspect? The idea of a woman performing a deed only brutal men were thought capable of and, more generally, that of a woman claiming the right to intervene in history were transgressions of the ideology of sexual difference which brought excitement to the narrative of Marat's murder. Nor can the sadistic dimension of the event be minimized as a factor explaining the haunting quality of the image of Marat's agony, as it recurs from eighteenth-century prints to nineteenth-century paintings, in the cinema of Abel Gance or in Picasso.

There was however another kind of dimension to it, rooted in what Marat came to symbolize. The event of Corday's killing Marat, I would argue, stimulated on the level of the narrative order notions and emotions which middle-class intellectuals were reluctant to conceptualize, namely, the fears of working-class politics.

To explore this issue, I shall interrelate visual images, the language of nineteenth-century historians and that of art critics. My objective in doing so is to show how this interdependence structured the nineteenth-century discourse on the French Revolution. I also want to argue that what have often been catagorized as questions of style or technique in art and literary criticism – I think in particular of narrative, realism, popular art – are means of codifying political language whenever the issue at stake is 'history'.

REALIST SCENARIO AND HISTORICAL TRUTHFULNESS

It was for its contribution to the recording and the teaching of history that Madame Tussaud's Museum claimed its intellectual respectability when it opened in Baker Street in 1833. To implement its objectives the Museum provided visitors with guidebooks consisting of short biographies of the historical figures they portrayed, assuring them that the information 'will not only greatly increase the pleasure to be derived from a mere view of the figures but will also convey to the mind of young persons much biographical knowledge – a branch of education universally allowed to be of the highest importance' (Madame Tussaud's 1830: 2).

The institution consolidated its contribution to historical knowledge five years later, with the publication of Madame Tussaud's *Memoirs and Reminiscences of France*, which, as its subtitle indicated, would constitute *An Abridged History of the French Revolution* (Tussaud: 1838). Written in the mode of reported speech by Francis Hervé, the book also purported to guarantee the authenticity of the collection of French eighteenth-century figures, by providing a detailed account of the circumstances in which they had been produced.

First, it confirmed that the creator of the wax figures, Madame Tussaud, had been an eyewitness to the Revolution: she had come to Paris in the 1770s and did not leave until the Peace of Amiens in 1802, whereupon she settled in England. The unusual range of acquaintances she had gained, Hervé explained, gave her a privileged position for an objective view of the French Revolution (Tussaud 1838: 3). At her uncle's, the wax modeller Curtius, she had met Necker, the Girondists and Jacobins alike, the latter group in particular as Curtius had sided with the Montagne, and this would counterbalance, Hervé asserted, her acquaintance with the Royal Family, where it had to be admitted, her own sympathy lay.

Second, the book attested that wax figures had been cast from the real historical figures. The head of Marat, we are told, was cast shortly after his death, upon David's request (Tussaud 1838: 340) (plate 11.1).[1] Whereas painting could only mediate the artist's visual observation of the sitter, the wax figures, the creation of which started from the imprint of the sitter's body, seemed to preserve some of the immediacy of the physical presence for future generations.

Third, the book demanded that the wax figures should not be considered as a mere record of physical appearance, for they emanated from the intellectual exchange which took place between Madame Tussaud and the French political leaders: the purpose of the book was to document such intellectual dimensions that gave historical significance to the Museum's collection.

Opened in 1882 with wax figures modelled at that time, the Musée Grévin likewise presented its Galerie de la Révolution as a History

Museum. Short of owning life-cast figures, they collected objects which the historical characters might have seen, touched or possessed. What had made the creation of *La Mort de Marat* (plate 11.2) possible at all, the catalogue explained, was the acquisition of the bath-tub and other such contemporary objects which entered the Museum collection (Musée Grévin 1894: 26). The catalogue also made it clear that the creation of each scene proceeded from historical research, referring to such sources as the collection housed in the Musée Carnavalet and the Proceedings of the Revolutionary Tribunal.[2] *La Mort de Marat* was modelled by the sculptor Léopold-Bernard Bernstamm, who had exhibited a low relief: *Charlotte saisie par Simone Evrard* at the Paris Salon of 1886.[3]

Even the briefest of perusals of iconographic documents would confirm that the Musée Grévin enlisted as its main source of evidence a history painting that had been shown at the Paris Salon of 1861: Paul Baudry's *Charlotte Corday* (1861) (plate 11.3).[4] In both cases Marat is positioned on the left foreground, with his head titled backwards, the knife stuck well in evidence, his facial features and the tension of his body expressing excruciating pain. Both portray Corday at the centre of the composition, standing quite composed against the map of France. The right-hand side of the composition, which shows a proletarian woman (Simone Evrard) holding Corday, while a *sans-culotte* enters the room, was inspired by an even more recent history painting, *L'Assassinat de Marat*, which Jean-Joseph Weerts exhibited at the Salon of 1880 (plate 11.4).[5] The Musée Grévin proudly acknowledged its relation to the high art of history painting by calling each show room a 'tableau'.

Beyond historical research, the wax museums also based their claim for authenticity on their commitment to truth: 'The faithful reproduction of nature and the respect for truth in its minute details, such are the principles which preside over all the creations of the Musée Grévin' (Musée Grévin 1894: 2). The process of make-believe engineered by wax museums, so as to induce the viewer into accepting the verisimilitude of the historical reconstruction, does not lack sophistication. Each tableau stage-manages a realist scenario which positions the visitor as eyewitness to a scene in its moment of occurrence. Its main principle consists in inviting the viewer to focus attention on the specificity of visual quality in an attempt to construct the real on the basis of an equation between the concrete and the true.[6]

Listing, examining, and commenting upon specific details helped establish the order of the concrete:

There is no doubt that when the viewer comes face to face with Marat's head tilted backwards and when he looks at the furniture of the closet, the bath tub, the heavy leaden inkstand, the fallen chair, the map on the wall – and these minute details reconstructed in the

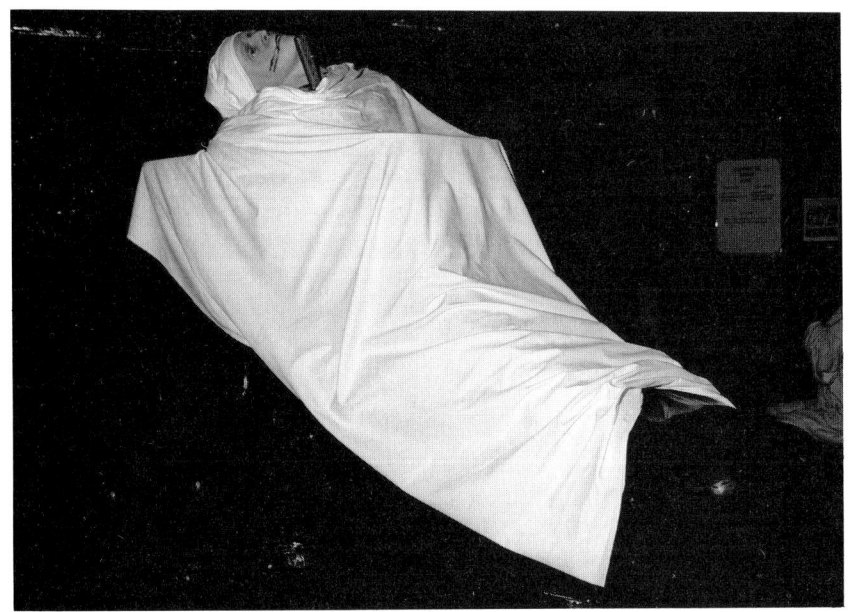

11.1 Death Mask of Marat, taken by Madame Tussaud on display in the Chamber of Horrors, London, Madame Tussaud's, courtesy Madame Tussaud's.

11.2 La Mort de Marat, Paris, Musée Grévin, courtesy Musée Grévin.

11.3 Paul Baudry, *Charlotte Corday*, 1861, oil on canvas, Ville de Nantes, Musée des Beaux-Arts, photograph by Patrick Jean.

11.4 Jean-Joseph Weerts, *L'Assassinat de Marat,* 1880, oil on canvas, Roubaix, Musée de l'art et d'industrie de Roubaix, photograph by Arnaud Delbeke.

realist manner of Balzac, he is bound to believe in the artist's absolute veracity.

(Dauban 1861: 15)

Commentators proceeded to apply such modes of reasoning to abstract categories, transposing notions of psychological identity, space or time, into the concrete order pervading the realist scenario. The description of Marat's agony seems to have been essential to this effect. Again and again, the critics emphasized that Marat had been pictured 'dying' rather than dead, how his head was 'turning backwards', his muscles 'tensed' with pain, or the knife still 'vibrating' in the wound. In contrast to David who had 'represented the impure victim ennobled in the majesty of death' as Henri Delaborde remembered (Delaborde 1861: 882) Marat had now been 'captured' in the last few seconds of agony. Such a degree of temporal precision helps to ascertain the overall specificity of the mode of representation. It also testifies the artist's scrupulous accuracy which gave the tableau its historical credentials.

Was the presentation of Marat's agony entirely devoid of sadistic pleasure? Was there not some satisfaction in being reassured that the

164

people's friend met such horrific death? Such questions did not arise in the context of the argument for Realism, and one was left praising the artist's quasi-scientific, medical power of observation.

The lighting effect also contributed to the veracity of the representation. In contrast to a tradition which associated Marat with darkness and its connotations of evil, the transparent light which falls equally, or nearly equally on Marat and Corday was perceived as a further commitment to historical truthfulness:

> Had the artist wanted to speculate on the horror of the subject, this was easy. All he had to do was to create one of these lighting effects which invariably captivate the gullible crowds of the exhibition: bathe Marat in sinister shades and throw a halo of light around Charlotte's head . . . The shadow which envelops Marat's corpse is a transparent veil which hides nothing, all the details of the action are revealed to the viewer's eyes as they must have appeared to the police inspector. The subject is not enveloped with these poetical images which make the charm and the defect of Mr Lamartine's narrative; it unfolds itself to the naked eye in the light of history.
>
> (About 1861: 231)

Even time, the most abstract of category, appeared to operate within the order of the concrete. The disorder of Marat's room purports to register the action in its momentary occurrence while the perception that Marat is 'dying' or 'has just died' contributes to make time specific.

The sense of immediacy secured by the realist scenario is highly contrived. On the one hand there is the moment depicted in the tableau: people rushing into the room and discovering Marat's corpse. On the other hand there is the viewer's own discovery of the scene. As the floor of the room on which the visitor walks towards the scene of *La Mort de Marat* is higher than that of the reconstituted room of Marat, her or his eyes are likely to perceive Charlotte Corday first, and Marat only by coming closer to the scene. The Musée Grévin, like Paul Baudry, has contrived to give the viewer the role of first eyewitness to the scene.

To strengthen this effect, the Musée Grévin provided their visitors with a written commentary which itself read as an eyewitness account of Marat's murder: 'it is half past seven in the evening. The heat is suffocating . . . Seated in his bathtub, here, in the room where we are, Marat is proof reading an article (Musée Grévin 1894: 27–8). In describing the material circumstances in which the event took place and in inviting the reader to enter the narrative space, the commentary followed the principles already described.

But the text was not as anodyne as its opening sentences made it seem. Within the plethora of details, it introduced a characterization of Marat and Corday which was far from neutral:

165

Marat . . . is proof reading an article and writing down the names of those to be sent to the *guillotine* tomorrow . . . his *snake's* eyes sparkle at the thought of new *victims* she is denouncing to him . . . Her gaze rests on the *monster's* hideous and lascivious eyes . . . the sinister work is carried out . . . and immediately she turns her head away standing calm, beaming and serene: she is indeed the *angel of assassination!*[7]

The text conveys a politically coded representation of Marat and Corday, easily unmasked once the description of circumstantial evidence is peeled off. Through the use of metaphorical language, Marat is portrayed as a bloodthirsty tyrant whose activity as a journalist had no other purpose than sending people to the guillotine. In contrast, the expression 'angel of assassination' construes Corday as some agent of Divine Providence who, like Saint Michael killed (the snake) for the salvation of mankind.

This quotation was reprinted in the Musée Grévin catalogues until the mid-1930s; a hundred years earlier the catalogue of Madame Tussaud's had used the same metaphorical language of the 1791–95 counter-revolutionaries:

he recommended revolt, pillage, and murder; he excited the soldiers to assassinate their generals, the poor to seize the property of the rich . . . *Delighting in blood*, he promoted the murders of September . . . required . . . 300000 more lives . . . a young *heroine with the spirit of Judith*, determined to rid the world of such a *monster* . . . on the 14th [*sic*] of July 1793.

(Madame Tussaud's 1830:30)

The violence and imagery of the 1830 Madame Tussaud's catalogue echoes the language of the counter-revolutionary Couet de Gironville who drew this portrait of Marat during the Thermidorian Reaction:

Marat never ceased to order lootings, and murders, he incited disorder in the army, broke the trust in the generals, lit the torch of civil war . . . All good citizens knew that Marat was the murderer of the nation . . . Marat was a national plague growing from within, sending off infectious emanations which spread the delirium of the most violent anarchy amongst the citizens . . . Marat's men spread the terror of his deletions from one extremity of France to the other . . . and became in no time rich land owners.

(Couet de Gironville An IV: 71,14, 17, 20)

Marat and his followers were alternatively referred to as *Septembriseurs* 'men of carnage', *anthropophages* or 'throat-cutters', images which placed the blame for the September Massacres on Marat. They were also called 'anarchists' and 'agrarians', a terminology which referred to the dismantling of the hierarchy of power and the proposals for the reform of the system of ownership of the land. The imagery of cannibalism could encompass both sets of references.[8] In their struggle against Marat in 1793, the Girondists had systematically used an imagery of cannibalism and animal monstrosity to refer to his politics. Corday was speaking as one of them when, in her letter to the Girondist Deputy Barbaroux, she refers to Marat as 'a ferocious beast which was about to devour France by the fire of civil war'.[9] The image of the murdered Marat with blood dripping from his gaping wound, his rolling eyes, and the reptilian connotations of his mutilated body, translated into visual terms the politically coded language forged by his enemies.

The same principle operates in Gillray's *The heroic Charlotte la Cordé.* (1793) (plate 11.5).[10] In dislocating the human body, his technique opens up a series of connotated meanings about Marat's monstrous nature. The triangular shape of the nose, the exaggerated elongated chin, make his mouth look like the beak of some bird of prey; thin, elongated and flaccid, the right arm is reminiscent of a snake, while the abnormally protruding thorax evokes some beast of prey digesting its victim. This image of Marat can be usefully compared to the rendering of the *sans-culottes* as actually committing cannibalism in the print which Gillray produced in response to the Massacres of September 1792, entitled *Un petit Souper a la Parisiènne* (plate 11.6).[11] Note how the *sans-culotte* depicted in the centre of the composition sits on a bag of stolen jewels bearing the inscription *Propriété de le Nation*: Gillray's print also associated the imagery of cannibalism with the threat placed on the system of ownership.

The metaphorical language of the late eighteenth century construed the pair Marat–Corday as the duality between evil and good. It was then customary to call Corday the 'new Judith', a reference which Gillray picked up in the speech attributed to Corday – note how the words 'Judith of Bethulia' are printed in darker tone and spaced out at the end of the text to make them clearly legible.

The image of the murdered Marat still conveyed the same kind of associations during the nineteenth century, amongst the right. Commenting on Paul Baudry's painting, in a right-wing Catholic paper, Ernest Vinet seemed able to recreate this vocabulary anew:

> The President of the Jacobin Club evokes the idea of a reptile unrolling himself to digest his victim . . . There stands the new Judith [against] the map of France, this admirable France which Marat and his friends were dismembering . . . What a Republican energy and willpower mastering terrible emotions can be read on such an innocent lovely face . . . In her hands stiffed with tension there seems to shine the sword of vengeance.
>
> (Vinet 1861: 438)

The Realist scenario of nineteenth-century visual art disavows the existence

11.5 James Gillray, *The heroic Charlotte la Cordé, upon her Trial at the bar of the Revolutionary Tribunal of Paris, July 17th 1793*, published 17 July 1793 by H. Humphrey, coloured etching, London, British Museum, Trustees of the British Museum.

11.6 James Gillray, *Un petit Souper a la Parisiènne – or – a Family of Sans Culotts refreshing after the fatigues of the day*, published 20 September 1792 by H. Humphrey, coloured etching, London, British Museum, Trustees of the British Museum.

of any symbolic order and attempts to neutralize its narrative categories within the specificity of its time-scale. The puzzling phenomenon is that so many intellectuals accepted the identification of Marat and Corday with categories similar to those already expounded. Theophile Gautier's description of Baudry's *Charlotte Corday* parallels that of Vinet, though he would not have wished to share his political identity:

> Baudry gave all the importance to Corday, the interest having to focus on the heroine and not on the *monster*. Marat's head, wrapped in a cloth tilts backwards in the supreme convulsion of agony . . . the left hand clings nervously to a wooden plank, the *fierce leveler's* pulpit whom death itself could not stop in his *monstrous* undertaking. On the other side, standing against the wall there is Charlotte Corday, *the angel of assassination* as Mr de Lamartine calls her . . . She is like a petrified *Nemesis*! . . . Later, the thought of having delivered her country from a *tyrant* will probably kindle anew the courage of the chaste maiden . . . She will be able to applaud this *abstract murder reborn from Roman times*.
>
> (Gautier 1861: 38–9)

The symbolism of space, the fact that Corday was given precedence over Marat at the centre of the composition and her proximity to the map of France was enough for a connotative system to operate within the order of the concrete, with the result that the map of France becomes a signifier of Corday's professed intention: to restore peace and unity in France.

Reflecting on the power of the images which he had brought together for the exhibition *The Shadow of the Guillotine: Britain and the French Revolution* David Bindman concluded:

> If we still think of the French Revolution in terms of the guillotine, innocent aristocrats and brutish sans-culottes, then this represents the triumph of visual images which have a virtually unbroken history from the propaganda campaigns of the 1790s through the Victorian period to the present day.
>
> (Bindman 1989: 78)

The Marat myth has proved peculiarly resilient. The image of the dismembered Marat, I shall go on to argue, embodied at a primary level, a politically coded language, which maintained its significance during the struggles of the nineteenth century.

THE ANGEL OF ASSASSINATION

Translated by T. Ryde within a year and published in London in 1848 Lamartine's *History of the Girondists* (1847–8) contributed the most seductive portrayal of Charlotte Corday. In a tissue of connoted meanings, Lamartine's text construed her as a creature of superhuman charm and power. To explain how a woman could re-enact in 1793 the heroic deeds of Roman men who sacrificed their life to their country, Lamartine called upon Corday's lineage: she happened to be a descendant of Corneille and therefore a 'natural' Cornellian heroine. Her education too was enlisted to justify the heroine: she read Plutarch, Raynal and Rousseau and came to espouse Republicanism after much mature and solitary meditation which gave her a strength of mind that commanded 'admiration and respect'. The writer dwelt at length on Corday's physical appearance, as manifesting her inner personality. Her youth, beauty, fair hair and complexion, her translucent eyes and angelic voice were all enlisted to signify the purity of her mind and visions. Her resolute chin and muscular arms, on the other hand, indicated a strength only men were thought capable of. Lamartine invited his readers to make an equation between Corday's chastity and the purity of her action, pointing out what revealed this in her physical appearance: the absence of curve in her bust, and what made it apparent in her mode of behaviour: her tendency to blush in men's presence and her insistence to hide her body from men's sight. There was, moreover, a tale of repressed romance, which showed how Corday took the resolution to renounce earthly bonds so as to dedicate herself to the love of her country: 'the passion with which she would have been inspired for some one individual consumed her in her ardour for her country and the desire of immolating herself to this had wholly possessed her' (Lamartine 1848: III, 59). Lamartine dwelt on the issue, thinking it would provide a psychological explanation of heroic crime.[12] Writing from Corday's viewpoint, Lamartine stated that she killed Marat 'for the sake of liberty and humanity', describing her resolution in the manner of divine inspiration: 'She saw the loss of France, saw the victims, and believed she discerned the tyrant. She swore an inward oath, to avenge the one, punish the other and save them all' (Lamartine 1848: III, 61). The text seeks to identify Corday with a reincarnated Judith – had not the Bible been found opened at the Book of Judith on her bed? (Lamartine 1848: III, 66). Her semi-divine nature was revealed to all during her trial: 'Men deemed they saw divine justice, or the antique Nemesis, substituting conscience for law, and appearing to demand from human justice, not to absolve, but to recognise her and tremble' (Lamartine 1848: III, 86).

To give historical credentials to his interpretation, Lamartine integrated within his narrative carefully selected contemporary sources. These were first of all a series of writings by Corday herself. Corday had intended to leave to posterity a statement of her reasons in an 'Address to Frenchmen friendly to the Laws and Peace'. The access of the Montagne to power, she wrote, was to precipitate France into civil war and self-destruction:

The Montagne triumphs by crime and oppression, a few monsters

171

bathed in our blood, lead these detestable plots . . . Already the fire
of discord and civil war consumes half of this vast empire; there is
but one means to extinguish it . . . Let the destruction of the Montagne leave nothing but brothers and friends . . . their repose depends
upon the execution of the Laws. I do not infringe them by killing
Marat.

(Lamartine 1848: III, 80)

The narration of the circumstances in which Corday came to kill Marat
was based on the detailed account she gave in her letter to the Girondist
Deputy Barbaroux. The image of Corday as the angel of peace was
grounded in Corday's repeated statements that her objective in killing
Marat was to see peace restored in France. She wrote as much to Barbaroux: 'May peace be established as speedily as I desire . . . I enjoy this
peace for the last two days. The happiness of my country is mine' (Lamartine 1848: III, 84). The letter Corday addressed to her father, spoke of the
happiness of avenging innocent victims, and gave modern readers the
assurance of Corday's integration within patriarchy, opening as it did with
the submissive sentence: 'Pardon me for having disposed of my existence
without your permission' (Lamartine 1848: III, 85).

The other pieces of evidence the historian made use of were the tran-
scripts of Corday's interrogations and trial. Neither the police nor the
public accuser had been able to make Corday admit that she was a
Girondist agent or that she had acted for the love of a Girondist. Nor was
the President of the Tribunal successful in making Corday pass for insane.
On the contrary, the transcript of the trial showed Corday answering with
calm and clear mindedness.

Lamartine did not altogether invent Corday, he focused and worked
upon the image Corday wanted posterity to have of her, down to her
quotations from Roman history in the linguistic mode of the 1780s and to
the portrait she requested should be made of her. In *The History of the
Girondists*, the portrayal of Charlotte Corday did not exist independently
from that of Marat: they had been articulated together on the axis of
opposition between good and evil, perpetuating that metaphorical language
of the eighteenth century discussed earlier.

Lamartine's treatment of Marat was appallingly crude, not a consistent
portrayal but a leitmotif which linked all other images of blood and violence
in the text. Book 44 entitled *Charlotte Corday* opened with the following
appraisal of Marat and the French Revolution in 1793:

It was at this moment that the Girondists were struggling with
daring courage and prodigious eloquence against their enemies in the
Convention. The Jacobins only desired to wrest the republic from
the Gironde, in order to precipitate France into a bloody anarchy.
The convulsive throes of liberty, the hateful tyranny of the mob of

Paris substituted for the legal sovereignty of the nation, represented by its deputies; arbitrary imprisonments; the assassinations of September, the conspiracy of the 10th of March, the insurrection of the 30th and 31st of May, the expulsion and proscription of the purer portion of the Assembly, their scaffold in perspective, where liberty would ascent with them . . . in the place of these men, interesting or sublime, who appeared to defend in the breach the last ramparts of society, and the sacred hearth of every citizen, a Marat, the dregs and leprosy of the people, triumphing over the laws by sedition, crowned by impunity, carried into the tribune on the arms of the faubourgs, attaining the dictatorship of anarchy, spoliation, assassination, and threatening every species of independence, property, liberty, and life in the departments.

(Lamartine 1848: III, 59–60)

This heavily coded passage summed up Lamartine's political position. In Lamartine's text Marat is never envisaged as an historical figure but a symbol, that of the people's power. Unwilling to conceptualize a notion of working-class politics, Lamartine used instead a series of images of disruption. The politics of the bourgeoisie could be exercised through the democratic means of rationally organized institutions; the Legislative Assembly of October 1791 showed how well it could, as Lamartine stated. The people's power, on the other hand, could only manifest itself in acts of violence. Whereas the institutions of the bourgeoisie embodied the principle of justice, the people's power was necessarily a breach of the moral order motivated by envy. The September Massacres of 1792 were presented as the paradigm of the people's intervention in history.

Marat's access to power was described as the ability to manipulate the people and orchestrate their thirst for blood. As he made the September Massacres the turning point of the Revolution so Lamartine made Marat the main instigator of violence. Without giving any evidence of Marat's activity in the period of August and September 1792, Lamartine stated 'The idea belongs to Marat . . . in Marat it was a thirst for blood, the last remedy of a society he wished to destroy' (Lamartine 1847: II, 118). In his account of the year 1793, Lamartine exaggerated the influence Marat had on the Convention to secure a portrayal of the dictator as one who uses the people's power to frighten all other politicians into obedience:

Marat thus constituted himself, alone, after his triumph, the plenipotentiary of the multitude. He assumed the dictatorship. His policy had, for its only theory, death. He was the apostle of assassination *en masse*. He spoke as the master, not as the counsellor of the nation.

(Lamartine 1847: II, 487)

The term 'triumph' refers to Marat's acquittal by the Revolutionary Tribunal on 24 April 1793, subsequent to the accusation the Girondists had placed on him. The vignette of the people carrying Marat back to his Deputy's seat and later on a chair, through the streets of Paris, confirmed in nineteenth-century imagery, the power Marat had over the working class. 'The importance and authority over the people' as Lamartine (1848: III, 61) said, that is what most terrified about Marat. No explanation could possibly be given of Marat, except to reject him amongst the insane (Lamartine 1847: I, 116).

The image of the sanguinary Marat was multi-level. It concerned the 'people', their rights, the sacred rights of private property, perhaps just as much as the memory of the Revolutionary bloodshed. In the absence of any conceptualization of what working-class politics could entail, of what could constitute a political institution which recognized the working class the right to take control over the social order, the fundamental and irresolvable questions Marat raised about Revolutionary situations and the advent of democracy could not even begin to be heard.

MADAME TUSSAUD'S AND THE DISMEMBERING OF MARAT

The political upheavals of the nineteenth century explained in a large measure the endurance of Marat as a terrifying symbol of the people's revolution. In June 1848, the Republican Government, which had recently taken power with the fall of Louis Phillipe's monarchy, had to make decisions about working-class political aspirations: they killed and they repressed. The English editor of Lamartine was in no doubt that the present revolutionary situation in France had made the publication of *The History of the Girondists* compulsory reading for all European nations. The book opened with a review of the Revolution of 1848 which paid homage to Lamartine, then Foreign Minister of the Provisional Government of the Republic, and his peers, for having spared France 'from the immediate horrors of anarchy and bloodshed' (Lamartine 1848: III, xx).

Hervé, as editor of Madame Tussaud's *Memoirs* similarly thought that the Revolution of 1830 had made the publication of his book timely. Describing himself as an eyewitness to the 'Three days of 1830', he explained that much was to be learned by comparing the two revolutionary situations (Tussaud 1838: 89).

Madame Tussaud's *Memoirs* related two French Revolutions. The year 1789 is accounted for because it brought to its end a state of appalling tyranny commonly symbolized by the Bastille. Its actors and its heroes are the people: 'On 14 July the Bastille was taken over by the people after a tremendous conflict, in which the mob displayed a heroic courage which would have done credit to a better cause' (Tussaud 1838: 92). But, for Hervé, history collapsed in 1791 as the French Revolution degenerated into 'the tyranny of the mob,' the responsibility for which, it was argued, rested entirely with the leaders of the Montagne:

> The principal blame must ever rest with the instigators who urged a victorious mob, whose hands were still stained with the blood of their victims and by false representations excited their fears and engendered an implacable hatred against the unfortunate beings who had become their captives.
>
> (Tussaud 1838: 263)

Hervé's preoccupation with 'the people' cements together a text which would otherwise have remained a mosaic of biographical sketches. But who were the people beyond a series of attributes reflected in the inflexions of meaning of the seven words alternatively used to designate them? The people have no individual identity, no facial features in Madame Tussaud's *Memoirs*, and perhaps the term *populace* acknowledges the difficulty to comprehend. One characteristic is the position at the bottom of the social hierarchy: *the low orders*; another is their total lack of culture: *the uneducated*. They constitute a mass *the multitude*, and that is what makes them so dangerous. They have a tendency to disorderly conduct *the rabble*, and no other psychological identity than the animal force that motivates them, their *appetites*. When history keeps this instinctive force under control, they can behave admirably – they are *the people*. But when they are subjected to the wrong kind of leadership they become the machine of destruction of the social order, 'the mob'. The questions raised around the persona of Marat concerned working-class leadership.

In Madame Tussaud's *Memoirs*, Jacobin politics are sketched out in the same crude terms as in Lamartine: their strategy, we are told consisted of raising the people to a pitch of violence and in channelling it against their own political enemies. They were 'the sanguinary party' to which Marat belonged together with Robespierre, Legendre, Santerre. What distinguished Marat from the others was the uncanny power of fascination he could exercise through the use of language:

> In Marat there was a something which must have excited attention wherever he went, his discourse and his delivery were not of the common order, his arguments were full of force, his imagination often wild and poetic, whilst his manner was ardent, impassioned, impressive, well calculated to captivate the mob.
>
> (Tussaud 1838: 248–9)

If, in this passage, the portrayal of Marat is not devoid of a certain degree of admiration, elsewhere in the text, his exceptional talents as orator and journalist seem demoniac: 'he appeared almost superhuman to the populace ... he resembled one who was under the influence of some demoniacal possession. This contributed to awe the multitude with whom he attained the utmost celebrity' (Tussaud 1838: 195). What scared most about Marat was his ability to manipulate the people, to succeed as their 'arch instigator'. What infuriated most was the love he inspired in them, 'a rude and barbarian kind of affection' (Tussaud 1838: 365).

The Marat narrative could not end with Corday's action in 1793. In Madame Tussaud's *Memoirs*, the French Revolution reached its terminal point in 1795, when the people decided to desecrate the remains of he who had once been their idol (Tussaud 1838: 433–4). Such is the notion of the French Revolution the wax museum set out to impart in its guidebooks. The spatial organization of the showrooms of the museum made it tangible too, first by disassociating Marat from the category 'history', to include him, instead, in that of 'criminality'.

This policy was already implemented in 1830, when the severed head of Marat cohabitated in 'the separate room' with that of Ravaillac, Henri IV's murder in 1610 and, next to them, a contemporary English criminal, Steward, who had been executed in 1829 for having robbed and poisoned the Captain of a trading vessel. During the course of the nineteenth century the Chamber of Horrors extended its collection of English criminals, all of whom were members of the working class. As for 'History', it was represented by a succession of Kings and Queens, those who were believed to have moulded the course of history, and amongst whose ranks Henri IV, Marie Antoinette, Louis XVI and Louis XVIII belonged. Charlotte Corday could not figure in either category since she was a 'heroine', not a leading political figure.

By grouping together the severed heads of the leaders of the Montagne and those of contemporary English criminals, the wax museum invited visitors to draw a parallel between the efficiency of the Police and the Judicial system of the English State and the course of Providence which brought the leaders of the Terror to the same horrific end.

The architecture and spatial organization of the Musée Grévin imposed a similar interpretation of the French Revolution. As one follows the visit of the Galerie de la Révolution, *La Mort de Marat* has to be viewed last, for it is situated in a transitional area that leads to the lower level of the Museum and is separated from the main gallery by a wall partition. As the four main tableaux of the gallery represent the suffering of the Royal Family in prison, and the fifth tableau the Revolutionary Tribunal which the nineteenth-century guidebook described as the very opposite of Justice (Musée Grévin 1894: 15–21), one could infer that Marat's murder fulfilled the course of Providence, which reenacted on him the same kind of violence he had inspired against the Royal Family.

The lower gallery of the Musée Grévin presented, until the end of the century, *l'Histoire d'un crime*, which narrated in eight tableaux the fate of a working-class man who, having robbed a bank, ended up on the guillotine.

11.7 E. M. Ward, *Charlotte Corday Going to Execution*, 1852, oil on canvas, whereabouts unknown.

As *The Six Stages of Wrong* in the Chamber of Horrors at Madame Tussaud's, it contributed to locate Marat within the category 'criminality'.

The fear and hatred of Marat had its roots in the fear of working-class politics and the visual arts did not need to take on as dramatic an appearance as the Chamber of Horrors or Baudry's *Charlotte Corday* to convey such emotions. We often find them embedded at a latent state in the Corday iconography. E. M. Ward's *Charlotte Corday Going to Execution* (1852) which was inspired by Lamartine's text, betrays some of these political preoccupations, mostly in the figure of the proletarian woman standing in the right foreground (plate 11.7).[13] The task of situating the depicted scene within the context of the French Revolution in a large part rests with her, for the medieval architectural setting, the heroine's timeless gown, her neat hair free from the cap which women wore on their way to execution, all work to the opposite effect.

Ward's composition operates a series of contrasts and oppositions between the working-class woman, Corday and the group of Robespierre, Danton and Desmoulin who lurk in the dark and hollow space of the prison gate. The abusive behaviour of the woman of the *sans-culottes* is

177

contrasted to Corday's self-composure to signify that the heroine's actions are guided by reason and moral principles. With her powerful physical presence, her darkness of skin, coarse features and dishevelled hair, the proletarian woman is, on the contrary, anchored in the sphere of instincts. Her counterpart can be found in the image of the enormous and therefore dangerous dog which, for the present moment, is kept under control with a mere pat on the head. The absent Marat is thereby signified as the people's leader, loved by a 'rude and barbarian kind of affection', the instigator and manipulator of the powerful instinctive force the people represent. In spite of its anodyne appearance, Ward's painting integrates some of the preoccupations exemplified by Madame Tussaud's *Memoirs* or Lamartine's *Charlotte Corday*.

Marat entered the realm of indestructible mythologies in the context of the bourgeoisie's perceptions of their Other – the working class. The political upheavals of the nineteenth century also generated a bulk of revisionist and sympathetic research on Marat. In 1847, Lamartine was demolished point by point in a terse pamphlet by Constant Hilbey. Significantly Hilbey defined his political standpoint by proudly adding after his name the term *Ouvrier* – working class. The major biography of Marat was researched during the dictatorship of the Second Empire by Alfred Bougeart who published his two volumes of *Marat, l'Ami du peuple* in 1865.

In the first two hundred pages of volume I, Bougeart explained the writings of Marat, what they consisted of, what their philosophic principles were, what impact they had on the evolution of the French Revolution. Marat was an erudite, and a distinguished political philosopher; his writings influenced the course of history; and his newspaper *L'Ami du peuple*, in spite of what Michelet wrote, reflected a genuine concern for the poorer members of society; Marat was not an 'anarchist' but a lover of social justice, concluded Bougeart. In the 600 following pages Bougeart reviewed Marat's political action from August 1789 to his death. He wanted to apologize for him, even for the September Massacres of 1792:

> For the past three years the People's Friend had put forward the only means capable of avoiding insurrections and saving innocent lives in case of revolt; they did not want to listen to him; the people rose up in anger, violent and without a guide.
>
> (Bougeart 1865: I, 108)

Bougeart was also concerned to explain the source of the Marat myth which he recognized as an inheritance from 'modern historians' and which he wanted to dispel. He accounted for it in terms of the thirst for power which maintained social hierarchy:

> If Marat counts so many enemies it is because tyranny is not only

exercised on the throne; at all levels of the social ladder and in all kinds of social groupings there are those who aspire to dominate, and there is no domination without passive obedience.

(Bougeart 1865: II, 67–8)

Both Hilbey and Bougeart were sent to prison for their work on Marat.

Members of the nascent socialist movement in England used Bougeart's writings in their attempt to define the nature of working-class politics. The *Gentleman's Journal* published Bax's article on Marat in 1877, paving the way to his full-length biography of 1900. François Chèvremont devoted his entire scholarly life to Marat and his bibliography of Marat's writings, published in 1880, has remained an indispensable source for contemporary historians. Chèvremont opted to give his collection to the British Museum library which is, as a result, one of the richest archives for study on Marat.

Was it sheer irony of Providence that the first book published in England subsequent to Chèvremont's gift, should have been devoted to Charlotte Corday? Its author, Mrs Van Alstine, well aware of contemporary research, thought she could recognize in Marat's writing 'arguments which have since gained such a wearisome familiarity in the mouths of modern Socialists' (Van Alstine 1890: 93). Though the language of Lamartine or Carlyle could no longer seem objective, the term 'poetic' was now being used to disqualify the writings of Bougeart, Chèvremont or Bax (Van Alstine 1890: 94).

The images of guillotine and severed heads, the narratives of crime and punishment, belong to the spectacles of fear and sadistic pleasures which the wax museums made their business to orchestrate. What I have offered here, is a wider context of explanation, arguing that such spectacles of horror emerged from the fear that the people's power inspired in the bourgeoisie, which found its foremost expression in the nineteenth-century conception of the French Revolution as 'the tyranny of the mob'. Perhaps, the saddest aspect of this whole subject does not concern Marat but 'the people', and the way the so called Popular Arts have subjected them to the mythologies of those who deny them political rights.

NOTES

1 *Death Mask of Marat, taken by Madame Tussaud on display in the Chamber of Horrors*, Phillipe Curtius or Madame Tussaud, wax model of head and shoulders set in a tin bath 1,230mm; listed in Madame Tussaud's 1803: 41–2; see Bindman 1989: 147, no. 127.
2 Introduced in the 1894 Musée Grévin catalogue as 'reconstituted in all its details with religious exactitude, from contemporary evidence and documents (Musée Grévin 1894: 30).These data were accepted at their face value by Claude Cézan in his *Le Musée Grévin* (1974: 101–5).
3 *La Mort de Marat*, Musée Grévin, since 1886 in La Galerie de la Révolution, listed in Musée Grévin: 1894: 26–36, no. 28.

4 Paul Baudry, *Charlotte Corday*, 1861, oil on canvas 2.03 × 1.54, Musée des Beaux-Arts de Nantes, bought in 1861 for 12,000 francs.

5 Jean-Joseph Weerts, *La Mort de Marat*, 1880, oil on canvas 272 × 360, Musée de Roubaix, Schulman 1989: no. 31.

6 The following argument is based on research I carried out on Paul Baudry's *Charlotte Corday*. See my 1985: 91–125.

7 The Musée Grévin catalogue gave its sources as Comte d'Ideville, *Maisons et jeunes souvenirs*. This text, it seems, was already included in the 1886 catalogue.

8 In 'L'homme de sang: l'invention sémiotique de Marat', Philippe Roger subtly draws attention on 'la plume de sang', but minimizes, I believe, the fears associated with Marat's speeches and writing about the reform of the system of ownership, see Roger 1986.

9 See the 1989 Versailles exhibition *Charlotte Corday* catalogue for Corday's writings (Delaporte et al. 1989: 207–14). During the nineteenth century, the most accessible source would have been Du Bois *Charlotte Corday* (1838). Du Bois also published the transcript of Corday's trial. Corday's writings were first published under request of Fouquier Tinville.

10 James Gillray, *The heroic Charlotte la Cordé, upon her Trial at the bar of the Revolutionary Tribunal of Paris, July 17th 1793*, published 29 July 1793 by H. Humphrey, etching, coloured, 310 × 358 mm, BMC 8336, Bindman 1989: 148, no. 132.

11 James Gillray, *Un petit Soupér a la Parisiènne – or – A Family of Sans Culotts refreshing after the fatigues of the day*, published 20 September 1792 by H. Humphrey, coloured etching, 252 × 353 mm, BMC 8122, Bindman 1989: 124, no. 81.

12 With the expression 'angel of assassination' Lamartine sought to introduce the case of Corday as an insoluble moral dilemma. See Benrekassa 1986, especially pp. 313–14.

13 E. M. Ward, *Charlotte Corday Going to Execution*, 1852, whereabouts unknown. In his monograph Dafforne de-politicized Corday's action by explaining her motives as those of revenge for her lover whom Marat had killed (Dafforne 1879: 31).

BIBLIOGRAPHY

About, E. (1861) *Dernières lettres d'un bon jeune homme*, Paris. Levy.

Adhémar, J. (1978) 'Les Musées de cire en France', *Gazette des Beaux Arts* 92: 203–14.

Bax, E. (1879) *Jean Paul Marat, The People's Friend*, London, Modern Press.

—— (1900) *Jean Paul Marat, The People's Friend*, London, Grant Richards.

Benrekassa, G. (1986) 'Histoire d'un assassinat – La mort de Marat dans l'historiographie du XIX Siécle', in Bonnet 1986: 311–33.

Bibliothèque nationale, éstampes series PB1 and N2.

Bindman, D. (1989) *The Shadow of the Guillotine: Britain and the French Revolution*, London, British Museum.

Bonnet, J. C. (ed.) (1986) *La Mort de Marat*, Paris, Flammarion.

Bougeart, A. (1865) *Marat, l'Ami du peuple*, 2 vols, Paris, A. Lacroix and Verboecken.

Cézan, C. (1974) *Le Musée Grévin*, Paris, Edouard Privat.

Chéron de Villiers, P.-T. (1865) *Marie-Anne-Charlotte Corday d'Armont, sa vie, son temps, ses écrits, son procès, sa mort*, Paris, Amyot.

Chèvremont, F. (1880) *Jean Paul Marat orné de son portrait. Esprit politique accompagné de sa vie scientifique, politique et privée*, 2 vols, Paris, Chez l'auteur.

Couet de Gironville (An IV) *Charlotte Corday*, Paris, Chez le Citoyen Gilbert, 1795.

Dafforne, J. (1879) *The Life and Works of Edward Matthew Ward*, London, Virtue & Co.

Dauban, C.-A. (1861) *Journal géneral de l'instruction publique*, June: 15–17.

Delaborde, H. (1861) *Revue des deux mondes*: 882–3.

Delaporte, J., Fallay d'Este, L., Gendre, C., Desile, P. et al. (1989) *Charlotte Corday*, ed. Musées Départementaux de la Seine – Maritime, Versailles, Musée Lambinet.

Du Bois, L. (1838) *Charlotte de Corday, essai historique, offrant enfin des détails authentiques sur la personne et l'attentat de cette héroine, avec pièces justificatives, portrait et fac-similie*, Paris, Librairie historique de la Révolution.

Gautier, T. H. (1861) *Abécédaire du salon de 1861*, Paris, Dentu; 32–44.

Gottschalk, L. (1974) *Jean Paul Marat: A Study in Radicalism*, Chicago, University of Chicago Press.

Hilbey, Constantin Ouvrier (1847) *Marat et ses calomniateurs, séance de la convention nationale du 25 Septembre 1792. Extrait du Journal de Marat précédé d'une introduction et accompagné de notes*, Paris, Chez tous les libraires.

Lamartine (1847–8) *History of the Girondists, or, Personal Memoirs of the Patriots of the French Revolution. From unpublished sources*, 3 vols, trans. H. T. Ryde, London, Henry G. Bohn.

Madame Tussaud's (1803) *Biographical Sketches of the Characters composing the Cabinet of Composition Figures executed by Curtius of Paris and his Successor*, Edinburgh.

—— (1830) *Biographical and Descriptive Sketches of the Distinguished Characters which compose the Unrivalled Exhibition of Madame Tussaud*, London.

—— (1897) *Madame Tussaud's and Sons' Exhibition* catalogued by George Augustus Sala.

—— (1913) *Madame Tussaud's and Sons' Exhibition*, catalogued by George Augustus Sala.

Marat, J.-P. (1988) *Ecrits*, ed. Michel Vovelle, Paris, Editions sociales.

Massin, J. (1960) *Marat*, Paris, Le Club français du livre (Portraits de l'histoire).

Michelet, J. (1847–57) *Histoire de la Révolution Française*, 7 vols, Paris, C. Marpon and E. Flammarion.

Mitchell, C. (1985) 'The problems of the representation of time', unpublished doctoral thesis, University of Leeds.

Musée Grévin (Archives Musée Grévin) (1894) *Catalogue illustré*, 94th edn, catalogues reprinted until 1935.

Roger, P. (1986) 'L'homme de sang: l'invention sémiotique de Marat', in Bonnet 1986: 141–66.

Schulman, D. (1989) *Jean-Joseph Weerts*, Musée de Roubaix.

Tussaud, Madame (1838) *Memoirs and Reminiscences of France Forming an Abridged History of the French Revolution*, ed. Francis Hervé, London, Saunders & Otley.

Vatel, C. (1861) *Procès criminal de Charlotte Corday devant le Tribunal Révolutionnaire*, Paris, Poulet-Malassis.

Vermorel (1869) *Oeuvres de Marat, l'Ami du peuple*, Paris, Décembre-Alonnier.

Vinet, E. (1861) *Revue nationale et étrangère*: 437–41.

Van Alstine, Mrs J. (1890) *Charlotte Corday: A Biography*, London, W. Allen & Co.

12

Breaking the code: interpreting French Revolutionary iconoclasm

Richard Wrigley

Art historians concerned with the French Revolution have been predominantly preoccupied with the problems of artistic production, asking questions along the lines of: was it hospitable to the support and encouragement
of High Art, and did it produce a new revolutionary art? The answer has
tended to be a somewhat disparaging 'No'. The reasons usually given for
this paucity are the inhibition of the relatively slow process of pictorial
production which history painting or monumental sculpture required. More
generally, the custom provided by traditional clients – the Church, the
State and social élites – rapidly dried up as a consequence of the Revolutionary hiatus. Moreover, pictures which connect specifically with political
issues were repeatedly rendered obsolete or compromising because of
changes in the status quo, if indeed they were not left as sketches or
plaster maquettes. In some cases, there is also displacement of time and
commitment from the business of painting to active political engagement,
best known in the exemplary case of J.-L. David, who for a time became
a leading member of the Revolutionary government. In another sense, art
historians have spilt much ink over interpreting and reinterpreting a very
limited set of works – especially those of David – as if they in some way
contained certain essential clues to the cultural politics of the day. Finally,
the Revolution has tended to be treated as starting and ending rather
abruptly, thus restricting the space within which some kind of cultural
settlement was to be achieved.

Thinking about iconoclasm is a useful way of broadening our enquiries
regarding the role of the visual arts within the Revolution. This is because
it requires us to make sense of the diverse forces which lay behind such
moments of censure. In so doing our attention is shifted from reconstructing
or decoding individual artists' intentions, in so far as they are predicated
as being responsible for a given image or object, towards a consideration
of what we might call crises of effectivity, during which audience response
became active to the extent of reworking the image or object in question.

To address the problem of audience is to enquire about the currency of
visual cultures in eighteenth-century France. In order to open up reflection

on this question it is helpful to look to recent work on the politics of language in effecting a culturally defined representation of social difference. From the work of Eugen Weber (1977), Michel de Certeau, Dominique Julia and J. Revel (1975) on governmental attempts to establish French as the national language, we know that there was considerable resistance to such ambitions to impose linguistic standardization: until well into the nineteenth century, local patois was the first language for most French people (Weber 1977, Certeau, Julia and Revel 1975). This immediately throws into question how successfully official ideologies were inculcated across France. Whilst there is no visual equivalent to a purified, normative French language, the fact that there might be tensions between the local and constructions of the 'national', should, I think, alert us to a vacuum in our perception of the currency and diffusion of forms of visual culture during the Revolutionary period. Looking at moments of conflict between visual or emblematic manifestations of official discourse, whether of the *ancien régime*, or of the new Revolutionary period, leads us to consider what was at stake in each instance, for whom, and for which social and political constituencies.

Discussions of Revolutionary iconoclasm have tended to reproduce the absolute terms of proscription and prescription that habitually characterize Revolutionary discourses themselves. This is most immediately the case in the terminology employed. For, above all in France, it has become normal to talk not of iconoclasm, but of vandalism, an inherently derogatory term whose usage implies censure of the 'vandalism' in question, linking it to the Dark Ages, the epoch that gave vandalism a bad name.[1] In terms of the evolution of constructions of the meaning of vandalism, we need to confront and disentangle successive versions of what has been claimed for this aspect of the Revolution. Most relevant here is the persistent reactionary reading of the Revolution that places it at the head of a threatening genealogy of insurrection and anarchy that contaminated the nineteenth century. It is an irony of history that the Jacobin Republic, which acted comprehensively to prevent the opportunistic depredations of vandalism, has been singled out as the sole agent of Revolutionary violence against property and images. In part, this reflects a negative reading of the Revolution as a new monolithic state remorselessly applying a dual policy of propaganda and iconoclasm, destroying the old and enforcing the new. Thus Louis Réau, in his book *L'Histoire du vandalisme. Les monuments detruits de l'art français* (1959), claimed that, during the Revolution:

> The ravages of jacobinism spread across the whole of France and her civil and religious monuments . . . The revolutionaries' *idée fixe* is the abolition of the past, as if the past, always alive in each of us, could be effaced by a stroke of the pen. The men of the extreme left have

183

preferred to conceal revolutionary vandalism and the conflagration of the Commune.

(Sprigath 1980: 533–4)

Such comments echo the categorical denunciations of the Jacobin Republic that were articulated immediately after its fall, defining vandalism as a specifically Jacobin form of intolerance. For the *Journal des arts* in *an VIII* (15 pluv. an VIII (4 February 1800), no. 39:6) the spirit of iconoclasm was inimical to the French people; the ravages of vandalism had been *largement salariés* by England, aided and abetted by a destructive and puritanical republican ideology which condemned the arts as aristocratic. Under the Consulate, apologists for the Revolution played down Revolutionary activities in this area by pointing out that France had seen worse under Louis XIV, who had been responsible for the destruction of 'Calvinist temples' after the Revocation of the Edict of Nantes.[2] Exaggerated provincial rumours of mass destruction could hardly be taken seriously given the existence of the Louvre and the Musée des monuments français (D.1801).

By contrast, in what follows, rather than offering an historical survey of Revolutionary iconoclasm, I wish to consider the phenomenon in relation to questions of legibility. What interests me is the relationship between changes to the physical appearance of an object or image and the effect this has on its revised conceptual message. As far as possible, observations are drawn from individual incidents so as to suggest a range of possibilities, rather than any larger, more ambitious generalizations.

One line of enquiry into iconoclasm as a Revolutionary phenomenon would be to follow the decrees and official reports which record and attempt to prevent the phenomenon. Such texts probably tell us only a limited amount about the effectiveness of such bureaucratic orders from above, and how they were adapted, received and actually applied. All the accounts we have of iconoclastic acts – journalism, government officials' memoes, police reports – are inherently partial, if not explicitly partisan. Descriptions of iconoclastic acts that identify single causes, and which see them as symptoms of either dominant or repressed political forces – whether Jacobin megalomania or counter-revolutionary subversion – tend to obscure the inevitable polysemic resonance that such acts and their results would have had within a given community, and as perceived by local governmental representatives, and in due course as reported through the channels of journalism and official, public and confidential reports.

The *tabula rasa* envisaged by Revolutionary euphoria, on which the new political agenda was to be written, could not, in practice, be wiped clean instantaneously. This is an important point because it exemplifies the inherently eclectic nature of Revolutionary imagery, drawing heavily and not always critically on established models as a means of creating a novel but still comprehensible visual and conceptual vocabulary. As Mona Ozouf has demonstrated, local variations of the same notionally uniform *fêtes* reveal unpredictable, *ad hoc* interpretations at work, as in the case of the various attributes employed across France for the principle female allegorical figures in the *fête de la Réunion* (Ozouf 1976: 116). This echoes the point made above concerning the diversity of visual cultures with which any nationwide analysis of imagery contends.

Usage of the term 'iconoclasm', and more especially 'vandalism', suggests complete destruction, total eradication. However, in practice, we find that acts of iconoclasm are commonly exercises in compromise, usually resulting in hybridized or synthetic results which succeed in making of the object concerned a vehicle for a message utterly different to its original meaning. Derrida's concept of *rature* comes to mind here as a potentially useful tool in thinking about the kind of legibility that can result from iconoclastic acts, and the interplay between old and new meanings. According to Derrida, when a word is under *rature*, that which has been erased none the less remains visible, and therefore in dialogue with the superimposed marks (Derrida 1967: 38, 90). The term also has a technical philosophical origin in Heidegger which is part and parcel of its appeal for Derrida.[3] Clearly, there are problems in applying a concept that deals with texts to the realm of two-dimensional images or three-dimensional objects, but nevertheless it seems an apposite way of considering many characteristic Revolutionary semantic hybrids. Moreover, in French the word *rature* brings with it echoes of *rater*, to fail or misfire, and *gratter*, to scrape, both of which carry associations that fit well with iconoclastic practices in suggesting respectively failed communication, and interference with a (legible) surface. Indeed, there is perhaps more scope for recoding visual images by means of physical alteration than is the case with texts. Different media have specific possibilities and problems in this respect. We might start, however, with a subject that is weighted towards the textual by considering the role of inscriptions as part of the urban fabric of Paris.

Before the Revolution, French towns and cities did not rely much on textual signs to identify their constituent parts. Paris seems to have been no exception to this. Residences of the nobility were identified by coats of arms; inns relied on large pictorial signs to attract custom, neither of these contrasting vocabularies required a literate observer. When an innovative scheme to systematize the means of locating addresses by numbering houses was introduced in Paris in the 1770s, it was actively repulsed by the inhabitants who feared that it was to do with a scheme for collecting taxes (Hillairet 1985: 34). Monograms on royal buildings were habitually added as a kind of natural dynastic accretion. The architectural decoration of the Louvre, for example, is generously sprinkled with such markers. Following the demise of the *ancien régime*, the evident expendability of consuls, emperors and monarchs in nineteenth-century France found its

185

logical expression in Charles Garnier's decision to design bolted-on metal 'N's for his new Opéra, suitable for rapid removal in the not too distant future (Wagner 1986: 229).[4] However, in that they did not constitute royal insignia they were not attacked as part of the practice of effacing the signs of royalty. For example, when news broke of the Royal Family's attempted escape from Paris in June 1791, royal arms were spontaneously smashed and battered (*Feuille du jour*, 174 (28 June 1971): 719–20).[5] Alarmed reports of such outbreaks give the impression that they were exhaustively thorough. But this was far from the case. Over two years later, following a decree of 4 July 1793 that painted and sculpted attributes of royalty on public monuments should be effaced, it was further decreed on 9 October of the same year that parks, gardens and houses still bearing 'signes de la royauté' would be confiscated.

New labels were a replacement for such obsolete emblems. The city increasingly acquired informative textual elements. Alexandre Lenoir had taken the initiative to mark the house where Molière had been born with a stone inscription, and been accused of abrogating civic responsibilities for his pains. Such didacticism was not always welcomed. In 1795, the *Magasin encyclopédique* (1795: 470–88) recalled with horror the proposition to subjugate through sloganizing by inscribing 'La Liberté et la Mort' on all houses.

The Revolution's aftermath was hardly likely to leave vestiges of official inscriptions unmolested. In August 1802, Sir John Dean Paul was one of many British visitors in Paris profiting from peaceful relations between Britain and France following the Peace of Amiens to examine the art works amassed in the Louvre. He noted that on all official buildings, the inscriptions such as 'Liberté, Egalité, Fraternité' ending in 'ou la Mort' had had the final word scratched out and replaced by 'Justice' or 'Humanité' (Lacombe n.d.: 57).[6] Such incomplete emendation left a reminder of the Republic's years of crisis; only the offensive part of the motto was replaced so as to signal its supercession.

Revolutionary didacticism made full use of the common belief in the power of images to propagate new ideas by virtue of their direct impact on the spectator's sight. But explanatory texts are always in attendance. In October 1793, Fabre d'Englantine reported to the Convention on the efficacity of the new Revolutionary calendar's metaphoric imagery: 'We conceive of nothing except by images; in the most abstract analysis, in the most metaphysical combination, our understanding only progresses by images (Herbert 1972: 7, lxxii). Yet, even with elaborate commentary on the calendar's new terminology, it was the source of much confusion and scepticism. It represents a cautionary tale regarding the absorption of new visual and verbal vocabulary, for despite its obligatory usage on official stationery and documents, there was considerable popular resistance to a ten-day week with new names for days and months. In the case of Jacques-

Louis David's colossal statue of *Le Peuple français*, the figure was covered with anatomical programme notes: 'sur son front, *Lumière*; sur sa poitrine: *Nature, Vérité* sur ses bras, *Force, Courage*' (Delécluze 1855: 156–7).

The heavy-handed textuality of David's statue was an insurance against misreading the otherwise imposing colossal figure. If we turn to the appropriation of already existing objects for Revolutionary ends, labelling seems to have been less important than the strategic addition of key emblems. This fits well with a narrative of Revolutionary culture as being made up of a dialectic between continuity and discontinuity. Within these terms, however, the synthesis was often improvised and unresolved.

On 20 April 1792, the *Gazette de Paris* reported that at Molsheim near Strasbourg, a group of national guards had committed 'toutes sortes d'abominations' on a statue of the Virgin, decapitating it and substituting a police cap for the head. The Molsheim incident represents an example of what we might call punitive iconoclasm: the *bonnet de police* substituting for the smashed head and giving a crude legitimation to the surviving body. Such incidents combine the violence associated with 'vandalism' with a positive desire to appropriate the object. As reported here, the actions were those of members of a new albeit sometimes unpredictable Revolutionary institution, the national guard, which might legitimately see itself as offering exemplary instances of new forms of behaviour. Acts of iconoclasm are also associated with the arrival of members of the Revolutionary armies.

To some degree, the indiscriminate application of iconoclasm might well depend on an absence of local ties – defacing or destroying objects and monuments that had been familiar as part of local topography was perhaps easier for outsiders. The collision between new style Revolutionary rituals, badges and established local traditions and practices is equally if not more evident in relation to new features intended to reinforce Revolutionary iconography. The widespread substitution of liberty trees for May poles and shrines was effected in order to harness communal associations of respect to new ends. The appositeness of this strategy is illustrated when we observe the reversion of sites of Revolutionary veneration back to their earlier local purpose. A Liberty Tree was dismantled at Raismes, near Valenciennes in *an V* to make way once again for the playing of *longue paulme* – an early form of tennis (*Journal des hommes libres*, 23 vend. an V (14 October 1796): 32). The elision effected here by the implantation of the Liberty Tree is not the familiar – indeed, central – one between religious sensibility and political consciousness, but rather the potentially contentious exploitation of an important site of collective leisure and sociability in the interests of focusing attention on a new national symbol. It goes without saying that such appropriations were heavily tied up with local political power play, and are not to be taken at face value as simply functional alternatives. For example, the municipal authorities at Falaise substituted a weathercock for an *emblème de la liberté* – presumably a liberty cap – but the Department ordered this to be put back at their own expense (*Journal des hommes libres*, 8 brum. an V (29 October 1796), no. 23: 92). Removal of emblems prompts us to suppose the determining involvement of political motives. But this is not necessarily so. The removal of liberty caps from the lightning conductors of the *maison commune* in Paris might be interpreted as a provocative challenge to one of the Revolution's most revered emblems. This was in fact the subject of lengthy discussion. The desire to keep up Revolutionary appearances eventually gave way in favour of the more down to earth inclination to diminish the likelihood of being electrocuted by lightning (*Thermomètre du jour*, 7 August 1793, 306).

There are other instances of a more discreetly synthetic approach to overhauling religious images than was applied at Molsheim. In Chartres cathedral, Bridan's sculpture of the *Assumption* was converted into a figure of Liberty by doing no more than adorning the Virgin with a *bonnet rouge* (Combes n.d.: 139). While the scale of the sculpture probably discouraged any more radical solution, it is none the less remarkable that this huge figure borne heavenward amongst thick clouds could be abruptly accepted as a quite different entity. The mystical nature of Catholicism perhaps facilitated belief in such a miraculous transformation – or revelation. Similarly at Bayeux, where the cathedral was redesignated a Temple of Reason, a statue of Faith was given a *bonnet rouge* and a cockade, the crucifix held in the statue's hand replaced by a pike with tricolour oriflamme, so as to create a Liberty-Republic hybrid.[7] Both cases might be seen as falling into an alternative iconoclastic mode, which we might call redemptive, suggesting that the statues' symbolism was radically shifted not by doing violence to them, but rather by integrating key Revolutionary emblems which recast the whole semantic context in which they were perceived. In the secular sphere, the re-use of socles retained both a significant material element, and also suggested the replacement of old values by new. Bouchardon's bronze *Equestrian Monument to Louis XV* in the Place royale was abruptly removed on 11 August 1792, and subsequently replaced by Lemot's *Liberty* of painted plaster, seated on the same base, stripped of its reliefs, which survived until June 1800 (Hillairet 1985: 375–6).

We should also see these examples of sculptural renewal as manifestations of the collective desire for a form of monumental permanence by which to enshrine and commemorate the Revolution. Such appropriations often have the character of *ad hoc* improvisations in place of the expensive and lengthy business of originating new Revolutionary imagery. Detractors of the Revolution have repeatedly drawn attention to its failure to produce monuments in bronze and marble, and the reliance on the ephemeral wood and plaster props used in *fêtes*, as if this was in itself a measure of political superficiality. For the *Journal des arts* (20 frim. an VIII (12 December 1799), no. 28: 8–9), the succession of 'autels de carton, des libertés de plâtre, des Arcs triomphaux en fils d'archal et de toile granitée, des obélisques de sapin' had done more to enrich a few entrepreneurs than to commemorate the Revolution. For the *Abréviateur universel* (18 pluv. an III (6 February 1795); Ozouf 1976: 158, n. 5) they were the 'symboles imposants et fragiles de nos théories éphémères'.

By taking over churches and Church property, it was hoped to redirect the respect and subjective sentiments such buildings commanded into new political channels. The enlightenment of the Revolution was to be demonstrated by its philanthropic conversion of the edifices of superstition to the purposes of social welfare and for housing the institutions of the new political culture. When churches became the premises for political clubs and other official bodies, imagery and symbolism had to be adapted (or concealed) accordingly where it was part of the fabric and not removable to depots prior to conveyance to the Musée des monuments français.

The Panthéon represents the most monumental example of this process of symbolical reclamation. A new sculptural programme illustrating Revolutionary themes was substituted for the original religious subjects (Luke 1987). The Panthéon is also the largest instance where the building's new function was broadcast by means of a simple French inscription across its portico's frieze. By 1796, the deliberately abstract allegories of the scheme that Quatremère de Quincy had overseen were criticized as being illegible. But here illegibility implies as much a refusal to decipher a sculptural relief as it describes the image's lack of effectiveness (*Mes Tablettes*, 2 brum. an V (23 October 1796): 256-7).

The most comprehensive exercise in simultaneously destroying and reclaiming a building is that of the Bastille. As the site of the Revolution's first victorious *journée*, and in consequence the symbol of *ancien régime* 'despotism' par excellence, the lowering mass of the Bastille was ripe for some special commemorative treatment. Later proponents of the conservation of historic buildings were to denounce destructive profiteering by entrepreneurs who were eager to demolish and re-use materials, but Palloy, the mastermind behind the demolition of the Bastille, succeeded in making a profit and retaining his Revolutionary credentials. The stones were carved into miniature replicas of the fortress. These were distributed across France and were treated in the same manner as religious relics, transubstantiated into emblems of liberty, especially useful for *fêtes* (Schama 1989: 408-19). One of Leseur's gouaches in the Musée Carnavalet, Paris, shows one of these objects being ceremoniously carried like some sacred tabernacle. The appeal of this kind of indexical memento seems to be particularly strong in the aftermath of political and military victories. In 1651, at Bartholomew fair, a brass founder sold tobacco boxes supposedly made from a statue of Charles I which had been pulled down by order of Parliament (this turned out to be a hoax, for the statue was in fact hidden and re-erected after the Restoration).[8] Many French memorials to the First World War were

189

made from melted down German guns, taking up the biblical injunction to turn swords into ploughshares. A notorious modern equivalent is the monument in Baghdad to the Iran–Iraq war which incorporates thousands of Iranian helmets and melted down enemy guns (Khalil 1991). The most compelling and politically apposite parallel to the case of the Bastille's having been razed to the ground, but reconstituted in atomized form out of its own fabric, is that of the Berlin wall. On this occasion demolition was not monopolized by a Palloy, but none the less the redundant use value of broken bricks and chunks of concrete was instantly replaced by dramatically enhanced exchange value as they became highly desirable commodities available by mail order.

As well as rejigging buildings, the Revolution was also responsible for creating new institutions whose purpose was to protect France's cultural heritage. Attempts to conserve *patrimoine* were directly related to the problem of 'vandalism' (Poulot 1988: 201–37). This is exemplified if we return to the case of Bayeux Cathedral. Although one particular statue was salvaged, many others had been damaged, and almost all of the paintings here and in other churches in the town had been destroyed. Indeed, in this case, we find well illustrated the close causal connection between the perception of a threat to disenfranchised religious monuments and the compensatory desire to establish a legal and political framework to protect not so much the churches themselves, as the works of art they contained. Nationalization of Church property accelerated the need to act on this, and was institutional-ized in the form of a national committee which was to oversee the making of inventories of objects worthy of protection before they were consigned to depots for safekeeping. This expansion of curatorial activity coincides with an evolution towards newly empirical historiographical tendencies. The Revolution not only gave a dramatic new momentum to the writing of alternatives to the hitherto dominant orthodoxy of monarchical chronicles, but also engendered a productive debate on how to understand works of art, and particularly architecture, as a form of historical evidence. In 1802, J. J. Leuliette argued that, although they were disagreeable from the point of view of taste, medieval cathedrals were appropriate to their age and effective in fulfilling their intended aim: 'elles impriment une terreur religi-euse, une auguste mélancolie. Leur caractère sombre semblait convenir parfaitement à l'usage auquel on les destinait.' This historicist view of architecture was taken to extremes in the proposal in 1799 to transfer the Musée des monuments français, which had been set up in a convent, to Notre-Dame cathedral (Tuetey 1915–17b: 128).

One offshoot of this discovery of the historic nature of the city's fabric was the beginning of what might be called the cult of scenes from the lives of great men – where they lived and worked, places where significant events had occurred. Lenoir's initiative regarding Molière's house, already mentioned, is a perfect example of this. Prompted by F. M. Granet's painting of *The Interior of Michelangelo's House*, exhibited at the 1806 Salon, Amaury-Duval wrote how fascinating it was 'à retrouver les lieux situés, bâtis et décorés tels que le génie les habitait il y a trois siècles' (Chaussard 1806: 398). In *an II*, when statues of saints were being stripped from Notre-Dame, it was pointed out in the *conseil général* of the Commune that Charles François Dupuis had been inspired to conceive his planetary system by the sculpture of the 'deux portes collatérales'. Dupuis was to be consulted on what should be spared (*Courier républicain*, 24 brum. an II (14 November 1793), no. 15: 116).

A further perspective on the question of how far iconoclasm was consensual or popular also comes from Bayeux. Worries about destructive 'ravages' gave impetus to official attempts to stem indiscriminate acts of vandalism, and the elaboration of a policy of conservation.[9] Such a policy had to resolve political demands – images of monarchy and religious superstition were at best redundant and at worst provocation to counter-revolution (especially relevant in the royalist Vendée in the north-west, scene of bitter conflict throughout the Revolution) – with a desire to demonstrate that the Revolution was a better guardian of civilized values than the *ancien régime*, and that Liberty was the friend of art. In this sense, news of widespread vandalism was bad publicity for the Revolution; proscription of politically offensive images, it was argued, had to be tempered by a discrimination that some works were worthy of preservation when considered in the light of a canon of cultural value no matter what their subject matter or associations. Antipathetic associations could be neutralized in so far as objects were relocated within an edifying narrative of French cultural history – generically we can recognize this conceptual if not physical space as the museum. When J. A. Dulaure visited the Musée des monuments français in its early days, he reported that artists were annoyed to find images of kings excluded, for they believed that 'un vrai républicain pourroit voir en peinture, même en nature, tous les rois de la terre, sans éprouver la moindre tentation en faveur de royalisme' (*Thermomètre de jour*, 584 (6 August 1793): 300). But he still had his doubts on the advisability of displaying such objects and images. The creation of museums saw them as leading a process of sifting through the nation's artistic and monumental *patrimoine*, and, further, engaging in a didactic form of presentation that would order objects according to an historical narrative. The museums' need for reasoned didacticism points to a tension inherent in much Revolutionary discourse between a belief in innate virtue liberated by the Revolution, and the acknowledgement of the need for regulatory surveillance aimed at repressing counter-revolutionary sentiments.

Pictures in the public spaces of churches were consigned to depots. They were transferred from individual ownership, or that of institutions, to that of the nation. What has perhaps not been taken into account is that during the Revolution, privately owned, domestically located pictures also became

191

the focus for denunciation in the public interest, and could become subject to the strictures of the political surveillance associated with the Terror. Hitherto, under the *ancien régime*, possession of collections of paintings had signified a degree of affluence in material terms, and also a level of cultured sensibility. In a political culture where *sans-culotte* philistinism was for a time the norm, it therefore made sense to include them in 'anti-aristocratic' proscriptive rhetoric. With the creation of a new public political culture, private activities were opened out to public scrutiny: pictures were marked as belonging to the *ancien régime* and all too easily construed as signifying an allegiance to old, reactionary values. This intrusive iconoclasm could be ruthlessly applied. In Beauvais on October 1793, a Parisian mechanic Antoine Botte was denounced to the *comité de surveillance* by two citizens for being guilty of possessing a picture of 'The Judgement of Solomon'. Although Botte wished to keep the picture he was forced to *barbouiller* it (Dommanget 1918: 46).

Faced with this kind of threat, other luckier pictures might be treated to more subtle protective measures. An *Offering to Saint Nicholas* originally painted by Pierre-François Delauney was altered at some point after his death in August 1789 to form an *Offering to Liberty* by the very careful erasure of the saint and his replacement by an allegorical figure (Wrigley 1980: 745–7). Given the great care taken to implant the figure of Liberty, so as not to disrupt the composition, this seems to have been an essentially protective strategy by the picture's owner, rather than some coarser, more punitive form of re-painting or damage. The sophisticated medium of oil painting had the advantage, as in cases like this of allowing an image to be created that revealed no visible traces of its alteration, in contrast to the combined effects of dressing up and mutilation of statues. However, we are left to speculate as to whether this was the consequence of sincere Revolutionary sentiment, or anxious prudence designed to safeguard the picture from any iconoclastic intervention. In another case from the later 1790s, we know nothing of the circumstances of the alteration, but are left with a revison that might be deemed resourceful or desperate in which Saint Ursula was over-painted to create a post-Themidorean allegory, *Concord, or the Directoire Putting an End to the Old Government* (Lossky 1968: 181–2). Clément Belle's *Temple of Thetis*, although originally an official commission from the very end of the *ancien régime*, can be mentioned here because of the similarity of the new subject that was arrived at. In 1794, it was converted into *Minerva Giving to Hercules the Decree which Abolishes the Vices of the Old Government* reflecting the repressive anti-republican mood of the Directoire, and the utility of mythology in a period of chronic political euphemism.[10] The facility with which a seamless join could be effected when introducing a new or replacement figure in a painting courtesy of the finesse and opacity of oil paint was equalled by the relative ease with which engravings could be updated. It is in the nature of prints that, however much work has been done on the plate to create a series of states, the image that appears on the paper is of a piece. Thus numerous prints' revised states are only known to us as such since we have both, or all, states of the print.

The continuities of visual culture that had sustained artistic production during the *ancien régime* were comprehensively thrown into question by the political innovations of the Revolution in a way that precipitated a profound reassessment of the value of past and contemporary imagery. Revolutionary debates threw into question the role of the arts within the new political culture. A concrete conclusion emerged in the form of the Louvre and the Musée des monuments français, institutions which protected those objects in which the pre-eminent values of France's national culture were enshrined. If, during the nineteenth century, 'vandalism' remained an element in periods of rebellion, redemptive iconoclasm became almost a matter of bureaucratic procedure. This was never to be more so than during the Restoration, when the Bourbon monarchy was faced with the problem of what to do with the ubiquitous imprint of Napoleon's dynastic aspirations.

NOTES

1 There is an extensive literature on Revolutionary iconoclasm. For an excellent overview see Sprigath (1980: 510–35) and for a wide-ranging account of non-revolutionary iconoclasm see Freedberg (1989).

2 The author of the article in question assumes the appropriate name of 'A. Mnemon', *Journal des bâtiments civils et des arts*, 13 pluv. an X (2 February 1802), no. 148: 197–202.

3 The idea of applying the concept of *rature* to a discussion of iconoclasm came to seem plausible after reading Orton 1989.

4 Wagner (1986) treats the detail as unconfirmed, and refers to Darcel 1870–1: 415.

5 An exception to the tolerance of royal *monogrammes* occurred at the royal porcelain manufactory at Sevres. The interlaced 'L's which had been used as a hallmark were ordered to be replaced by RF standing for 'Republique française' in July 1793 (Béalu 1989: 27). I am grateful to Mme Tamara Préaud for kindly drawing this article to my attention, and for providing me with a copy.

6 Lacombe adds that such a revised inscription was still visible in 1880 on the pediment of the Ecole de droit, citing his source as *Bulletin de la société d'histoire de Paris et de l'Ile-de-France* (1880): 153.

7 Ozouf (1976: 117) further notes the conversion of a Virgin into a Liberty by the Société populaire de Rodez.

8 See the Victoria and Albert Museum decorative art galleries: 'Continuity and change 1640–1660'.

9 Tuetey 1915–17a: I, 504. A commissioner in Bayeux reports an 'irruption vandalique' in a letter of 26 October 1794.

10 A. C. Belle, *Minerve remet à Hercule le décret qui aboli lex vices de l'ancien gouvernement*, 3.56 × 3.86. *Musée national du Louvre. Catalogue des peintures, Ecole française*, Paris, 1972, 27, Inv. 20297. This was the central part of a triptych on the theme of

the temple of Thetis, commissioned as a cartoon for the Gobelins in 1788 to provide a tapestry for the Palais de Justice, and transformed in 1794 into an *Allégorie de la Révolution*.

BIBLIOGRAPHY

Béalu, C. (1989) 'Les Porcelaines révolutionnaires', *Art et curiosité* April 27, 10–39.

Certeau, M. de, Julia, D. and Revel, J. (1975) *Une politique de langue: la Révolution française et les patois: l'enquête Grégoire*, Paris, Gallimard.

Chaussard, P. J. B. (1806) *Le Pausanais français*, Paris, F. Buisson.

Combes, L. (n.d.) *Episodes et curiosités révolutionnaires*, Paris, Madre.

D. (1801) 'Au citoyen G. Artiste correspondant de L'Institut national, à s . . . , département de la Meurthe', *Journal des bâtiments civils et des arts*, 23 prairial an IX (2 June 1801), no. 79: 12–14.

Darcel, A. (1870–1) 'Les Musées, les arts et les artistes pendant le siège de Paris', *Gazette des beaux-arts*, series 2, I (4): 415.

Delécluze, E. J. (1855) *Louis David, son école et son temps, souvenirs*, Paris, Didier.

Derrida, J. (1967) *De la grammatologie*, Paris, Minuit.

Dommanget, M. (1918) *Le Déchristianisation à Beauvais et dans l'Oise 1790–1801*, Besançon, Bibliothèque d'histoire révolutionnaire.

Freedberg, D. (1989) *The Power of Images. Studies in the History and Theory of Responses*, Chicago, University of Chicago Press.

Herbert, R. L. (1972) 'Neo-Classicism in the French Revolution', *The Age of Neo-Classicism*, London, Royal Academy and Victoria and Albert Museum: lxxii-lxxv.

Hillairet, J. (1985) *Dictionnaire historique des rues de Paris*, vol. 1, Paris, Editions de Minuit.

Khalil, S. al (1991) *The Monument: Art, Vulgarity and Responsibility in Iraq*, Berkeley, University of California Press.

Lacombe, P. (ed.) (n.d.) *Journal d'un voyage à Paris au mois d'Août 1802 par Sir John Dean Paul*, Paris, Marcel Dreyfous.

Leuliette, J. J. (1802) *Journal des bâtiments civils et des arts*, 9 vent. an IX (1 October 1802): 340–2.

Lossky, B. (1968) 'Une image religieuse mutée en allégorie révolutionnaire', *Gazette des beaux-arts*, 71: 181–2.

Luke, Y. (1987) 'The politics of participation: Quatremère de Quincy. Theory and practice of "concours publiques" in Revolutionary France, 1791–1795', *Oxford Art Journal*, 10, no. 1: 15–43.

Orton, F. (1989) 'On not being bent blue. An introduction to Derrida and a note on Johns', *Oxford Art Journal*, 12, (no. 1): 35–46.

Ozouf, M. (1976) *La fête révolutionnaire 1789–1799*, Paris, Gallimard.

Poulot, D. (1988) 'La naissance du musée', in P. Bordes and R. Michel (eds), *Aux armes et aux arts! Les arts de la Révolution française 1789–99*, Paris, Editions Adam Biro: 201–37.

Schama, S. (1989) *Citizens. A chronicle of the French Revolution*, London, Viking.

Sprigath, G. (1980) 'Sur le vandalisme révolutionnaire (1791–94)', *Annales historiques de la Révolution française*, 52: 510–35.

Tuetey, A. (1915–17a) *Procès-verbaux de la Commission temporaire des arts*, 2 vols, Paris 1912–18.

—— (1915–17b) 'Un projet de transfert du Musée des monuments français à Notre-Dame', *Bulletin de la société de l'histoire de l'art français*: 128–39.

Wagner, A-M. (1986) *Jean-Baptiste Carpeaux. Sculptor of the Second Empire*, New Haven and London, Yale University Press.

Weber, E. (1977) *Peasants into Frenchmen: The Modernization of Rural France 1870–1914*, London, Chatto & Windus.

Wrigley, R. (1980) 'Pierre-François Delauney, liberty and Saint Nicholas', *Burlington Magazine*, 122: 745–7.

Index